Management Strategy and Information Technology

Text and Readings

MANAGEMENT STRATEGY AND INFORMATION TECHNOLOGY

TEXT AND READINGS

Christopher Barnatt

Lecturer in Organizational Behaviour, Computers and Management
University of Nottingham, UK.

INTERNATIONAL THOMSON BUSINESS PRESS
I ⓣ P An International Thomson Publishing Company

London • Bonn • Boston • Johannesburg • Madrid • Melbourne • Mexico City • New York • Paris
Singapore • Tokyo • Toronto • Albany, NY • Belmont, CA • Cincinnati, OH • Detroit, MI

Management Strategy and Information Technology: Text and Readings

Copyright © 1996 Christopher Barnatt

First published 1996 by International Thomson Business Press

I(T)P   A division of International Thomson Publishing Inc.
        The ITP logo is a trademark under licence

British Library Cataloguing-in-Publication Data
A catalogue record for this book is available from the British Library

First edition 1996
Reprinted 1996

Typeset by Christopher Barnatt
Printed in the UK by The Alden Press, Oxford

ISBN 0-412-74950-5

International Thomson Business Press
Berkshire House
168–173 High Holborn
London WC1V 7AA
UK

International Thomson Business Press
20 Park Plaza
14th Floor
Boston MA 02116
USA

Contents

5 Systems Development and Implementation

6 Reengineering Work and Organization   71

THE READINGS

PREFACE

This book is intended to fulfil two objectives. Firstly, like all textbooks, it seeks to provide a concise and structured set of notes concerning its chosen subject area — in this case the managerial issues arising from the operational and strategic application of information technology. Secondly, *Management Strategy and Information Technology* furnishes its target audience with a selection of accessible and up-to-date journal papers. We all know that students are supposed to read journal articles of relevance to the courses and modules upon which they enrol. However, in practice, restrictions of time, library resource, and even the curse of apathy, prevent this noble pastime occurring. Hopefully, with about half of this volume dedicated to quality journal reprints, readers will be able to gain at least some exposure to research-informed academic thinking on the cutting edge.

Within the following pages there are no flowcharts or project control diagrams; no schematics of mainframes or explanations of binary mathematics. Rather, the focus is upon how the worlds of business and IT are evolving, and the fresh challenges that are arising out of such change. No longer do businesses need to be convinced as to the importance of using computers. Instead, issues meriting study and further investigation concern the range of application of existing and emerging computer technologies toward the pursuit, and the attainment, of competitive advantage. Technical concerns are being replaced by managerial dilemmas, whilst networks of personal computers are challenging the mainframes of tradition *and winning*. Partially as a result, organizations are witness to power struggles between end-users keen to exploit their new desktop machines, and IT personnel sceptical of 'distributed' computing with its less-structured methodologies. There are 'disconnects' to heal, new mindsets to embrace, and innovative means of reengineering work *through* computer application to take on board. It is precisely such *management* challenges that are explored within this book.

Much of the content of the text is derived from my second and final year undergraduate and MBA modules in business computing and information systems taught within the School of Management & Finance at the University of Nottingham. It should be appreciated that this is not an 'introduction to computing' book, and therefore that some basic computer knowledge, in addition to some general business understanding, is assumed from the outset. But fear not! For undergraduate students, this background knowledge is likely to have come from an introductory computing/IT 'skills' module, and from subjects core to degrees with titles such as Management Studies and Business Economics. All MBA students should find themselves perfectly comfortable with the business concepts required. In addition, readers undertaking an MBA will be able to draw upon previous work experiences when evaluating many of the concepts and controversies addressed, especially within the readings.

Chapter 1 provides an introduction to a range of important concepts and definitions — such as management information systems, groupware, downsizing and business process reengineering. Chapter 2 then begins analysis in earnest, with an exploration of how computer systems may empower competitive advantage. Subsequently, Chapter 3 addresses the traditional 'rift' between 'business people' and IT personnel — the so called IS/IT 'disconnect' — and how it may be managed and averted.

The remaining three text chapters address more specific managerial concerns. Chapter 4 examines the downsizing trend towards the application of smaller, distributed and cheaper computer and communications technologies. It also weighs the advantages and disadvantages of outsourcing IT provision, an option now being chosen, or at least considered, by many large organizations. In Chapter 5, the age-old problem of successful systems development and implementation is discussed. Finally, Chapter 6 examines the current buzz-terms of business process reengineering (BPR), 'management by wire' and 'virtual organization' as business operations increasingly become translated into the datasphere of 'cyberspace'.

Readings 7 through 13, chosen to complement the text, have been selected based upon a number of key criteria. Firstly, all papers included had to be accessible to a wide readership and as up-to-date as possible. None of the included readings therefore resort to deep statistical or other complex research analysis; nor are they steeped in lexical complexity. All the readings were also first published in the 1990s. Granted, some 'classic' business/IT papers exist from the 1980s, yet many of their paragraphs now read as rather dated when considering recent developments in computer hardware and software.

In addition to the above selection criteria, all readings chosen had to serve as integrated, wide-ranging resources to the text chapters. Each paper included is clearly directed toward a specific topic area, yet the reader will also find its case examples valuable in fleshing out concepts from several of the text chapters. Links to the readings are indicated throughout the text, with the index also covering both the text and the readings. Management Strategy and Information Technology may be a book in two parts, yet it needs to be viewed as an integrated whole in order to derive the greatest value from its content. After all, a knowledge of how to gain managerial and strategic advantage from business computer application should not just advance a route of academic study. Perhaps more importantly, it should also prove invaluable when embarking upon any individual journey in pursuit of personal business success!

Acknowledgements

Finally before we get underway, a few 'thank yous' to others whose efforts have helped this book progress from idea to hardcopy reality. Firstly, thanks to the anonymous reviewers (whoever you may be!) whose enthusiastic feedback spurred this project forward. Secondly, a big thank you to Joanne Ball, Geraldine Spurr and Sandra Mienczakowski for their assistance during the overly-hot summer of 1995. Thirdly, thanks to Viv Toye for her work as Production Editor, and to Stephen York as Copy Editor. Last, and by no means least, many, many thanks to my Commissioning Editor, Ingmar Folkmans. Back in the spring of 1993, a chance meeting between Ingmar and myself led to the offer to write a book on business computing. For some reason, books came to be conceived, written and published with several other publishers before we settled on the content — and the design — and the title! — for *Management Strategy and Information Technology*. Hopefully, after such a long fermentation process, Ingmar's unwavering support and enthusiasm for this project will be rewarded with success. With best wishes also to my parents, sister, other family and friends,

Christopher Barnatt

There are 30 OHP masters available for instructors from the publisher. Please contact Caroline Law at International Thomson Business Press for details (fax 0171 497 1426 or e-mail caroline.law@itpuk.co.uk).

1 INTRODUCTION: THE COMPUTER IN BUSINESS

KEY CONCEPTS INTRODUCED

Data processing systems ■ Management information systems ■ Decision support systems ■ Executive information systems ■ Office automation systems ■ Communications systems ■ Downsizing ■ Client/server computing ■ Groupware ■ Business process reengineering.

A large proportion of business organizations are now dependent upon information technology (IT) to maintain the efficiency and effectiveness of their operations. In fact, many companies could no longer function without their computer systems. From accounts work to stock control, document processing to database management, banking to the creation of virtual reality graphics simulations, IT now plays a crucial role in the accomplishment of many 'mission critical' task processes. Indeed, Charles Wang, Chairman of multi-billion-dollar Computer Associates, argues that today information technology 'doesn't support the business, it *is* the business', with computer application changing 'everything you have ever learned about business management' (Wang, 1994: 188-189).

As a concise resource for students of business computing, management information systems (MIS) or the management of IT, this book has two interlinked objectives. Firstly, it sets out to examine how, why, and for what purposes, computers have come to be employed across business today. Secondly, and as a consequence, *Management Strategy and Information Technology* also seeks to explore the impact of widespread and increasing IT adoption upon the managerial function, the reengineering of organizational processes via computer application, and the resultant managerial challenges and dilemmas that lie ahead. With its content mix of both explanatory chapters and journal article reprints, the book presents students with a cohesive text, whilst avoiding the common pitfall of reporting the views of only one contributor. Computer technologies and associated working practices are evolving so rapidly that *nobody*, however eminent, can hope to paint the full picture. The derivation of information and concepts from a variety of sources is consequently a vital pillar upon which any mature academic analysis has to be based.

The role of this first chapter is to introduce a range of concepts and definitions which surround business computer application and the management thereof. As a consequence, it is a less analytical chapter than the five which follow. However, by getting its basic spectrum of material out of the way early on, Chapter 1 does serve as an important resource for the rest of the book, which is freed to proceed unencumbered by the 'messy' pauses often required for definitions.

COMPUTER SYSTEM CLASSIFICATIONS

As illustrated in Table 1.1, modern business organizations are complex conglomerations of a great range of activity functions. Companies today also operate within complex global marketplaces, need to compete harder than ever before for customers and finance, and are forced to comply with a myriad of legislative requirements. It is therefore hardly surprising that the range of computer systems used to handle the information flows that tie business functions and their environments together come in a very wide variety of guises. Many analysts of business computer application subsequently choose to sub-divide the family of IT business systems into a manageable number of classifications. Usually, resultant lists of business computing system categories delineate between:

- Data processing systems
- Management information systems
- Decision support systems
- Executive information systems
- Office automation systems, and
- Communications systems.

DATA PROCESSING SYSTEMS

A large proportion of the computer systems used in business today are employed for the basic task of data processing (DP). Data processing systems involve any combination of computer hardware and software used to process the routine transactions of organizational life. Across most companies, functional departments such as accounts, purchasing and personnel now rely heavily on IT to process data. In the accounts department, for example, ledgers are no longer tabulated in paper volumes, but are instead keyed directly into a computer system. Accounts data, invoices, cheques, reminders and statements can subsequently be displayed on a screen or printed out as required. In some instances, facilities may even allow for the direct communication of data between DP systems within different organizations — a process known as electronic data interchange (EDI).

Table 1.1 Typical business functions

FUNCTION	SUMMARY OF MAIN ACTIVITIES
Purchasing	Determining and securing competitive sources of raw materials
Production	Scheduling, batching, sequencing and controlling the manufacture of goods and services
Research and Development	Devising, designing and testing new products and services
Personnel	Assessing manpower requirements and achieving them via employee recruitment, selection, payment and administration
Marketing	Promoting, advertising, selling, and possibly exporting, the outputs of the production function

In the purchasing department of many organizations, stock taking is now also computerized, with each component bar coded and checked into and out of an automatic data processing system. This negates the need for laborious manual stock checking. Similarly in personnel, computer systems will be used to store and to update employee records, and to produce wage and salary slips and tax documentation. In short, (data processing systems are used to take the drudgery out of monotonous and repetitive data handling tasks. When it comes to straight number crunching or repetitive information storage and retrieval, computers are far more cost-effective and far more reliable than human beings.)

MANAGEMENT INFORMATION SYSTEMS

Whereas a data processing system is used to automate the handling of data transactions, a management information system (MIS) is employed as an operational management tool. Basically, management information systems use DP system data to generate summary information pertaining to business performance. A manager of an accounts office, for example, may use a management information system to extract a report detailing the number of transactions processed per day, together with their overall value. Increases or decreases in performance can be monitored as a result. Similarly, a retail chain's management information system may provide aggregate data relating to individual stores in the chain in addition to sales figures on a product-by-product basis. Example 1.1 examines the use of a management information system which extracts data from the EPoS (electronic point of sale) DP system within the retail chain Boots the Chemists.

Example 1.1 EPoS and MIS in Boots the Chemists
(adapted from De Looze, 1994: 61-70).

Boots the Chemists (BTC) operates over 1000 high street stores in the UK, all of which employ an EPoS (electronic point of sale) scanning system on their checkouts to enable bar codes to be read off the items purchased by their customers. A complete stock inventory can therefore be updated continually as sales are made, negating the need for staff to count the actual number of products left upon the shelves at the end of the day.

BTC EPoS inventory data is linked into an automated stock replenishment system which requests fresh deliveries from the 116 Common Stock Rooms (CSRs) which provide overnight stock provision for BTC's top-selling 2500 lines. As a result of the installation of its EPoS DP system, BTC has been able to reduce its stock levels by 20%, whilst service levels have improved.

To take advantage of its EPoS scanning data, BTC has established an MIS database which provides merchandise information upon a variety of levels. Sales can be monitored not only by store or geographic region, but also on the basis of display-space utilization, selling costs per line of merchandise and competitive activity. As a result, BTC has been able to streamline its product ranges. The performance of new product lines can now also be monitored more quickly, allowing poor performers to be rapidly withdrawn from costly sales space.

In the run up to one Christmas period, monitoring of MIS data from Sound and Vision departments alerted management to slow sales volumes in audio hardware. By comparing the MIS sales data with stock levels in the supply chain, BTC were able to undertake a series of one-day promotions on audio hardware. As a result BTC was not left with large stocks of unsold audio hardware after Christmas, unlike other retailers whose traditional stock-checking systems had not alerted them to a general decline in demand for consumer audio products.

DECISION SUPPORT SYSTEMS

Whereas a management information system allows organizational data flows to be aggregated for static analysis, a decision support system (DSS) provides tools that enable data to be manipulated in order that it may be utilized within the decision making process. In many instances, decision support systems are extended management information systems into which hypothetical or projected information may be input in order to enable scenario analysis and hypothesis testing. Other DSS variants will have no MIS links, perhaps because they relate to data on potential new projects or which is only available from other organizations. Either way, any decision support system will be highly interactive in operation, with user inputs playing an important role alongside available hard facts.

Decision support systems are used in either unstructured or semi-structured business situations, and serve a key role in isolating the areas in which human judgement and expertise are required (Alter, 1992: 133). Commonly, decision support systems provide 2-D and 3-D graphical outputs of data, representing likely decision outcomes in an easy to evaluate fashion. Functions such as 'what-if?' analysis are usually also available. When deciding upon the opening bid in a takeover battle, for example, a decision support model containing financial data upon the target firm may be utilized. The manager responsible for making the decision would be permitted to change variables within the model (such as projected sales figures, asset depreciation and interest rates), to find out what would happen to the viability of the target if these variables altered. Similarly, what-if? decision support models may be used to discover the sensitivity of costs for a new product in relation to possible changes in expenditure on raw materials, electricity, advertising and fixed overheads.

Sometimes listed as a separate computer system category, various *expert systems* are now also becoming commonly applied in various areas of decision support. These combine a data set derived from many real-world cases with a base of rules or heuristics which are applied to the data set in order that 'expert' knowledge becomes available. Although traditionally utilized in extremely narrow yet highly technical fields such as geological forecasting and chemical analysis, expert systems are starting to be used within some broader business functions such as financial analysis. For example, as reported in Reading 11, American Express have embedded the knowledge of their best credit authorizers into an expert system whose application that has led to a substantial reduction in credit losses. The drawback of expert systems is that they lack basic common sense, as well as having no knowledge of anything outside of their programmed technical specialism. As a result, the systems are not really 'expert' at all. Inform a medical expert system that a patient has spots all over and it may well pronounce a case of measles. However, if the patient happened to be a Dalmatian rather than a human being, then the diagnosis may be entirely incorrect!

EXECUTIVE INFORMATION SYSTEMS

An executive information system (EIS) is a highly flexible, highly interactive and very user-friendly management information and decision support system intended for use by the upper echelons of management. Therefore, whilst most management information and linked decision support systems will provide only summary operational information and data modelling functions at a grass-roots, operational level, executive information systems will be programmed with a much more strategic capability. EIS data aggregation is therefore likely to be available at the level of divisions or SBUs (strategic business units), in addition to being categorized by individual departments, products or retail outlets.

The use of an executive information system should negate the need for top managers to continually plod through mountains of paper reports, or to rely too heavily upon the data analysis skills of their subordinates. As a result, executives using an EIS will become empowered to spend the majority of their time making quality strategic decisions. EIS interfaces tend to be highly graphical in nature, permitting even those with very basic computer skills access to a wide range of information. Indeed, it has been suggested that executive information systems are simply previous management information systems re-badged and with a friendlier interface such that they can finally deliver to technophobic top managers what the original MIS systems promised in the first place (Martin and Powell, 1992: 187-188).

OFFICE AUTOMATION SYSTEMS

Hardly surprisingly, the term office automation system (OAS) refers to any combination of computer hardware and software employed to automate a general office task. The use of a personal computer (PC), a printer, and word processor software, therefore constitutes an OAS for document processing, allowing letters, reports and so forth to be typed, processed, stored and retrieved electronically. Similarly, a PC and a database software package may be used to construct an electronic address book, rather than having to rely upon on a box of cards to store customer and supplier contact information.

Because office automation systems involve the 'computerization' of basic office tasks, many analysts simply include them under the general heading of data processing systems. When the two terms are used distinctly, an OAS is usually defined as involving the small-scale application of personal computer hardware and software to aid in the accomplishment of ad-hoc 'desktop' office work. In contrast, DP systems tend to exist on a much broader scale, are concerned with far more structured business processes, and will involve substantial hardware and software investment. In other contexts, the term OAS is applied to label networked computer applications enabling project scheduling, diary management and similar groupwork planning facilities.

COMMUNICATIONS SYSTEMS

Ever since Alexander Graham Bell developed the telephone in the late 1870s, business organizations have relied upon information technology for communications purposes. Whilst telephone services and exchanges are becoming increasingly versatile, the use of computers themselves as information communications systems is also increasing. The use of electronic mail (e-mail) is spreading daily, allowing employees to send each other messages and data files without the hassle of first having to print out their keyboarding for dispatch into a postal system or facsimile machine. Indeed, between 1987 and 1994, over 26 million new e-mail addresses were registered in the USA alone (Tetzeli, 1994: 34). As discussed in Chapter 6, there are now approaching 50 million users of the worldwide computer network known as the Internet. According to Dataquest, by 1995 over 60% of business PCs in Europe were connected to some form of network and hence were capable of being used for communications purposes (Taylor, 1995: 11).

Voice-mail systems are now also proliferating. These allow telephone messages to be digitally stored and re-routed. Voice and e-mail technologies are also destined to converge, with systems already in development which will allow both audio and text-based messages to reside in a single computer-based mailbox which the owner may access from anywhere in the world. EDI communications systems are also now of vital strategic importance for many organizations, allowing both data, and models for data analysis, to be shared between their respective computer systems. Computer-mediated communication (CMC) is one of the fastest growing areas of business computer application, and arguably the one driving most other developments, as discussed within subsequent chapters.

KEY TRENDS AND DEVELOPMENTS

Computing and communications technologies continue to evolve at a rampant velocity. We are therefore fortunate that the majority of the key developments and conceptual trends regarding their business application remain deep-routed enough to make it worthwhile isolating them for detailed analysis. Many of the developments and trends we may delineate are also so wide-ranging that they carry with them implications right across the spectrum of business operations. It is therefore worth highlighting some current 'buzz-terms' in this introductory chapter, as they will reappear as recurrent themes across the rest of this book. The remainder of Chapter 1 will therefore concern itself with an introduction to:

- The downsizing revolution
- Client/server computing
- Groupware application, and
- Business process reengineering and new working practices.

THE DOWNSIZING REVOLUTION

Over the past five to ten years there has been a fairly dramatic shift away from mainframe-based business computing infrastructures. In the place of the traditional *dumb terminals* used for mainframe access, PCs now occupy the majority of office desks. The term 'downsizing' is used to refer to this trend, where at the most basic level centralized mainframe computers are being replaced by 'distributed' armies of 'mere' PCs.

Arguably the most significant trend sweeping business computing today, downsizing has been argued to increase an organization's IT flexibility. Downsizing also brings computer power closer to its end-users, and hence provides one means of breaking down the long-standing barrier (or 'disconnect') between the IT department and the rest of the company, as explored in Chapter 3. Dan Trimmer, a radical exponent of the downsizing 'revolution', notes that it is a comprehensive concept representing far more than just the occasional use of a PC to do jobs, such as word processing, that a mainframe cannot service. Rather, downsizing has the potential to become a corporate-wide computing initiative whose legacy will be vastly reduced costs in hardware, software and personnel. Downsizing will also make end-users far more aware of the potential of computer technology to enable business growth and/or to promote competitive advantage.

The downsizing trend has fairly obviously been technologically driven, with the concept only becoming feasible now that high-performance, low cost and user-friendly PCs are widely available. Until the 'PC revolution' organizations had no choice but to rely upon a central data processing facility based around a small number of mainframe or minicomputers. In the mid 1990s, however, it can reasonably be argued 'that a major threshold has been crossed such that many large organizations over time will be able to dispense with mainframe computing entirely' (Trimmer, 1993: 3). A more comprehensive exploration of downsizing developments is provided in Chapter 4.

CLIENT/SERVER COMPUTING

Client/server computer solutions attempt to combine the advantages of operating a centralized computing resource, such as a mainframe or minicomputer system, with the freedom and flexibility reaped when employees are allowed to work on smaller, individual, stand-alone machines. Under such an 'architecture', many 'client' computers, although capable of operating independently, are provided with access to additional centralized facilities offered from a larger 'server' machine. Client/sever computing is therefore dependant upon a network cabling infrastructure being available to link client machines (usually PCs) to their server or *host* computer.

In many circumstances, servers are themselves high-specification PCs. In other situations, servers will be minicomputers (such as the AS/400 from IBM), or even centralized mainframes. It should be noted, however, that when the server is a mainframe or a minicomputer it will be offering very different functions to its client machines than those traditionally provided by a centralized machine to range of dumb terminals. Whereas the latter had no internal processing capacity and were totally dependant upon the mainframe, clients are always independent computers in their own right. They therefore call upon their mainframe, minicomputer or PC server for additional rather than primary data access and applications support.

Under most client/server architectures, the server computer is used to store databases of information to be used by all client users (such as accounts or personnel records). The server usually also stores many of the applications programs which clients will utilize, as well as providing electronic mailboxes through which e-mail and voice-mail for its clients will be directed.

As a large number of PCs tend to be involved as clients, the growth of client/server computing is very much associated with the downsizing trend. This said, the two concepts should not be confused. To delineate, downsizing is concerned with adopting many small machines in place of larger computers. Client/server computing, on the other hand, is concerned with linking smaller client computers to larger servers so that users may utilize a greater number of services. A fully downsized computing solution would therefore get rid of a central mainframe. However, under a client/server architecture, an 'old' mainframe could well be preserved as an 'information warehouse' to service the data requirements of its new PC clients. Indeed, some analysts today now talk of 'rightsizing' rather than downsizing, with client/server solutions involving integrated mainframe, minicomputer and PC IT architectures. The delineation of downsizing/rightsizing is also discussed in Chapter 4.

GROUPWARE APPLICATION

Once computers are linked together across networks, possibilities for the application of 'groupware' abound. The term groupware simply refers to any computer application specifically designed for the use of groups rather than isolated individuals. This contrasts groupware with the traditional 'individual-ware' that has been used upon stand-alone PCs since their conception in the late 1970s. Groupware is a product of the new age of computer 'connectivity', reflecting the fact that computers are now devices to be used for information communications as well as for information processing, storage and retrieval. As software systems enabling users to share information across organizations, groupware applications are now the perfect tools for newly-cooperative corporate cultures. Indeed in mid-1995, there were already around 100,000 groupware users in the UK spread across 700 organizations (Glyn-Jones, 1995: 83).

The most basic form of groupware is electronic mail, which simply permits one-to-one and one-to-many text-based computer communications. More advanced groupwares offer users entire 'virtual' working environments. In the highly popular groupware package *Lotus Notes*™ for example, common data stores are available to all users in addition to messaging facilities. What's more, it is also possible for multi-user, interactive on-screen dialogues to occur between remote users. Different people, in different offices and potentially even different countries, can therefore work on the same documents simultaneously. At the time of writing there were claimed to be at least 1.35 million *Notes* users worldwide, with Lotus estimating that there would be 20 million users by 1997.

Even when employees share a common location, groupware application can greatly improve productivity. No longer do office workers have to ferret for lost invoices or other documentation buried within the desktop paper-stacks of their co-workers. Instead, every member of a team is able to have access to every document at the same time, regardless of whether it was created electronically (in the form of an e-mail correspondence, for example), or instead arrived as a physical piece of paper whose image was subsequently scanned into the groupware database for common electronic retrieval.

BUSINESS PROCESS REENGINEERING AND NEW WORKING PATTERNS

As increased computer connectivity continues and groupwares abound, organizations are increasingly being afforded the possibility to redesign their business processes, and hence to specify new forms of working and reporting relationship. No longer do the members of a project team have to meet in the same location to have a meeting. Instead, they can use groupware systems such as *Lotus Notes,* or perhaps video-conferencing links, to hold meetings even when the participants involved are dispersed across many locations.

The concept of business process reengineering (BPR) relates to the fundamental rethinking and redesign of business processes in order to achieve dramatic improvements in performance (Hammer and Champy, 1993). Such performance improvements are frequently achieved through the adoption of downsized, client/server computing infrastructures running groupware applications. Computer-based communications systems now frequently short-circuit traditional hierarchical structures, whilst providing the glue to hold together flatter, more dynamic and increasingly project-centred organizations. The teams that work on such projects even have the opportunity to become 'virtual' in nature, being tied together via CMC infrastructures rather than due to their proximity to a common working location. In future many employees may no longer have to travel to a place work, instead connecting into their organizational computer system from either a home PC or via a portable computer link whilst out in the field.

Even for those employees who will continue to work in an office, the computer-enabled reengineering of business may hold many changes in store. As managers come to appreciate that office buildings constitute their most expensive and most under-utilized asset (Lloyd, 1990), pressure will mount to use workspace more effectively. As illustrated in Example 1.2, one possible model for the reengineered 'office of the future' has already been created by the Digital Equipment Corporation. Within, no longer do workers 'own' a particular desk or PC. Instead, such

Example 1.2 Reengineering the office at Digital
(adapted from *Business Update* DEC 1993).

When designing its new Stockholm office, Digital Equipment Corporation (DEC) created what many have termed the 'office of the future'. Recognizing that the office is a place to meet others and to exchange information, and that such activities may be constrained by placing employees in individual offices, the company opted for a large, open-plan environment. Within, permanent desks have been abandoned, and instead computer terminals are freely available to anybody who wants to use them. Rather than occupying permanent desk space, however, the workstations pull down from the ceiling on 'flexibars', to sail back out of the way when they are not required.

Glassed-in 'quiet space' is available in areas set aside for client meetings, whilst personal sets of drawers are used to store any individual possessions. All other space is communal. A large console known as 'the bridge' is located at one end of the office where desk-bound secretaries are seated at eye-level to those who may stroll up to them. Finally, all chairs are mobile and available in a wide variety of sizes and styles, with all telephones being cordless so that people can take calls where they like. In short, Digital's Stockholm office has re-thought everything from scratch. Office space has been cut by half, with sharing having permitted the level of desktop equipment to be cut by 60 per cent.

facilities are simply used as required within an airy, open-plan environment carefully festooned with the latest technological innovations. A more detailed exploration of computer-driven business process reengineering, and resultant new working practices, is provided in Chapter 6 and within Readings 11 and 13.

OVERVIEW

This chapter has reviewed the adoption and classification of computer systems across business today. It has also introduced the concepts of downsizing, client/server computing, groupware application and business process reengineering. Whilst each of these topics is returned to in depth in subsequent Chapters and Readings, it is important that readers feel comfortable with a general understanding of the terms before they progress further. Business IT is a discipline awash with technobabble. However some of it is important, and actually needs to be understood!

Computers now play a highly significant role within the key business functions of all large and the majority of small and medium-sized organizations. The working environments of many office employees, together with the nature of the tasks they execute, have and will continue to change as computing advances accrue across modern business. Managerial roles are also starting to evolve as IT enables new working practices, with fresh patterns of employer–employee relationship already starting to come on-line. As a result, organizational strategies and structures are evolving to ensure that the maximum competitive advantages may be reaped from increased computer adoption across all levels of organization. In the next chapter, the ways in which IT may be exploited as a competitive weapon in order to empower 'competitive advantage' come to be explored.

REVIEW AND DISCUSSION QUESTIONS

1. Distinguish between:

   - A data processing system
   - A management information system
   - A decision support system, and
   - An executive information system.

2. Identify the links between downsizing, client/sever computing, the development of groupware and business process reengineering.

3. Discuss the role(s) that computers may play within the following types of business organization:

   - A large supermarket chain
   - A mail order retailer
   - An airline
   - An insurance company.

REFERENCES

Alter, S. (1992) *Information Systems: A Management Perspective*, Reading MA:McGraw -Hill.

Barry, M. and Barr, B. (1994) 'The Electronic Frontier: Exploring and mapping Cyberspace', *Futures* 26(7): pp.699-712.

De Looze, S. (1994) *The Strategic and Cultural Impact on Business of Developments in Information Technology*, Dissertation presented in part-consideration for the degree of MBA.

DEC (1993) 'A More Natural Way of Working', *Business Update*, Issue 7: pp.6-7.

Glyn-Jones, F. (1995) 'The Groupware Grapevine', *Management Today* (April).

Hammer, M. and Champy, J. (1993) *Reengineering the Corporation*, New York: Harper Collins.

Lloyd, B. (1990) 'Office Productivity: Time for a Revolution', *Long Range Planning*, 23(1): pp.66-79.

Martin, C. and Powell, P. (1992) *Information Systems: A Management Perspective*, London: McGraw-Hill.

Taylor, P. (1995) 'Revolution in Computer Networking', *Financial Times Review: Information Technology* (7th June).

Tetzeli, R. (1994) 'Surviving Information Overload', *Fortune International*, 11th July.

Trimmer, D. (1993) *Downsizing: Strategies for Success in the Modern Computer World*, Wokingham: Addison-Wesley.

Wang, C. (1994) *Techno Vision: The executive's guide to understanding and managing information technology*, New York: McGraw-Hill.

2 EMPOWERING COMPETITIVE ADVANTAGE

KEY CONCEPTS INTRODUCED

Automation and augmentation ■ Routine and creative work
■ Competitive advantage and Porter's competitive
strategies ■ The value chain ■ Cost reduction ■ Product
differentiation ■ New purchaser–supplier relationships ■
Increasing switching costs ■ Raising entry barriers ■ New
product genres ■ Changing industry structures ■ The
computer applications matrix ■ Balancing the applications
mix.

Increasingly, information technology is being used to position companies within their marketplaces so that they may outperform their competitors. In order to understand how IT may be used to reap such 'competitive advantage', it is first necessary to investigate how computers empower increases in both the *efficiency* and the *effectiveness* of business operations. Increases in efficiency due to computer adoption occur when tasks — such as preparing a set of accounts or wage slips — can be fully or partially *automated*. Increases in effectiveness, on the other hand, occur when non-automatable activities — such as decision making — come to be assisted or *augmented* by IT application.

AUTOMATION AND AUGMENTATION

In their investigation of the differences between task process automation and augmentation within the 'computerized workplace', Larson and Zimney suggest the consideration of an activity spectrum ranging from work that is wholly 'routine' to that which is totally 'creative'. They note that routine work activities are highly repetitive, accommodate large volumes, have a high frequency of use, and as such are highly predictable. In contrast, creative work has a craft-style, 'one-of-a-kind appearance', with each creative activity having a low volume and frequency of occurrence (1990: 10).

The significance of isolating work activities into the routine and the creative is that, whilst routine work may be automated via the application of a computerized data processing system or OAS, creative work is incapable of being automated.

This said, creative work may be augmented via the application of computerized systems for decision support. There is still a myth, however, that routine work is the only type of work to exist within many businesses (Larson and Zimney, 1990: 9). Clearly if such a belief is not dispelled, then problems will arise in reaping benefits from computer application, as attempts will be made to automate creative task activities that can in reality only be augmented.

OPERATIONAL COMPUTER CAPACITIES

In a purely operational capacity, there are three key benefits that may result from computer application. These may be listed as being:

- To improve cost-effectiveness
- To increase business growth potential, or
- To assist in the decision making process.

The role of computers in improving cost-effectiveness is clear and straight-forward. As discussed in the first chapter, all OAS and DP systems are designed to automate routine, repetitive tasks such as document preparation, accounts processing, order entry and stock control. Further examples of *strategic* computer application for cost reduction are examined later in this chapter.

When it comes to increasing business growth potential, computers come into their own over human beings by being able to increase their throughput capacity with little or no cost overhead. As an example, consider the processing of a payroll run. For an accounts clerk working manually, the time needed to process 200 wage slips would probably be nearly double that needed to process 100. Run the payroll on a computer, however, and it may only take 10% longer to process the extra 100 slips. This would be due to the fact that most of the time involved in running payroll would be spent in setting-up the system (threading the printer and so forth), rather than in actually printing the output (Barnatt, 1994: 97). It should therefore be clear that with key organizational systems computerized, administrative restrictions upon the growth of the business are greatly curtailed. Additionally, as discussed in Chapter 6 and Reading 13, computer-mediated communication (CMC) technologies may now be employed to allow thousands of people to work together cohesively either nationally or internationally. Indeed, as businesses become larger, it becomes impossible to coordinate their functioning without complex communications infrastructures. As noted by Haeckel and Nolan in Reading 12, computer systems are increasingly becoming the tendons that hold the skeleton and muscles of many companies together.

Finally, the capability of computers to help out in decision making, returns us to the poles of routine verses creative work. Many decision tasks — such as reordering supplies when stocks fall to pre-determined levels — may be isolated as routine work processes. As such they may be fully automated by rule-based decision support systems. Other decision types, however, are creative, and may only be augmented. For example, decisions regarding the choice of colours, graphics and typeface for a book cover are subjective, and will *never* be able to be automated. They can be augmented, however, with graphics and desktop publishing (DTP) software used to assist the designer, editor, and other personnel, in the production of mock-ups from which they may select their final choices. To cite an entirely different kind of example, in Reading 10 a Director involved in the implementation of a new hospital information system explains how:

> . . . management rests so much on good information. And if we get the information right in terms of content, accuracy, and above all its timeliness and relevance, then that gives us a much better basis for making good decisions (Reading 10, p.149).

COMPETITIVE ADVANTAGE AND COMPETITIVE STRATEGIES

Now that their basic operational business capabilities have been detailed, it becomes possible to examine how computers may be employed in a strategic capacity in order to bestow competitive advantage. The concept of competitive advantage relates to the strength of each firm's particular profile of competencies within its marketplace. This set of competencies will determine what makes that company's products or services stand out from those of its competition. It may be, for example, that the firm offers the cheapest goods available, that its products are technically the most advanced within its market, or that it excels in reliability, customer service or after sales support.

The most famous analyst of competitive advantage is Michael Porter, whose books *Competitive Strategy* (1980) and *Competitive Advantage* (1985) are required reading for all serious students of strategic management. Porter contends that, in order to make its products or services outperform those of its competitors, a business needs to choose between three basic (or 'generic') competitive strategies, by either:

- Becoming the lowest-cost producer within its industry,
- Differentiating its products/services from those of its rivals, or
- Targeting its products/services within narrow market niches, which may be selected either on the basis of cost or via product/service differentiation.

Taking the computer industry as an example, hardware manufacturers adopting each of the above competitive strategies are fairly easy to isolate. Consumer electronics giant Amstrad, for example, has long played a lowest-cost competitive strategy, firstly with its highly successful PCW word processor range, and subsequently by offering a variety of basic but cost-effective IBM compatible PCs.

Apple Computer, on the other hand, has played a product differentiation strategy. Apple's Macintosh and PowerMac PCs are largely incompatible with the industry-wide IBM PC standard, yet are differentiated by the superb, user-friendly 'feel' of their graphical operating system, a very high build quality, and high-performance graphics. A company playing a target-niche strategy selected on the basis of cost has been Commodore, with its range of Amiga PCs. Especially suited for desktop video (DTV) work, Amiga hard and softwares have been offered at a fraction of the price of those of other DTV platforms. As a result, the Amiga has been extremely widely used to enable low-cost graphics production on TV shows such as *Babylon 5*, *Star Trek: Deep Space Nine* and *SeaQuest DSV*. Finally, hardware manufacturer Cray continues to target a niche market by product differentiation rather than by price, supplying multi-million dollar supercomputers for extremely high-power applications.

COMPUTER TECHNOLOGY IN THE VALUE CHAIN

Another critical concept from Porter is that of the value chain. This refers to the progression of activities within a firm which may be isolated as adding specific value to its outputs. The more value added at each stage, the more competitive a firm's resultant products or services are likely to be. Furthermore, if a firm can add value at any stage that cannot be added by its competitors, then it is likely to attain significant competitive advantage. Figure 2.1 illustrates a simple three-stage value chain for a manufacturing firm.

Using value-chain analysis, the significance of particular technologies (including computer technologies) in the attainment of competitive advantage may be highlighted. As Porter notes:

> A firm, as a collection of activities, is a collection of technologies. Technology is embodied in every value activity in a firm, and technological change can affect competition through its impact on virtually any activity . . . [as] . . . every value activity uses some technology to combine purchased inputs and human resources to produce some output (Porter, 1985: 166).

Today, computer technology may be employed by most firms within most stages of their value chains. With reference to the three value processes isolated in Figure 2.1, computer aided design (CAD), and/or virtual reality (VR) systems, may quite possibly be applied to augment the first stage of innovation and design. The production process may then be automated via computer aided manufacturing (CAM). Finally, marketing and distribution may benefit from the application of electronic data interchange (EDI) linkages. A more detailed explanation of each of these three areas of computer application in the value chain is presented in Example 2.1. The application of CAD, CAM and other advanced manufacturing technology (AMT) systems in reaping competitive advantage is also discussed by Senker and Senker in Reading 7.

Figure 2.1 A manufacturing value chain.

STRATEGIC COMPUTER APPLICATION

Now that the concepts of competitive advantage and the value chain have been introduced, the strategic application of computers in business may be more fully explored. Today, the use of computers in a strategic, in addition to an operational, capacity, is rapidly increasing. Arguably, this is because computer systems may be used to create competitive advantage in so many ways. As has already been noted, at the most basic level computer technology may simply be employed in order to reduce costs across different value chain stages. As a result, the use of computers may also come to enhance the differentiation of a company's products. Furthermore, computer systems may permit a proliferation of new purchaser–supplier relationships, build-in switching costs, raise barriers to entry, permit the development and distribution of new product and service genres, and, as a consequence, impact upon the structures of industries themselves.

ENABLING COST REDUCTION

As highlighted by Porter, one strategy for obtaining competitive advantage is to decide to become the overall lowest cost producer within an industry. Another is to target a niche market on the basis of a low final selling price. If either of these competitive strategies are adopted, then computer technology is invariably applied to reduce costs across the value chain. In manufacturing firms, cost reductions most usually arise from the automation of routine processes in production and from routine office work automation, as previously discussed. However in service orientated industries, whilst OAS and DP systems can again reduce basic administrative costs, other forms of computer application also need to be considered.

Over the past decade, computer systems have been widely applied within many service sectors. In banking and financial services, employment levels have plummeted in recent years, due in no small measure to the growing use of cashpoint ATMs (automated teller machines) and computer network facilities. In retail chains, examples of cost-cutting IT application most notably include the introduction of EPoS bar code scanners to reduce costs and to improve customer through-flow, as discussed in the last chapter. In creative industries such as design,

Example 2.1 Computer application across the value chain.

Augmenting innovation and design

Computers may augment the creative processes of innovation and design by allowing people to freely experiment, to conceptualize their ideas more easily, and by enabling the rapid realization of accurate drawings and plans. Spreadsheet software can be used to run 'what-if?' cost scenarios for new production ideas to test their feasibility, whilst drawing and modelling programs allow designers to present clients and/or management with stylish concept visuals.

Most computer aided design (CAD) software packages now allow for the translation of 2-D plans into 3-D models, which may subsequently be viewed from any angle. Some packages additionally permit 3-D models to be coloured, textured, and rendered as photorealistic images. A few can even place the designer within their model as part of a virtual reality (VR) simulation.

Automating production

Computer aided manufacturing (CAM) systems integrate computer technologies with mechanical robots and manufacturing plant in order to automate the physical labours of production. Many CAM systems are capable of using data directly from CAD software to control production. As a result, specification changes may feed through directly from the design office to the factory floor with no human involvement required in the resetting or recalibration of machinery.

Programmable robotic car assembly lines are perhaps the first form of CAM to spring to mind, and have indeed greatly reduced production costs, and increased operational flexibility, for many automobile manufacturers. However, CAM systems are common across many forms of industry, with computers now controlling the manufacture of items as diverse as pharmaceuticals, food, white goods, and even computers themselves. Even when the actual process of production is not itself automated, CAM systems often direct the flow of components around a factory by controlling the stocking and movement of robotic conveyors.

Assisting marketing and distribution

The dominant computer technology for assisting product marketing and distribution is electronic data interchange, or EDI. EDI systems allow for the transfer of structured data between computers in two or more companies in a directly usable format (Peppard, 1993: 145). Sharing data via EDI removes the necessity for its rekeying when it is passed between organizations. In the UK, Tescos has long been an EDI pioneer. When stocks in its warehouses run low, orders are now dispatched electronically to the majority of its suppliers via EDI, from whom they are directly dispatched with minimal human involvement.

publishing and television, computers have also come to play a major role in cost reduction. Specifically, the introduction of DTP and DTV systems have rendered many past craft skills and cumbersome manual processes obsolete, particularly within smaller organizations. In other industries such as tourism, travel and entertainment, advanced on-line information systems have enabled cost reduction by optimizing the most effective utilization of capacity. Undoubtably the most cited example of the latter concerns the introduction of the SABRE computerized reservation system (CRS) at American Airlines, as detailed in Example 2.2. A more thorough evaluation of IT application across different industrial sectors is again provided by Senker and Senker in Reading 7.

AIDING PRODUCT DIFFERENTIATION

If a company chooses not to go down the road of reducing costs in order to gain competitive advantage, then it will need to differentiate its products either across the whole marketplace, or within a specific sectorial niche. Usually this involves producing the highest quality products or services possible, and/or providing them through novel distribution channels. Again, these are both areas of activity in which computer application can play a significant role.

The development of the SABRE customer reservations system at American Airlines not only served to reduce the company's costs. Additionally, SABRE permitted the airline, together with travel agencies accessing its system, to offer higher quality of service than their competitors by improving their provision of information to travellers. As a result, American Airlines' services were differentiated from those of other market players. In a similar vein, worldwide tourist operator Club Med invested in a state-of-the-art reservations booking system to integrate information flows across its hotel, travel and holiday village operations. The computer system is viewed by its directors as strategic, in that it increases the flexibility of Club Med's prices and products, hence differentiating them from those of its competitors (Daniels, 1994: 61-62).

Computer application may also empower the development of new sales and distribution channels or means of customer service. Banking, shopping and insurance services offered over the telephone are a prime example here, as they have only been made possible due to the development of real-time computer databases capable of processing customer queries upon demand. The international conglomeration of computer networks known as the Internet is also starting to be used as a new retailing and information distribution medium. With the development of the world-wide web graphical interface to the Internet, companies such as the Internet Bookstore can differentiate their products from those of their competitors by offering on-line search and sales facilities. A more detailed discussion of the business implications of the expansion of the Internet is provided within Chapter 6.

Example 2.2 SABRE reservations at American Airlines
(sourced from Hopper, 1990 and from Rochester and Rochester,
1991: 247).

The computerized reservations system, SABRE, was developed in the late 1950s by American Airlines in order to cope with a volume of reservations beyond the capacity of any manual system. One major function of the system is to improve the company's *yield management* — the process of establishing different price tariffs for different seats on a flight, and their allocation for revenue maximization. In order to keep aircraft as full as possible, SABRE is programmed to carefully control the number of discounted seats available in the months, days and hours before each take-off. All reservations and seat price amendments are updated in real time, and as such are continuously available on-line to all travel agents and airline personnel.

When first up-and-running in 1963, the system annually handled data derived from 85,000 telephone calls, 40,000 confirmed reservations, and 20,000 ticket sales. By 1990, SABRE was handling nearly 2000 messages per second and creating more than 500,000 passenger records per day. Yield management software had also been developed to a point where historical booking patterns were being reviewed up to a year in advance, with constantly updated analysis of competitors' fares and bookings.

American Airlines' reliance on SABRE was demonstrated in 1987 when a programming error was inadvertently introduced into the system coding. For a period of three months, discounted seats were not properly reported, and passengers chose cheaper seats on other airlines. Over the period, estimates placed American Airlines losses due to the programming error at around $50 million.

EMPOWERING NEW RELATIONSHIPS

Via the use of EDI and other computer-mediated communications (CMC) media, the nature of the trading patterns between organizations may also be drastically upgraded. Since the mid-1980s, the capacity to transmit on-line data between companies has allowed for the development of automated order processing systems, automated materials handing and warehousing, and the restructuring of distributions channels (Porter, 1985: 321). Additionally, in the 1990s, we are witness to time-saving, real-time processing links between firms and their clients, and to the sharing of *knowledge* in addition to information via common data models. In the UK insurance industry, for example, a system called *BrokerNet* allows for the direct transfer of quotes and policy details between insurance providers and the independent financial advisers (IFAs) who liaise with customers. Such 'live business transfers' remove the need for participating IFAs to fill-in and mail paper documents to the insurer. The speed and quality of the service provided to their customers is thereby increased (Wheeler, 1993).

In the USA, retail chain Wal-Mart has gone a stage further in applying computer technology to change the nature of its relationships with supplying firms. As detailed by Haeckel and Nolan in Reading 12, Wal-Mart and jeans manufacturer Wrangler now electronically share not only sales data, but additionally 'learning loop' software to interpret it. The knowledge derived from this system enables inventory operations to be optimized, with the occurrence of stock outs greatly reduced.

As well as permitting new relationships with other firms, CMC developments are also supercharging patterns of organizational interconnection with domestic consumers. Home banking and interactive home shopping services are just two of the developments contingent upon the provision of highly advanced computerized systems. Further discussion of the application of computers to realize new organizational relationships appears in Chapter 6, and within Readings 11, 12 and 13.

INCREASING SWITCHING COSTS

Whilst systems for EDI and common data analysis may permit new and more cost effective supplier–purchased relationships, they can also lead to a greater dependence upon increasingly captive supply channels. In short, the more closely two organizations interlink their computer systems, the less likely they are to cease trading together.

Setting up EDI or other CMC links between two organizations invariably involves the upfront commitment of considerable technical and administrative resources. Once such as link is up-and-running, both parties will therefore wish to use it for a reasonable period of time in order to recoup their set-up costs. A retail chain that has just initiated an EDI link with one drinks manufacturer, for example, may find that the costs of switching to supplies from another firm become prohibitive due to the time and resources they have invested.

By increasing the switching costs of retailers or other purchasers of their products, companies may be capable of reaping long-term competitive advantages over other firms within their industry. Once a purchaser is 'tied' to a supplier via EDI or other CMC investments, the supplier's bargaining power to raise their prices, or to alter product specifications, is almost invariably increased. After all, purchasers will be loathe to write off their investment in the EDI or other link, and hence will tolerate small price rises or other changes that would previously have made them think about switching to another supplier. This sort of example clearly illustrates the potential strategic benefit of first-mover investment in IT for many organizations. In the short-run costs may be considerable. However, in the medium- and long-term, the competitive benefits may be even greater.

RAISING ENTRY BARRIERS

IT purchaser–supplier alliances, such as that previously noted between Wal-Mart and Wrangler, not only render the involved suppliers competitive advantages against existing competitors by raising switching costs for their customers. Additionally, they also raise entry barriers before others wishing to enter the market.

Barriers to entry exist where there are impediments to new firms wishing to commence trading in markets already successfully exploited by others. Clearly, if existing market players have invested heavily in IT, then organizations keen on entry to their market will also need to do so. In practice, however, this can prove extremely difficult. Just imagine the costs and logistical problems that would be faced by a new bank or building society trying to set up its own, independent cashpoint network. Even if this feat *could* be accomplished in every high street, customers would still have to be enticed away from their *existing* banks. Just as firms find that their switching costs increase as their reliance on computer technology grows, so consumers today get increasingly 'hooked' into high-tech relationships with cutting-edge organizations. As another example, by putting computers into cars, manufacturers have not only improved performance, but have also guaranteed on-going business for their dealers. When vehicles need servicing, it is increasingly likely that only garages tied to the original manufacturer will be equipped with the computerized diagnostic tools necessary to access the data contained within today's sophisticated automobile electronics.

NEW PRODUCT GENRES

As with the introduction of many new forms of technology, the application of computers in business has led to the development of entirely new forms of products and services in addition to the improvement of existing ones. For example, companies who build up large customer databases may be able to sell on such information to other firms for use in product mailings. Similarly, newspapers, magazines and libraries can now offer access to their archives and information over computer network links. Already developments in multimedia are changing the world of publishing, with the latest generation of school children expecting encyclopedias and other references sources to exist upon CD-ROM rather than as mighty paper tomes.

By the turn of the century, the provision of most technical and academic information is likely to be in an electronic format, rather than relying upon the distribution of forest-guzzling pulp. Many opportunities to innovate new forms of product and service will be developed as a result. One looming growth industry is likely to involve the creation of *software agents* — personal electronic 'slaves' that will seek-out information based upon the evolving 'profiles' of their human 'masters'. News International hopes to have such 'retriever' agents to search its vast libraries of 'digital product', whilst Apple Computer spin-off General Magic has conceived a control language —*Telescript* — to permit software agents to work together in ensembles in order to undertake electronic transactions on behalf of either people or organizations. Other software agents will be able to sort electronic mail messages so that their masters only need to read the ones in which they will be most interested (Barnatt, 1995: 99-105). Further information upon software agents is provided within Chapter 6.

As already noted, the Internet's world-wide web interface is already fostering novel, differentiated forms of product, advertising and retailing. Innovative working genres, bringing with them their own unique competitive advantages, are also being developed. In particular, the adoption of sophisticated computerized home-working (or 'telecommuting') systems, together with video conferencing links, will permit services to be rendered across previously unsurmountable geographic boundaries. Many firms will reap considerable cost advantages by having some or all of their employees distributed in remote locations. Virtual reality modelling is also expected to be a boom industry early next century, opening up entire marketplaces for its cyberspace pioneers. The discussion of such developments is taken further in Chapter 6, and in Readings 12 and 13.

CHANGING INDUSTRY STRUCTURES

As noted by Porter in his famous 'five forces' model (1980), industry structures will evolve — usually to the advantage of those firms driving such evolution — as and when customer and supplier relationships change, raised entry barriers exclude potential new entrants, and differentiated substitute products alter the balance of power against existing competitors. All of the strategic applications of computer technology outlined to this point therefore have the potential to change the very *nature* of the industries within which all market players compete. Computers change the rules of business, levelling some playing fields, whilst raising mountains and sinking gullies across others.

Computer application is also enabling competition on an increasingly global basis. CMC systems provide the only efficient means of linking teams of workers, distribution channels, information flows, and other value chain elements, across countries, geographies and time zones. For most organizations, a strategy of globalization is contingent upon advanced computer application.

By permitting the development of *programmable* CAD/CAM and AMT systems, computer technology is also playing a critical role in shifting industrial structures away from those based upon *mass production,* and towards new structures contingent upon *flexible specialization.* For many years, the only option for companies wishing to service large markets was to produce a narrow range of products mass-produced in bulk by dedicated plant. Now that plant is programmable, smaller runs of more differentiated product are possible. Whereas Henry Ford produced his model 'T' in 'any colour so long as it was black', cars on modern product lines are now often tagged and customized to individual customer specification. The reengineering of business away from mass-production is eating away at the very pillars of traditional industrial logic. Both driven by, and driving, more and more advanced computer application, the industries of tomorrow are almost certain to appear very different from those we all know today.

THE COMPUTER APPLICATIONS MATRIX

With so many potential strategic applications for computers in business, it becomes important to find a means of classifying the role played by each IT system within its organization. To enable such classification, a portfolio matrix categorizing IT systems into one of four quadrants is often utilized. Such a grid is illustrated in Figure 2.2, and classifies systems as being either *core operational*, *strategic*, having *future potential*, or as providing business *support*. The basis of this matrix is derived from the work of McFarlan (1984), although numerous other writers (for example Edwards et al, 1991 and Peppard, 1993) have presented their own variants. The use of a strategic grid for information resource management is also detailed by McFarlan and Nolan in Reading 9.

Core operational computer applications are those which have become vital to the running of the business. They will therefore include DP and MIS systems for inventory and production control and order management. Moving up, strategic systems are those reaping the greatest competitive advantages, and which will prove most vital to continued business success. Strategic computer systems provide for the greatest product differentiations, or the largest degrees of cost competitiveness.

In the top-right quadrant of the computer applications grid, future potential systems are those which are innovative, and which as such are likely to be developed to reap key strategic benefits. They are the strategic stars of the future, today including systems for advanced video conferencing and for the exploitation of virtual reality. Finally, support systems improve operational and managerial effectiveness, but are not critical to organizational survival. Payroll and accounts systems are likely to be listed in this quadrant (Peppard, 1993: 68). If such systems temporarily fail, whilst a degree of chaos and internal dissatisfaction may ensue, production, design and customer service functions will not be immediately disrupted and business is unlikely to be lost.

As within the similar Boston Consulting Group (BCG) quadrant grid, applications are expected to rotate around the computer applications matrix over time. Achieving a *balance* of systems across the grid is therefore of greatest strategic importance. To take banking as an example, twenty years ago the development of a network of cashpoint ATMs could only be viewed as having future potential. A little under ten years later, and cashpoint systems were strategic, differentiating the services of one bank or building society from another. Today, cashpoints systems are core operational — vital systems upon which all banks and building societies depend. In ten or twenty years time, however, cashpoints may be little

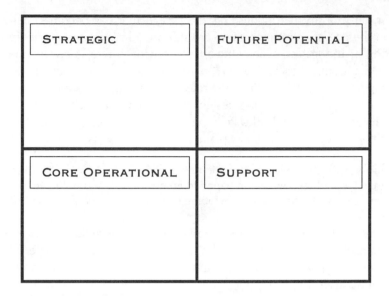

Figure 2.2 The computer applications matrix.

more than support systems. After all, if (as many analysis predict) the majority of consumers come to conduct the majority of their transactions electronically via debit cards and over the telephone and computer networks, then the failure of a bank's cashpoint system would become an annoyance rather than a major inconvenience to its customers.

BALANCING THE APPLICATIONS MIX

Hardly surprisingly, maintaining effective core operational and support computer systems, whilst simultaneously reaping competitive advantage from the latest strategic systems, *and* innovating those with future potential, may well become a nightmare. With computer and communications technologies evolving so quickly, nobody can predict with any degree of certainty which future potential applications to endorse, and hence which systems will become strategic and subsequently core operational in the years ahead. Standards wars continue to proliferate in computer software, hardware, digital communications and multimedia. Many firms are therefore destined to plump for the wrong technological bandwagon. Perhaps for this reason, some successful organizations choose not to be first movers in the adoption of new computer technologies. Instead, large firms such as Asda, ICI and Grand Metropolitan are reported to be 'early followers' rather than pioneers on the cutting-edge (Management Science America, 1990: 42).

Even in an industry like publishing and design that has become totally dependant upon the use of computers, there are still mixed feelings as to the importance of investing in the fastest, state-of-the-art equipment. There is always the risk, for example, that companies taking on board new systems too far ahead of their clients' expectations are less likely to maximize the payback on their hardware. As the Managing Director of one design consultancy puts it: 'you have to tip-toe through all the bells and whistles keeping a very clear picture of what you need', whilst another Creative Director explains that:

> My philosophy is that I want to be a pioneer in every area . . . [of this business] . . . other than technology, where I'm happy to come second, and not have to pay for costly mistakes that others can make for me (*Creative Technology*, 1995: 27).

The above quote indicates how important it is to appreciate *where* within the computer applications matrix each of a company's systems is located. If *all* of a firm's systems can be classified as strategic or future potential (and in some high-tech industries this is not uncommon), then problems may well be in store. There is nothing wrong in using 'old' and 'obsolete' computer technology for core operational and support business functions. As an example, old 286 and 386 PCs running DOS-based word processors and spreadsheets continue to be the most cost-effective for a great many organizations. Such firms *could* upgrade all of their hardware and software to 'modern' 486 and Pentium systems running the latest *Windows*™ packages, yet this would be highly unlikely to prove cost–effective.

As discussed in Chapter 5, cost–benefit analysis is critical in new systems development, especially if the systems concerned are core operational or support, rather than of strategic or future potential value. In the former two categories, paybacks have to be immediate. Gaining competitive advantage from computer application should *never* involve investing in the 'latest' software and hardware gizmos for the sake of it. As Chapter 3 explains, business needs should *always* drive technological requirements, and not the other way around.

OVERVIEW

This chapter has outlined the main arenas of computer application associated with the attainment of competitive advantage. Reading 7 provides more detail upon several of the issues discussed, and should be consulted for an increased understanding of the topic area. As has been noted in the text, Readings 11, 12 and 13 also explore some of the concepts covered, as well as offering additional practical examples.

Whilst across many organizations, business computer application has undoubtedly proved critical to current success, the management of IT is most usually complex and often problematic. IT personnel and other members of staff invariably have different backgrounds and opinions as to what is best. Developments such as downsizing are also causing old traditions to be questioned, whilst new systems are often delivered late, over budget, and sometimes fail to meet specification. There is also increasing employee resentment of the technology-driven restructuring of many working relationships. These four sets of key managerial issues are addressed in sequence within the remaining chapters of the text. However, in a sense, each remaining chapter may be viewed as a sub-topic within the wider discipline of attempting to reap competitive advantage from computer application. If computer application did not bestow enormous business benefits, then it would not be instigated. That businesses now spend more on computer and communications technologies than on traditional production plant (Stewart, 1994), only serves to indicate how important IT systems are, and how critical the managerial issues arising from their application have become.

REVIEW AND DISCUSSION QUESTIONS

1. Distinguish between the use of computers to automate and to augment task processes.

2. Explain the concepts of 'competitive advantage' and the 'value chain'.

3. Provide examples of the use of computer technology to:

   - Enable cost reduction
   - Provide product differentiation
   - Raise entry barriers
   - Develop new product genres

4. Pick an industry or organization, decide how it may be applying IT to reap competitive advantage, and place each of its applications within a computer applications matrix grid.

REFERENCES

Barnatt, C. 1994 *The Computers in Business Blueprint*, Oxford: Blackwell Business.

Barnatt, C. 1995 *Cyber Business: Mindsets for a Wired Age*, Chichester: John Wiley & Sons.

Creative Technology (1995) 'Who Needs More Technology?', pp.24-27 (January).

Daniels, N.C. (1994) *Information Technology: The Management Challenge*, Wokingham: Addison-Wesley.

Edwards, C., Ward, J. and Bytheway, A. (1991) *The Essence of Information Systems*, London: Prentice Hall.

Hopper, M.D. (1990) 'Rattling SABRE — New Ways to Compete on Information' *Harvard Business Review* (May-June).

Larson, R.W. and Zimney, D.J. (1990) *The White Collar Shuffle: Who Does What in Today's Computerized Workplace?*, New York: Amacom.

Management Science America (1990) 'Excellence and the IT Factor: Information Technology Inside Excellent Companies in Britain' *Journal of Information Technology*, 5(1).

McFarlan, F.W. (1984) 'Information Technology Changes the Way You Compete', *Harvard Business Review* (May-June): pp.98-103.

Peppard, J. (1993) *IT Strategy for Business*, London: Pitman.

Porter, M.E. (1980) *Competitive Strategy*, New York: The Free Press.

Porter, M.E. (1985) *Competitive Advantage*, New York: The Free Press.

Rochester, J.B. and Rochester, R. (1991) *Computers for People: concepts and applications*, Homewood, ILL: Irwin.

Stewart, T. (1994) 'The Information Age in Charts', *Fortune International* (4th April).

Wheeler, R. (1993) *Brokers Monthly and Insurance Adviser* (November).

3 BRIDGING THE DISCONNECT

KEY CONCEPTS INTRODUCED

The disconnect ■ Information systems and information technology ■ Business/IT career structures ■ Supplier account control ■ The management of computer personnel ■ CEO/CIO complaints ■ The disconnect's increasing significance ■ IT on the front line ■ IT skills for managers.

UNIVAC, the first computer designed for business application, was delivered to the US Census Bureau less than half a century ago. Since those early, glowing-valve-technology days, there have invariably been tensions between the technical people charged with maintaining and programming computers, and the business managers eager to reap the benefits of computerization. Members of IT staff have often come to view employees in other departments as naïve and ignorant with regard to computer application. With parallel blinkers, managers in business functions, such as production, marketing and finance, have evolved an increasing scepticism towards 'techies with no business sense' who have so often failed to deliver highly expensive computing 'advances' on time and within budget. As Trimmer succinctly encapsulates, 'the relationship between the IT department and the rest of the company has not been a happy one' (1993: 1).

Within his entertaining and informative book *Techno Vision* (1994), Charles Wang of Computer Associates specifically explores the rift between 'IT people' on the one hand, and 'business people' upon the other. Wang goes on to label the gulf between these two groups as the 'disconnect', which he defines as:

> . . . a conflict, pervasive yet unnatural, that has misaligned the objectives of executive managers and technologists and that impairs or prevents organizations from obtaining a cost-effective return from their investment in information technology (Wang, 1994: 1).

This chapter explores the concept of the disconnect — its roots, its implications, and the importance of adopting strategies designed to heal its rift. No longer, as in days gone by, are computers located solely in hermetically-sealed back rooms. Instead, computers now occupy most desks, many briefcases, some jacket pockets, and in a few instances provide customers with their primary interface with an organization. It is therefore strategically suicidal to differentiate 'IT people' and 'business people' across the organizations of the late 1990s.

RIFTS AND TENSIONS

Reporting upon his detailed study of the 'office revolution' at the turn-of-the-decade, Robert Heller noted that there was already a cultural divide emerging within the workplace. Across its chasm, informed 'datacrat' IT evangelists were parading a flow of new electronic ideas, whilst 'uninformed conformists' failed to see the relevance, or at least the full potential, of computer technology (Heller, 1990: 9). Today, ignorance of the potential operational and strategic application of computers in business is still remarkably widespread, particularly within smaller organizations. Even in 1995, around half of small firms did not consider themselves to computer literate, whilst more than two-thirds admitted to problems in keeping up with IT advances (*Daily Telegraph*, 13th April: 33). Additionally, as Andrew D. Brown discusses in Reading 10, there is also often a problem of 'legitimacy' with IT systems, which are often viewed as 'expensive to purchase, difficult to implement, time consuming to operate, and of marginal significance to the well being of the organization and the pursuit of its mission' (Brown, 1995 — Reading 10, pp.143–144).

Even when there *is* broad agreement as to the importance of computer application within a business, tensions frequently emerge surrounding its management and implementation. Invariably, when new IT systems are to be introduced the stakes are high. Mistakes are likely to be costly not only financially, but also in terms of curtailed promotion prospects for those associated with the all-too-common failures of IT implementation. As detailed in Chapter 5, almost every company has a horror story to tell when it comes to systems development.

The paybacks from computer application also tend to be extremely unpredictable and hard to measure. With reference back to the computer applications matrix as presented in the previous chapter (Figure 2.2), it difficult to foresee when and if 'future potential' IT developments will become either strategic or core operational. This again can lead to tensions surrounding computer application, as it becomes problematic to decide where resources will be most effectively invested. Additionally, whilst most managing directors have some working knowledge of most other business functions (marketing, production, finance and so forth), many are ignorant and weary of the alarming complexities that surround computing advances. Managing directors therefore have to rely far more blindly upon the head of their IT department than upon the directors of most other business functions. The role of top management with regard to IT projects therefore tends to be far more 'hands off', with technical staff having to be highly trusted to make the right decisions. Once again, the potential for a strained and stressful business/IT relationship emerges, particularly when a project is failing to accrue the progress desired.

INFORMATION SYSTEMS
AND INFORMATION TECHNOLOGY

Whilst terms and definitions may be debated, few analysts with practical business experience would deny the existence of a 'disconnect' between IT and other departments across many organizations. As already noted, some tensions may be associated with the nature of IT itself. Others have resulted from more blatant mismanagement. To explore the latter concept, it is first prudent to distinguish between the oft-confused concepts of *information systems* and *information technology*.

In general, an information system (IS) may be defined as any 'combination of work practices, information, people *and information technologies* organized to accomplish organizational goals' (Alter, 1992: 7). From such a definition, it becomes immediately apparent that all forms of IT hardware and software constitute only one segment of the much broader categorization of IS. IT by itself is only a tool to be applied in a wider human and organizational context. IT by itself is of little value to a business. Rather, IT only comes to play a *useful* role when applied by human beings to enable the realization and completion of business processes that will further the goals of the organization.' Even in the mid-1990s, we have yet to witness a computer turning itself on, creating a new product or service, bringing it to market, and boosting profits as a result. A company's management of its IT facilities should therefore be contingent upon the operational and strategic IS requirements of all of its other departmental functions.

The above paragraph may appear to have preached the very, very obvious. It is therefore surprising that the message it contains has for years been largely ignored. For decades, the strategy and management of many companies' IT departments has been allowed to drive wider IS requirements. End-users have simply been informed of their computing requirements, rather than having their own requests for IS support fulfilled. In other words, technology and 'expert' knowledge in IT has driven the planning and implementation of information systems, and not the other way around.

In the largely cash-rich, 'never had it so good' days of the 1950s, mainframe computers with flashing lights and whizzing spools of tape became symbols of corporate success. Subsequently, year-on-year increases in computing expenditure went largely unchallenged. In the 1960s and 1970s, whilst most other business functions had to keep at least one eye on efficiency, cost–benefit analysis in IT was generally notable by its absence. Technical staff in isolated mainframe facilities were simply left to decide the 'appropriate' computing requirements of the rest of the organization. Indeed, in a very real sense, it could be argued that the gulf between IT managers and business managers widened to such an extent that the tail clearly came to be wagging the dog (Wyles, 1992: 495).

Origins of the divide

Charles Wang believes that many of the tensions and misunderstandings of the disconnect today are historical. In particular, he traces the development of the disconnect to the different evolutionary pathways that have traditionally been taken by business and IT managers (1994: 9). Seldom have there been sidesteps available between the career ladders of business versus technical personnel — with studies repeatedly showing that IS personnel rarely break into the upper echelons of management (Lacity and Hirshheim, 1993: 200). Differentiated employment subcultures for 'business' and 'IT' personnel have therefore emerged, each protected by, and entrenched within, its own values and vocabularies. Whilst the managers of most business functions will share a common lexicon involving terms such as profit margins, cost effectiveness and customer-orientation, those responsible for IT are more likely to be concerned with technical specifications related to network bandwidths, server storage capacities, programming code and so forth. With IT people generally not speaking the same strategic, market-driven financial language of the rest of the organization, the fact that they have become isolated as a discrete employee subset has hardly been surprising.

Historically, IT departments and personnel have also tended to be physically separated from the rest of the organization. Indeed, when constructed in the 1950s and 1960s, the first corporate data centres often had to be purpose built to adhere to the stringent physical and environmental conditions required by the mass of expensive hardware to be housed within them. With both their hardware and their armies of technical employees isolated from the rest of the company in cool, plush isolation, it is no wonder that IT departments came to be viewed in awe and to be surrounded with a certain veil of 'magic' and mystique. In their early days, computers *were* amazing, with most business managers, along with the vast majority of the general public, having no *concept* of their true capabilities or operation. In some instances, the legitimacy of the relationship between the IT department and the rest of the organization thereby came to be reversed — with the 'perception inside the glass house' being that the 'the organization only existed to ensure the data center's continued survival' (Wang, 1994: 11).

Supplier account control

The system of proprietary *account control* operated by IBM and other major hardware vendors in the early days of computing also fuelled the development of the disconnect. Monopolistic mainframe and minicomputer manufacturers effectively came to control many corporate computing facilities, with their clients locked-in to single sources of hardware and software supply. From the point of view of the vendors of closed-architecture mainframe systems, it made perfect sense to keep business managers as ignorant as possible when it came to making IT decisions. In doing so, they ensured that their customers became totally dependant not only upon their systems, but also upon their expertise. As a result of their ignorance, business organizations simply had to cough up and purchase whatever their mainframe supplier told them they needed to buy. As one Information Services Director has been quoted:

> Twenty, 30 years ago, people didn't have to be technologists because the vendors backed up a dump truck to the data center door and unloaded it. They told you when the next upgrade was coming and you took it (Warren Harkness, cited in Wang, 1994: 12).

Managing computer personnel

A final factor that fuelled the disconnect's adolescence was a perception in certain quarters that members of IT staff were, by their very nature, 'unmanageable'. This view stems from the fact that, in the early days of computing, technophobic business managers clearly had *no idea* what the job of most hardware and software engineers actually entailed. Rather than seeking to find out, they simply inferred that 'managerial interference' in IT was uncalled for and could even prove detrimental. The stereotypical, pale-faced, awkwardly-anti-social 'techy geek' hunched over clattering keyboard was often deemed to be an eccentric, creative individual who worked better if left to his own mysterious devices. Even today, such beliefs still hold true in some quarters. For example, it has been reported that a blind eye is turned towards drug use by some programmers in top Silicon Valley computer companies due to an understanding that psychedelics constitute an essential aid in the creative process for certain computer personnel (Rushkoff, 1994: 47).

Whilst in theory it could be argued that placing IT staff and their departments upon a revered and mysterious pedestal provides the ultimate evidence of their importance to the company, in practice it just marginalizes their contribution. Today no business function can be managed in isolation from any other. Indeed, with developments in computer-mediated communications, IT systems can serve as the glue to bring together *all* business departments in order to optimize their contributions in amalgamation. Computer systems constitute the arteries of modern business. As a consequence, strategy in IS and IT have to be intertwined. No longer a back room activity, IT has risen to become an essential umbrella function whose input is required by all other departments. Computer personnel therefore have to be embraced within the overarching corporate culture of the entire organization.

SOURCES OF COMPLAINT

The tensions of the disconnect may be manifested in a variety of guises. After spending a year talking to 200 chief executive officers (CEOs) and chief information officers (CIOs) in the USA, Wang came up with two lists of common disconnect 'symptoms' (1994: 26-27). Firstly, there were the complaints that CEOs ('business people') made about the CIOs (or IT managers). In aggregate, the CEOs questioned were fed up with CIOs who:

- Only communicated in technical rather than business terms
- Lost sight of business needs when making IT decisions
- Remained ignorant of the needs of the customers of the business
- Did not 'protect' their CEO from IT suppliers
- Didn't keep key systems operational, and
- Harboured negative judgements about 'non-technical people'.

Conversely, however, it was noted that CIOs were frustrated with CEOs who:

- Were not comfortable sharing strategic objectives
- Refused to explore how IT could help to solve business problems
- Would only think of IT as useful for accounts automation
- Neglected to give IT mangers expanded business responsibilities
- Treated IT professionals as inferiors, and
- Were too embarrassed or insecure to ask technical questions.

It does not take a great social scientist to deduce that the above two lists derive from very similar foundations. The groups on either side of the disconnect clearly view themselves as misunderstood, undervalued, and marginalized by the 'opposing' party. Both CEOs and CIOs obviously want their counterparts to speak the same language and to take their ideas seriously. Perhaps most importantly, both groups clearly show an understanding of the important role that IT has to play in fulfilling business needs. They also both have an appreciation of how IT is likely to become more and more strategically important in the future.

In amalgamation, the problems of the disconnect highlighted within Wang's lists of symptoms are those of stereotyped perceptions and a lack of communication. Like most problems surrounding business computer application, the disconnect is in the main a managerial rather than a technical dilemma. It is therefore up to management to put the organization's house in order. Indeed, the requirement to do so is becoming increasingly urgent.

BRIDGING THE DIVIDE

Tensions between the IT department and the rest of the business have been quietly festering since the dawn of the corporate mainframe. However, it is only now, with the turn of the century on the horizon, that the disconnect's gulf is finally starting to bite. No longer do computers just empower information systems to support other business functions. As discussed in the previous chapter, and in several of the readings later in this book, computer technologies may now also be applied to reap substantial competitive advantages. Increasingly, computers link customers and suppliers and allow for more flexible working arrangements. Most business transactions and communications also now take place electronically, whilst most business information is processed upon screen and keyboard. Any organization within which the disconnect is still prevalent therefore risks being seriously competitively challenged.

Business and IT managers obviously need to get together if the perceptual problems of the disconnect are to be solved. The value of every IT activity within the organization undertaken needs to be assessed, and in particular the value of each IT activity intended to be meeting an external client need. Exactly what such business/IT cooperation will entail will vary from organization to organization. However in all instances, it is important that business strategies come to precede IS strategies, so that all IT decisions come to be made on a sound business basis. As detailed in Reading 8, one way forward is for detailed information systems plans to be prepared. For these to be successful, however, they will need to find support across all managerial and organizational levels. All parties must come to put business and customer needs first, yet with an understanding that computer application is now potentially of value within *every* organizational activity.

Today there are no longer any IT-neutral business decisions. This is not to say that computers *must* be utilized within every business process. What is important, however, is that computer application should now be *considered* in every instance — and only then rationally ruled out if inappropriate, rather than simply ignored. If such an attitude comes to be adopted across all organizational levels, then the magnitude of the disconnect will be greatly reduced. However the disconnect will not be fully healed until IT and business *skills* come to be shared across the gulf of its divide, with IT fully integrated into front line operations.

A SHIFTING FOCUS

Increasingly, organizational computer applications and personnel have to be allowed to emerge from the gloomy darkness of the back room. The focus for IT application also needs to shift from internal delivery to customer support. Many customers now have their relations with many organizations mediated not by sales people but via computer systems. Take banking as an example. No more than ten or fifteen years ago, the majority of cash withdrawals took place over the counter within a customer's local high street branch. Nowadays, of course, most customers withdraw the cash they require from cashpoint ATMs. Computer systems are therefore coming to mediate the interface between customers and organizations. As developments in home shopping, home banking and interactive entertainment accrue, such a trend will accelerate. IT systems will therefore need to be designed with the customer in mind. No longer back-room techies never to see the light of day; programmers, hardware engineers and systems analysts will need a broader and broader training in, and appreciation of, a whole armoury of business skills. As Davenport and Short note in Reading 11, IT personnel are rapidly becoming many organization's 'new industrial engineers', and will require a high degree of interpersonal in addition to technical skills as a result. Indeed, with more and more organizations coming to rely upon information technologies to increase quality, to enhance product development, and to improve customer service, technical personnel will increasingly become front line workers whose efforts will be absolutely critical for their company's continued survival and future success (Richman, 1994: 44).

IT SKILLS FOR MANAGERS

For the disconnect to be eliminated, not only will it be important for IT personnel to have some degree of customer service training. In parallel, employees across all other business functions will need to be provided with a range of technical computing skills. As long predicted by science fiction writers:

> . . . in future those who understand corporate computer systems will wield the ultimate in organizational power. Times they are rapidly a-changing. No longer will an MBA, or many years working diligently up through the ranks, count significantly if you desire top-notch promotion. Almost certainly, it is those with the best technical, software and data handling skills who will become tomorrow's corporate executives (Barnatt, 1995: 189).

Accordingly, some organizations are now starting to make a degree of technical mastery in computing a prerequisite for career development. At Union Pacific in the US, for example, all aspiring managers must spend some time as a 'data integrity analyst'. Consequently, Union Pacific hopes to benefit from managers capable of being able to *handle*, rather than just to *oversee*, the processing of the data upon which the company's future growth and prosperity will depend (Richman, 1994: 47). Within many, many other companies, a good technical knowledge of IT is almost a necessity for business success. To cite Daniels:

> New managers today should have business and technology acumen. They need to be 'hard' diplomats in that they are willing to be flexible and include the use of IT in the job, yet firm in ensuring that the IT systems serve the business and not vice

versa. Managers need to be technologically comfortable . . . [for] . . . by becoming more technologically literate, they become increasingly opportunistic about the use of IT (Daniels, 1994: 128).

DEVELOPMENTS FOR INTEGRATION

Early computing technologies and infrastructures precipitated the disconnect's development. However, some of the more recent trends and technologies involved in business computer application now have the potential to help reduce the past segregations of business and technical personnel. The downsizing trend, as detailed in the next chapter, is making end-users more aware of the power of computer application within business processes. Technophobias are also being alleviated as end-user computing initiatives spread and groupware applications abound. The adoption of methodologies for business process reengineering (as explored in Chapter 6 and Reading 11) are also drawing together staff from both sides of the technical/business divide to engage in common organizational remodelling.

Often within business process redesign initiatives, the IT department ends up being transformed into a profit centre that sells its services to the other divisions of the organization. A fresh focus upon cost-effectiveness and customer service in IT results, whilst other organizational functions come to appreciate the necessity of their input to IS thinking and system specification. An alternative and more radical reengineering development may involve the outsourcing of all or part of the IT function to external contractors in the marketplace. However such a move, whilst likely to remove an internal IT/business disconnect, may simply serve to introduce new tensions between the organization and its IT outsourcing supplier. A far more detailed discussion of the advantages and disadvantages of outsourcing is provided in the next chapter. Reading 9 additionally addresses the issues concerning the management of an IT outsourcing supplier, with the suggestion that outsourcing agreements have to be treated as strategic rather than operational alliances.

OVERVIEW

The 'disconnect' — a perceptual divide between IT employees and those within other organizational departments — has been apparent since the dawn of business computing. However, like many business ailments, the disconnect is likely to be most damaging within those companies who remain unaware of it. As is so often the case with culturally and socially-rooted business problems, diagnosis can constitute a major step forward toward final cure and eradication. This said, corporate visions, computing skills, and business strategies, will have to be shared rather than hoarded if the problem of the disconnect is to be truly overcome.

Increasingly, a knowledge of IT will affect the way in which managers will choose to carry out their evaluation and management of the business as a whole (Daniels, 1994: 168). An increased knowledge of business and customer needs will also empower greater efficiencies and effectiveness within many IT department operations. As Sara Kiesler wrote exactly a decade ago:

> New technology has three orders of effects. The first is the intended technical effects — the planned improvements in efficiency that justify investments in new technology. The second is the transient effects — the very important organizational adjustments made when a technology is introduced but that eventually disappear. The third is the unintended social effects — the permanent changes in the way social and work activities are organized (Kiesler, 1994: 46).

Hopefully, whilst having existed in some form for almost fifty years, the disconnect will prove to be an effect of the second order — one stemming from a painful transition, but one which will soon disappear to have no lasting detrimental impact upon the organizations of the future.

REVIEW AND DISCUSSION QUESTIONS

1. Explain Wang's notion of the 'disconnect' and highlight ways in which it has and may become exhibited within a business organization.

2. Distinguish between 'information systems' and 'information technology'.

3. Discuss the similarities and differences between the views of the CEOs and CIOs on p.36, regarding their actual and apparent IT management role within their organization.

4. To what extent will it be possible to distinguish business managers from IT managers in the future?

REFERENCES

Alter, S.L. (1992) *Information Systems: A Management Perspective*, Reading, MA: Addison-Wesley.

Barnatt, C. (1995) *Cyber Business: Mindsets for a Wired Age*, Chichester: John Wiley & Sons.

Daniels, N.C. (1994) *Information Technology: The Management Challenge*, Wokingham: Addison-Wesley.

Heller, R. (1990) *Culture Shock: The Office Revolution*, London: Hodder & Stoughton.

Lacity, M.C. and Hirschheim, R. (1993) *Information Systems Outsourcing: Myths, Metaphors and Realities*, Chichester: John Wiley & Sons.

Kiesler, S. (1986) 'Thinking Ahead: The Hidden Messages in Computer Networks', *Harvard Business Review* (January-February).

Richman, L. (1994) 'The New Worker Elite', *Fortune*, 22nd August.

Rushkoff, D. (1994) *Cyberia: Life in the Trenches of Hyperspace*, London: Harper Collins.

Trimmer, D. (1993) *Downsizing: Strategies for Success in the Modern Computer World*, Wokingham: Addison-Wesley.

Wang, C. (1994) *Techno Vision: The Executive's Guide to Understanding and Managing Information Technology*, New York: McGraw-Hill.

Wyles, C. (1992) 'Put Information Technology in its Place', *Global Management 1992*, Management Centre Europe.

4 DOWNSIZING AND OUTSOURCING

KEY CONCEPTS INTRODUCED

Mainframe limitations ■ Downsizing advantages ■ Open v. closed architectures ■ Downsizing risks ■ Rightsizing and upsizing ■ The outsourcing alternative ■ Outsourcing advantages ■ Outsourcing options ■ Myths and drawbacks ■ Strategic partnerships.

This chapter concerns two distinct and innovationary developments in business computer application. The first is the 'downsizing' trend away from the use of centralized mainframes toward distributed, client/server PC networks. The second is 'outsourcing', whereby company IT operations are sub-contracted externally to specialists within the marketplace.

Neither downsizing nor outsourcing developments have yet to comfortably settle. In the late 1980s and early 1990s, each was strongly advocated as *the way forward* for corporate computer success. A few years on, however, and both downsizing and outsourcing have attracted substantial criticism. In place of downsizing, some analysts now refer to 'upsizing' or 'rightsizing', wherein PC networks coexist with mainframes for optimal corporate IS. Concurrently, several IT outsourcing ventures have also proved far more problematic than first anticipated. Within the following pages, neither downsizing nor outsourcing is therefore paraded as a panacea for future success. Rather, the *options* to downsize, or to outsource upon a range of levels, are examined as potential part-solutions that modern managers must be aware of when formulating IT strategy. This said, neither trend can be ignored — and in the case of downsizing in particular, the only sensible question today has to concern the *degree* to which new technologies and *new ways of thinking* need to be taken on board.

THE PC REVOLUTION

As already noted, downsizing involves the 'comprehensive replacement of mainframe functions by cheaper — and possibly smaller and distributed — types of machine, for both existing and new applications (Trimmer, 1993: 9). Fairly obviously, therefore, the 'downsizing revolution' has gone hand-in-hand with the adolescence and widespread adoption of PCs. Today's 486DX and Pentium™ IBM and compatible PCs are capable of performing tasks that once required room-consuming mainframes. The traditional, unassailable might of the mainframe is therefore inevitably coming to be challenged.

The first IBM PC was launched in the United States in 1981. Since that date, well over 200 million IBM or compatible PCs have been sold, and business computing has been transformed as a result. In a decade and a half, end-users have come to appreciate that computing power does not have to be concentrated within a central mainframe facility. Instead, an extremely wide variety of applications can be run upon standalone or networked PCs operated almost totally under end-user jurisdiction. Indeed, it should be appreciated that the sense of proprietorship that PCs can foster amongst end-users can prove a powerful determinant in favour of downsizing's success. Whilst initially apprehensive when presented with 'their own computer', most people soon rise to the challenge and enjoy the inferred status resulting from being a 'computer literate being' (Trimmer, 1993: 53). The move away from solely mainframe-based IS infrastructures can therefore play an important role in eliminating the traditional 'disconnect' between managerial and technical employees, as discussed within the previous chapter.

THE PROBLEM WITH MAINFRAMES

At first glance, mainframe computers would appear to offer several advantages for corporate IS. By being big, mainframes ought to be able to offer economies of scale. Mainframes also require the centralization of IT employees, which in theory should lead to benefits from staff specialization which would be lost by distributing IT support personnel across downsized end-user departments. Why is it, then, that many analysts still contend that the days of mainframe computing are numbered?

Firstly, mainframe hardware and the maintenance thereof is extremely expensive. Today, a top-of-the range system costs up towards £15 million (Bird, 1995: 72). Mainframes are also based around closed architectures, meaning that there are no market forces to drive costs down over time. In contrast, the architecture of the IBM PC is open, with any manufacturer free to 'clone' IBM PC compatible hardware. Not surprisingly, therefore, we have been witness to constant price wars in the PC marketplace, which have led to increasingly more and more cost-competitive personal computing. Indeed, with PC products being largely homogeneous, technical specifications freely available, and entry and exit to the industry largely unprotected, the PC market could be argued to be one of the most perfectly competitive in the world. Pound for pound or dollar for dollar, processing information upon a PC is far more cost-effective than processing it upon a mainframe.

The open architecture and widespread adoption of PCs has also led to literally thousands of high quality, low cost PC software applications becoming available. Standardizing on PC as opposed to mainframe hardware therefore does not limit a company to either purchasing software from one supplier, or being forced to write it in-house. Rather, with so great a range of PC software available off-the-shelf, the need to employ full-time specialist programmers to develop new PC IS applications is often unnecessary. In short, PC software is more flexible, and generally of much higher quality, than that run on most mainframe systems.

Even when bespoke applications do have to be written, PC systems designers rarely have to go completely back to basics as is the case when programming most mainframe applications. Often, off-the-shelf database software packages can be customized to a company's requirements. If not, rapid, object-orientated development languages are now widely available, most of which will easily interface with mainstream OAS applications. It should also be noted that is it currently *impossible* to run graphical user interfaces (such as offered under Microsoft® *Windows*™) over mainframe/terminal links. PC user interfaces are therefore almost always far more user friendly — and of a far higher quality — than those found upon their mainframe ancestors.

DOWNSIZING ADVANTAGES

As PC hardware advances continue to accrue, the potential advantages of downsizing are becoming more and more spectacular. Indeed, it is worth remembering that many of today's cutting-edge PC applications — multimedia and network video conferencing, for example — have *never* been available upon mainframe systems. Proponents of downsizing are adamant that today's PC systems offer business users lower costs, a wider range of higher quality hardware and software, and improved overall IS flexibility when compared to the mainframe alternative. PC-based client/server IS infrastructures can usually also be installed, operated and maintained by a smaller number of generally lower-skilled (and hence less expensive) personnel than required to manage a mainframe with similar functionality. There is also the possibility of taking PC applications out on the road (or home at the end of the day), due to the widespread availability of high-capacity, low-cost portable PCs. Indeed, it has been estimated that around one-third of all PCs sold today are portables.

CRITICISMS AND FALSE PERCEPTIONS

Despite the above list of apparent advantages, there are still many advocates of tradition who refuse to accept that cumulative benefits may be reaped by moving toward the increased adoption of PC systems. It should be appreciated, however, that many of the most vigorous anti-downsizing protestations are often based upon the maintenance of self-interest, rather than upon arguments that make the best technical or business sense. For a start, many computer manufacturers are not keen to see the rapid demise of the profitable mainframe market. IBM's $5bn losses in 1992 (the largest in corporate history) were largely attributable to its customers switching away from mainframe and minicomputer hardware to PCs sold in a competitive market with far lower profit margins (Wheatley, 1993: 67).

A great deal of resistance to the spread of downsizing also comes from IT professionals keen to defend their own territory. After all, the removal of a centralized mainframe facility invariably leads to the number of dedicated IT personnel in a firm decreasing. Even if this does not prove to be the case (with previous mainframe IT personnel distributed as support officers across user departments), then opportunities for career advancement in any previous central IT hierarchy almost always disappear. To put it bluntly, whilst good for the business, downsizing is usually perceived as bad for IT personnel. In fact, many IT professionals are still sceptical with regard to PC capabilities. Dan Trimmer, one of downsizing's most radical advocates, goes so far as to state that much of the resistance to downsizing is due to a genuine disbelief by IT staff of what is it now possible to achieve with PCs. He subsequently argues that:

> . . . downsizing is mostly a non-technical matter . . . [with] . . . many of the developments being those which help to demystify technology . . . [and indeed that] . . . those requiring the most education are generally the most specialist technicians. (Trimmer, 1993: 6-7).

Many of downsizing's most clear-cut successes would seem to support Trimmer's arguments. For example, the $500m Stealth Bomber was designed solely upon a network of desktop workstations, with software development alone making 32-bit PCs ninety times more cost-effective than a mainframe (Burrus, 1993: 171). As another example, many IT specialists long believed that only mainframe computer systems offered the processing power necessary for real time on-line transaction processing (OLTP) in industries such as banking. However, as detailed in Example 4.1, the Richmond Savings Credit Union in Canada is now just one of more than a hundred financial institutions running all of its IS operations over a PC network.

HURDLES AND RISKS

In terms of cost-effectiveness, flexibility and applications quality, downsizing may well find all the cards stacked in its favour. There are, however, other issues that need addressing when deciding upon the hardware platform to be adopted for business IS. Firstly, it takes a brave manager to make the decision to more from a tried-and-tested mainframe to an unknown downsized system based upon PCs, workstations and sometimes minicomputer servers. Even if technically feasible, a credibility threshold will always need to be crossed for downsizing's success to be guaranteed.

For many, downsizing is simply just not the traditional way of doing things. Downsizing initiatives may therefore not enjoy widespread support — particularly

Example 4.1 Downsized OLTP at the Richmond Savings Credit Union (adapted from Wheatley, 1993: 67-68).

The Richmond Savings Credit Union is a Vancouver-based bank-cum-building society with assets placing it within the top 10% of North American financial institutions. All of Richmond's computer processing is carried out over a network of standard PCs, which handles the on-line transaction processing (OLTP) for all of the bank's cashpoint ATMs, tone-dial phone banking and credit card operations. The software used at Richmond was written in a special language entitled Probe, and by 1993 was handling over 100,000 transactions a day for around 50,000 customers.

Probe was developed in the early 1980s by four computer programmers who realized the potential of the downsized computing power becoming available upon the desktop. In 1984 they formed a company called Prologic to further Probe's development. At this time, the Richmond Savings Credit Union had been hit hard by the recession and was finding its outdated mainframe to be highly inflexible. Desperate for a rapid solution, Richmond Savings gambled that a downsized PC system with software written by Prologic in Probe would be able to pull them back from the brink.

In order to minimize the risks as far as possible, a three-stage system development strategy was adopted. Firstly, Prologic created a PC-based decision support system that derived its information from Richmond's mainframe. Immediately this paid dividends by giving the bank a better understanding of its customers, hence allowing services to be more closely tailored to customer needs.

Phase two involved replacing all dumb terminals with PCs. These not only served to access the mainframe in place of the terminals, but additionally were available for spreadsheet operations and word processing. Finally, once PCs had replaced all dumb terminals, the mainframe system was removed entirely, with all customer accounts and transaction processing transferred to PCs on the network running Probe-based software.

within the IT department — with an army of sceptics all too eager to preach 'I told you so's' when the inevitable teething troubles begin to occur. There are potentially also complex logistical and retraining issues to be faced during any change-over from a mainframe to a PC-based system. This alone can kill any downsizing initiative in its tracks. However, as demonstrated by the Richmond Savings OLTP case in Example 4.1, one way around the changeover problem is to first implement PCs with mainframe links in place of terminals, before the final move to a totally PC-based system.

Other problems that can arise with downsizing are solely managerial. For example, if end-user IS requirements for downsized systems are vague and not clearly specified, then PC system implementation is unlikely to be a roaring success. Downsizing also inevitably increases the responsibility of end-users for system management. Arrangements for keeping files secure and backed-up will need to be organized on a departmental basis, an area of computing of which most non-technical specialists are blissfully unaware. Similarly, end-user departments will probably also have to take on legal and administrative responsibilities, such as the registration of many databases with the Data Protection Registrar.

If end-users are allowed to create their own spreadsheet and database systems, then care will also need to be taken to ensure that instruction and technical manuals are written and filed to accompany key applications. If the latter does not take place, then knowledge of how key systems operate may well be lost when employees move between positions or leave the organization. Additionally, with user departments creating their own downsized systems, incompatible databases and other files may be created, perhaps crafted for processing within different and incompatible software packages. In such instances, any benefits from downsizing may be obscured in a stroke if mission critical data cannot be readily communicated between desktops across the organization. Similarly, downsizing benefits may be weakened if two end-user departments create duplicate systems, or if too much end-user time has to be devoted to IS administration that could be more efficiently handled centrally en masse.

PARTIAL SOLUTIONS

Most of the above hurdles before downsizing's success can be lessened or removed by careful IS management. For example, central purchasing may be employed to ensure that staff across the organization all make use of the same PC hardware and software applications. This said, such moves do indicate why the 'unbounded enthusiasm' for downsizing exhibited by many of its early champions has now become more than a little dampened. The integration of IT systems across all business functions is now strategically critical for many companies' very survival. Partially as a result, and in order to avoid problems with duplicate or incompatible systems and curtailed IS career structures:

> . . . the pendulum is swinging back once again . . . [with organizations] . . . consolidating their data centers, beefing up the authority of their central IS staffs, and establishing company wide technical standards and work procedures (Simson, 1990: 158).

THE RIGHTSIZING ALTERNATIVE

As suggested within the above quotation, whilst the most radical advocates of downsizing insist that mainframe computers have had their day, some more liberally minded analysts now contend that the optimal solution for business computing requirements is to 'rightsize'. Proponents of rightsizing suggest that computer hardware platforms should be chosen with respect to the size and complexity of their primary applications. For OAS purposes, downsized PC networks may indeed represent the optimal solution. However, for more complex DP, MIS, decision support and EIS applications, it can be argued that mainframe systems still have an important role to play.

Under many rightsizing arrangements, old-fashioned, text-based mainframe terminals are replaced with PCs offering 'terminal emulation'. Most applications are then run upon these PCs, but with the mainframe maintained as their central server or 'information warehouse'. End-users hence enjoy the flexibility of being able to run high-speed, high quality PC software upon their desks, whilst still having the ability to access and to share secure, centrally-managed computing facilities.

Some companies have clearly become totally disillusioned with IBM PC systems, whose credibility was hardly bolstered by the fiasco of the Pentium™ microprocessor bug in 1994. Problems with duplicated systems and administration, and with ineffective local back-up and security, have in some cases prompted firms to simply abandon downsizing altogether. In 1993, for example, The Performing Rights Society decided to write-off an £8m experiment in distributed computing (Bird, 1995: 73). With mainframe as well as PC technology increasingly cheaper and more flexible, other companies still remain unconvinced as to downsizing's overall advantages. As the head of IT at Norwich Union has been quoted:

> You might be able to put the contents of a fleet of Minis into a juggernaut, but you couldn't necessarily carry a juggernaut's load in a fleet of Minis (Roger Stenson, cited in Bird, 1995: 74).

DOWNSIZING AND THE FUTURE

What should have become apparent from the above discussion is that the potential benefits to be gained from downsizing are controversial and still far from clear. Claims and counterclaims abound as to the *real costs* of widespread PC implementation and support, whilst the capability and reliability of PC systems is still arguably open to question. However, whilst recognizing that downsizing is no longer a panacea for corporate computing success, it is also important not to adopt too cynical an attitude toward some of the clear benefits that the trend undoubtably has to offer. Across the world, sales of mainframes are continuing to decline, with expenditures upon PC hardware and software continuing to increase. It is therefore quite possible that the 'rightsizing trend' some analysts are now reporting may prove to be no more than a transitory phase which will allow companies to continue to derive value from past investments in mainframe technology. However, once their old mainframes have been written off, companies may well replace them with more modern PC or minicomputer-based servers. Already, new generations of powerful PC 'super-servers' have entered the computing arena, whilst wider and more powerful bus standards are improving PC processing capacities (Manchester, 1993). Central data warehouses based upon PC rather than mainframe technologies are therefore likely to become dominant in the medium- to long-term. This said, the distinction between mainframes, minicomputers and PC super-servers is in itself becoming increasingly blurred.

THE OUTSOURCING ALTERNATIVE

In the previous chapter it was noted how there have long been tensions between the IT department and the rest of the organization. This chapter has already revealed how some companies may not come to reap the benefits of downsizing due to a hostility or disbelief towards its implementation by IT personnel. Further potential problems with IS/IT management during systems development and implementation are also highlighted in the next chapter.

One seemingly straightforward means of avoiding any tensions and/or conflicts of interest between the IT department and the rest of the organization is to subcontract — or to 'outsource' — some or all IS operations to an external specialist. In the early 1990s, outsourcing came to be heralded as the most prudent mechanism for IS/IT management by many well known organizations. Bucking the trend of the last forty years, American Standard, Eastman Kodak, General Motors, Metropolitan Life, Ford and others were no longer boasting about their internal IT provision, but rather were espousing the benefits of cutting it back and farming it out (Mandell, 1991: 51). Recently, as reported in Reading 9, other well-known companies have joined the outsourcing bandwagon, including Rank Xerox, Delta Airlines, British Aerospace and the Inland Revenue Service.

After making thirteen detailed case evaluations of firms considering IS/IT outsourcing, Lacity and Hirschheim (1993) concluded that such a strategy was usually chosen due to a desire:

- To increase efficiency by reducing operating costs in IT
- To acquire, or to reduce the cost of accessing, technical expertise, particularly during periods of system development or technological transition
- To duplicate the apparent successes of other firms
- To reduce uncertainty — typically via signing a ten year contract with a vendor
- To eliminate a troublesome department, or
- For IS personnel to enhance their credibility by demonstrating their commitment to corporate success.

Other commonly cited pressures to outsource include a desire for higher quality IT services, the more aggressive use of low-cost labour, and the better management of excess hardware capacity by vendors (McFarlan and Nolan, Reading 9). In terms of cost reductions alone in information management, savings attributed to outsourcing of 20—50% have been reported across both North America and Asia (Martinsons, 1993: 19). Such savings mostly result from the avoidance of large capital investment in new systems, together with ability of companies to reduce staffing levels and to run a leaner IT/IS management structure. Within British Petroleum's Exploration Operating division, for example, outsourcing has resulted in an IT department staff level of 1400 shrinking to just 150 people. What's more, the remaining employees are increasingly working with business managers in order to develop IT activities that add value to the company, rather than supplying processing power, help-desks and other more basic support services (Cross, 1995: 94).

THE RANGE OF OPTIONS

Outsourcing initiatives may be instigated across a range of IS/IT activities and adopted upon a variety of levels. With respect to the former, it may be that an organization only chooses to subcontract its data processing activities to the marketplace — an option frequently referred to as *facilities management*. At the other end of the spectrum, a company may decide to outsource all IT activities, including not only data processing, but additionally network management, telecommunications, and PC acquisition and maintenance.

With regard to the level of external IT vendor involvement, there are effectively three alternatives to consider. At the most basic level, firms may simply employ contract programmers to meet short-term demand as required. Moving up the scale, specific IT/IS projects may be contracted out. These may involve either new system developments, or the outsourcing of largely self-contained, discrete activities such as payroll processing. In former eventuality, the external suppliers concerned are usually referred to as *systems integrators;* their job being to deliver a working system within a preset timeframe for a pre-determined fixed price. A level up, however, the most common option is outsourcing in totality, which has been likened to 'turning over the keys to the kingdom'. With such total outsourcing, all hardware and software provision and support across an organization becomes the responsibility of an outside vendor. The company's internal IT department therefore either slims dramatically or ceases to exist, although transfer arrangements are often made for its staff to remain as employees of the supplying vendor organization.

What should have become clear from the above is that decisions to outsource are rarely as black-and-white as many articles would have their readers believe. Within Reading 9, McFarlan and Nolan discuss possibilities for outsourcing in more detail. They also suggest that a computer applications matrix or *strategic grid* (as discussed in Chapter 2) may prove useful in determining which activities and functions to outsource and which to retain in-house. It should also be noted that some companies have successfully chosen to outsource different IT activities to different vendor partners. In the case of British Petroleum as previously discussed, multiple IT suppliers act as one, yet are also in competition. BP therefore hopes to avoid becoming too dependent upon any one single IT outsourcing partner, as well as retaining some flexibility with regard to its IT provision (Cross, 1995).

EXPLORING THE ADVANTAGES

It is not difficult to present IT/IS outsourcing as a very attractive proposition. For a start, by servicing many organizations, external vendors should be able to offer economies of scale and specialization. What's more, firms that outsource their IS requirements will be free to concentrate more closely upon their core business activities. There will also no longer be any battles to recruit and to retain quality professional IT personnel (Martinsons, 1993: 18).

A degree of stability should also result from outsourcing, with most arrangements involving the signing of a ten year contract. The complexities of choosing the right present and future hardware and software from the myriad of potential options available will also go away. With its external vendor making the decisions, there will quite simply be no risk of the employing organization investing in inappropriate technology. After all, if inappropriate systems are installed, the company will simply be able to adopt a new outsourcing partner when the contract with their existing vendor comes up for renewal.

EXPLODING THE MYTHS

Increasingly, many of the above justifications for outsourcing need to be viewed with a certain degree of scepticism. When it comes to increasing efficiency by reducing operating costs, for example, most studies now suggest that there are few, if any, cost savings from scale and specialization that may be offered by an external vendor. Indeed, within all but the smallest organizations, internal IT departments ought to be capable of implementing most if not all of the efficiency savings that would be exploited by an external vendor.

Possibilities for duplicating the successes of other firms are also open to question. One of the first and most cited examples of a successful IS/IT outsourcing arrangement was that entered into by Eastman Kodak in 1989. However, it has been reported that Kodak enjoys a special relationship with its vendor partners — and in particular IBM — who were keen to use the company as a showcase for promoting the use of outsourcing in large companies (Lacity and Hirschheim, 1993: 21-22). More generally, it also has to be appreciated that only outsourcing success stories tend to be reported in the trade press and academic literature, hence giving a false perception as to the benefits that may be obtained. What's more, the reporting of IS/IT outsourcing ventures usually only occurs during their first months or years of operation. With outsourcing a relatively new phenomenon, and most contracts spanning a decade, we will therefore have to wait another five years or more to find out whether many arrangements prove successful (and are continued) after their initial 'honeymoon period'.

It also needs to be remembered that by no means all outsourcing decisions are made on a rational basis, and hence that seeking to copy them may prove unwise. Organizational politics and outsourcing usually go hand-in hand. As Lacity and Hirschheim concluded from their thirteen anonymous case studies, 'some decisions appeared rational, some political, most both' (1993: 188). As already noted, companies may outsource simply in an attempt to avoid the disconnect and hence to remove the powerbase of a troublesome IT department. Often upon the surface, outsourcing decisions appear to have been taken on rational grounds in order to reap cost-efficiency gains. However, with IS costs and efficiency being *extremely* difficult to either measure or to predict over time, it remains a relatively straight-forward task to justify a wholly political decision on an apparently rational basis.

POTENTIAL DRAWBACKS

Almost all the early proponents of outsourcing based their arguments upon the notion that the IT function within an organization merely provides a commodity service. Whilst this may have been partly the case up until the late 1980s, as discussed in Chapter 2 it may now be argued that computing and associated communications systems are key weapons to be wielded in the battle to reap competitive advantage. To outsource all IT operations to a vendor with no strategic knowledge or vision of an organization may therefore prove disastrous in the long term. For a start, expert technical personnel will almost certainly be lost when an outsourcing arrangement is entered into. Over time, an organization that has chosen to outsource therefore has the potential to become more and more out of touch with IT developments and the potential to exploit them for maximum business advantage.

Due to the loss of in-house expertise, outsourcing arrangements also tend to be difficult to reverse. Monitoring can also prove to be a problem if there is no internal pool of expertise available to check upon the validity of decisions taken by the external vendor. IS flexibility may also be lost through outsourcing, with organizations potentially becoming more and more wedded to their vendor's services and technology. Although contractual provisions may be instigated to enable changes in the system employed, additional software licence fees will invariably be passed on from vendor to client (Martinsons, 1993: 20).

Even if IS activities such as data processing can reasonably be viewed purely as commodity service activities, then security risks in outsourcing may still need to be considered. For financial institutions and research centres, data confidentiality and security is absolutely paramount. Any potential cost savings from outsourcing may therefore simply not be worth the risks incurred from increased data security and control vulnerabilities due to IT being in the hands of a third party.

There will also always be human resource consequences to consider. IT personnel who transfer to become employees of the vendor organization may be subject to split loyalties. Staff remaining with the outsourcing organization may also resent the descaling of their department — with the possible implication that they were inefficient — as well as their new role as vendor monitor and liaison rather than internal service provider. Whatever their attitude and final position, staff inevitably find being caught up in an outsourcing initiative unsettling. As Moran reports, most outsourcing contracts come complete with a 'double wammy': many staff getting a new employer they never applied to work for, whilst the vendor organization acquires employees it did not recruit (1995: 15).

STRATEGIC ALLIANCES

Undoubtably, IT now has a major impact upon corporate strategy, and no competent corporate leader should willingly let such strategy be conceded from their control (Lacity et al, 1995: 91). Because of this, a new strategically coopera- tive logic for IS/IT outsourcing is now emerging. Rather than the outsourcing firm and vendor organization entering into a standard, market-driven sub-contractual arrangement, they instead become partners in a less formal strategic alliance. Within such alliances, both organizations will find synergy and derive competitive advantage from working together. Open and honest lines of communication should thereby emerge, with the governance of the outsourcing relationship becoming easier as a result.

Strategic alliances allow each partner a greater understanding of each other's problems and objectives. For the outsourcing company, the early years of an outsourcing arrangement tend to be highly beneficial, as there is usually a one-off capital payment for transferred assets in the first year. Vendor organizations, on the other hand, face high costs in changeover within the first year or so, and hence are hoping to reap their benefits in the medium-and long-term. By treating vendors as allies rather than as market suppliers who may seek to bleed them dry, outsourcing organizations come to address conflicts of vendor/purchaser interests more amicably. However detailed contractual clauses specifying information disclosure and intent become, vendor motivations are always better gauged when outsourcing arrangements are based around a mutually beneficial contract between two allies (Martinsons, 1993: 24). Further discussion of the management of IT outsourcing strategic alliances is provided by Lacity and Hirschheim in Reading 9.

OVERVIEW

Downsizing and outsourcing, whilst quite distinct, almost undoubtedly encompass two of the most complex topic areas of business computer application with which most managers should be familiar. Increasingly, the adoption of a degree of downsized technology cannot be avoided; and once their competitors begin to outsource, organizations also need to carefully evaluate at least the *possibility* of following suit in order to remain competitive.

In taking a decision to heavily downsize, any organization is demonstrating a desire to make its own, internal best choices as to the optimum means of computer application. In other words, by downsizing, companies are trusting themselves to embrace the technology of the future. If a firm decides to outsource IS/IT operations, however, then at best it is deciding that it does not possess the expertise to make the best strategic decisions regarding computer application in house. At worst it will be reacting to political tensions to shift power bases and to remove a troublesome function. By downsizing, firms may get all of their employees 'mixed up with IT' and hence may *heal* the business/IT disconnect. By outsourcing, companies may instead seek to eradicate the disconnect by avoiding the issues that fuel its rift. In a sense, whilst technologically driven on the one hand, and economically driven on the other, downsizing and outsourcing may be seen as potential alternatives. For in the words of the President of Digital Consulting:

> If you become familiar with downsizing, you may avoid the task of becoming familiar with outsourcing (George Schussel, President of Digital Consulting cited in Wang, 1994: 148).

REVIEW AND DISCUSSION QUESTIONS

1. Explain the concept of downsizing and provide a set of arguments both for and against the adoption of such a strategy.

2. Distinguish between 'downsizing' and 'rightsizing'.

3. Highlight the potential advantages and disadvantages of the total outsourcing of IS/IT operations to an external market supplier.

4. How may the adoption of strategies to either downsize or to outsource key IS applications impact upon any perceived 'disconnect' between the IT department and other business functions?

REFERENCES

Bird, J. (1995) 'The Mainframe Attraction', *Management Today* (April).

Burrus, B. with Gittines, R. (1993) *Technotrends: How to Use Technology to Go Beyond Your Competition*, New York: Harper Collins.

Cross, J. (1995) 'IT Outsourcing: British Petroleum's Competitive Approach', *Harvard Business Review* (May-June).

Lacity, M.C. and Hirschheim, R. (1993) *Information Systems Outsourcing: Myths, Metaphors and Realities*, Chichester: John Wiley & Sons.

Lacity, M.C., Willcocks, L.P and Feeny, D.F. (1995) 'IT Outsourcing: Maximise Flexibility and Control', *Harvard Business Review* (May-June).

Manchester, P. (1993) 'Downsizing: A Case of Horses for Courses', *The Financial Times* (21st September).

Mandell, M. (1991) 'Corporate Computers: How Necessary?', *Across the Board*, XXVIII(3).

Martinsons, M.G. (1993) 'Outsourcing Information Systems: A Strategic Partnership with Risks', *Long Range Planning*, 26(3).

Moran, N. (1995) 'Ways to Reduce Staff Anxieties', *The Financial Times*, 5th July.

Simson, E.M. (1990) 'The "Centrally Decentralized" IS Organization', *Harvard Business Review* (July-August).

Trimmer, D. (1993) *Downsizing: Strategies for Success in the Modern Computer World*, Wokingham: Addison-Wesley.

Wang, C. (1994) *Techno Vision: The Executive's Guide to Understanding and Managing Information Technology*, New York: McGraw-Hill.

Wheatley, M. (1993) 'The Flight from the Mainframe', *Management Today* (June).

5 SYSTEMS DEVELOPMENT AND IMPLEMENTATION

KEY CONCEPTS INTRODUCED

Appraisal, development and implementation ■ The systems development lifecycle ■ Feasibility analysis and the systems study ■ Systems design and development ■ Implementation and maintenance ■ Prototyping ■ Packaged software solutions ■ CASE templates ■ End-user computing ■ Transformational leadership and the management of change ■ Niche marketing and IT legitimacy.

Even when IT and IS strategy is firmly linked to that of the business, the process of the development and the implementation of a new computer system is liable to be fraught with difficulties. Almost all companies have a horror story or two to tell concerning a project that went wrong, and there have been several extremely public 'disasters'. The abandonment of the UK Stock Market's Taurus trading system after the investment of over £400 million serves as just one illustration. Problems with the London Ambulance Service's new computer system in 1992 also made national headlines when lives were apparently put at risk. Indeed, in the majority of cases new systems usually only work ' . . . after a fashion . . . [with some operating] . . . just below the standards set by their original design specifications, while some respond well to heavy demand on certain functions but very poorly when it comes to others' (Eilon, 1993: 135).

The previous four chapters should have brought home the message that IS/IT is no longer an isolated business function. Computer systems now impact upon almost all modern business processes and can therefore not fail to prove complex to both develop and to successfully implement. Arguably, it has been because IS implementation has been viewed too simplistically as just a technological issue that so many problems with new systems have occurred. Only recently have the wide-ranging implications of IT/IS development and implementation upon people, cultures and organizational politics started to be more fully explored. In order to achieve success, those charged with managing systems development and implementation have to be just as concerned with 'soft' social, perceptual and cultural issues as with 'hard' technical specifications. Even the best computer hardware and software will fail to reap satisfactory paybacks if technophobic employees remain unconvinced as to its merits.

BUSINESS DECISIONS, TECHNICAL SPECIFICATIONS AND HUMAN RESOURCE MANAGEMENT

With almost constant IT advances and increasing business needs for process flexibility, systems development and implementation is never-ending in many medium and most large-sized organizations. Whenever the decision is taken to review and/or to sanction a new or revised information system, there ought to be three clear stages involved in the ensuring process. Firstly, there needs to be an appraisal of new system requirements. Secondly, once requirements have been decided, the new system will need to be developed — either internally, or externally by a systems integrator or outsourcing vendor as discussed in the previous chapter. Finally, the new system will need to be implemented and brought into successful operation. Figure 5.1 illustrates this simple model diagrammatically.

Across the following sections, various methodologies for appraising, developing and implementing computer systems will be explored. However, whatever methodology is employed, it is important to appreciate that all three of the broad stages of the involved process (appraisal, development and implementation) each involves three distinct decision arenas, namely:

- **Business decisions**, to address the need for, and the role of, the information system concerned.
- **Technical decisions**, to specify how IT will be used to fulfil new or revised system requirements.
- **Human resource management (HRM) decisions**, relating to how organizational change during the transition between systems be managed in order to achieve an implementation success.

Most traditional methodologies for systems development and implementation concentrate in the main upon technical issues. One of the primary purposes of this chapter, however, is to highlight the fact that many of the problems that arise during IS development and implementation are managerial rather than technical. Today it is up to managers as much as to programmers and systems analysts to ensure that new IS developments are brought into operation as smoothly as possible. As discussed in Reading 8, support by managers and employees across all levels of organization is vital for IS success:

> The people in the organization must believe that the information strategy is feasible. Similarly, the various user groups must believe that the results of the plan will help them to accomplish the company's goals and their own goals. (Adriaans, 1993 — Reading 8, p.99).

Figure 5.1 Stages in the creation of a new information system.

THE RANGE OF DIFFICULTIES

Several factors combine to make computer systems difficult to successfully appraise, develop, and to implement. Particularly within large-scale projects, problems can result simply in the battle to keep up with technological advancements and evolving business needs. For example, if a system will take two or three years to develop, then it may well be out of date or inappropriate by the time it is completed. New system specifications therefore have to be fluid enough to accommodate new technologies and user requirements unanticipated at the project's conception. On the other hand, system specifications also need to be rigid enough to ensure that the system ends up being implemented on time and within budget. Moon chasing is a common problem in computing, and whilst the latest bells-and-whistles may appear attractive, their bright new sparkle must not come to blind practicality. A basic, working system is of far greater value to an organization than any 'optimal' fairytale one that never quite gets finished.

Another problem in the pathway of successful development and implementation concerns IT's inherent inflexibility. Whereas human employees quickly climb a learning curve when introduced to a new range of activities and functions, any new IS technology with which they have to work will not similarly adapt to improve its performance over time. Therefore, when developing new computer systems, there is a necessity to get everything as near 'perfect' as possible from day one. The only realistic way to achieve this is to involve end-users as frequently as possible during the appraisal and development process. By doing so, their needs may be addressed as development progresses. As a result, end-users should not have to learn to compensate for inappropriate technology when a new system finally goes live.

THE SYSTEMS DEVELOPMENT LIFECYCLE

'Systems development' is frequently applied as an umbrella term involving the analysis of new system requirements, new system specification and design, end-user liaison, development and testing, and final implementation within an organizational setting (Martin and Powell, 1992: 193). As such, many paradigms for 'system development' extend across the three stages of new system creation as charted in Figure 5.1. By far the most common such model is the systems development lifecycle — or the 'lifecycle model' — which is usually reported to involve six phases as follows:

- The feasibility study
- The systems study
- Systems design
- System development
- Implementation
- Maintenance and review.

The lifecycle model was developed by the National Computing Centre in the 1960s as a structured methodology to aid in the development of mainframe and minicomputer-based systems by IT personnel. Whilst at first glance technological developments such as downsizing may therefore appear to lessen the model's value in the 1990s, its six stages may still provide us with a useful analytical framework. Analysis of lifecycle stages can help not only to indicate some of the technical difficulties to be encountered in systems development, but additionally to highlight many of the wider business and human resource issues involved in the creation and implementation of modern information and CMC systems. Each stage of the lifecycle model will therefore be detailed in progression.

THE FEASIBILITY STUDY

As the first stage of the lifecycle model, the feasibility study is concerned with an appraisal of the pros and cons of any new systems development. Even the best *ideas* for new computer applications may come to prove impractical in the cold light of day, and indeed it is important that such ideas are quashed before corporate resources are heavily invested. Feasibility studies inevitably involve some form of cost/benefit analysis, whereby financial estimates will be made in order to quantify the advantages of developing a new system. Such estimates may then be compared with the new systems's likely development and implementation costs. In some instances many new system scenarios may be evaluated — central mainframe versus downsized or outsourced options, for example — to enable the one with the greatest cost/benefit to be selected.

As discussed in Chapter 2, new system benefits may include efficiency savings in production, distribution or personnel, improved communications, an enhanced competitive position, customer or supplier lock-in, and increased entry barriers against potential new market players. All but the first of these benefits are likely to be extremely difficult to quantify in financial terms, thus complicating from the outset one side of the cost/benefit equation. Often potential losses that may arise from *not* going ahead with a new system also have to be considered, with several companies today not wishing to get left behind 'playing catch-up' in the race to re-engineer with IT.

Analysing the costs of a new system can also be somewhat problematic. Some IT costs — such as the price of new hardware and software, data conversion, computer consumables, IT staff salaries and maintenance — are explicit, and hence may be fairly easy to quantify. However, many other costs will be implicit — time spent in systems planning and implementation, for example — and are far more difficult to gauge.

Often, implicit costs are forgotten, with systems that will not prove cost effective ⌐⌐⌐⌐ for further development. It is therefore extremely ⌐⌐⌐ both explicit and implicit costs are ⌐⌐⌐ ⌐estments in new computer systems ⌐⌐⌐ With PC-based systems in particular, ⌐⌐⌐ Over a five year period, the Garter ⌐⌐⌐ hardware costs involved in running ⌐⌐⌐ ⌐ith technical support, administration ⌐⌐⌐ ⌐ment, formal training, casual learning ⌐⌐⌐ g 14%, 17% and 57% of expenditure

has passed its initial feasibility hurdle, ⌐⌐⌐ titled a systems evaluation, this stage ⌐⌐⌐ new system *should* do, often via an ⌐⌐⌐ y existing system if available. Many ⌐⌐⌐ der to determine the objectives, inputs ⌐⌐⌐ ems with the current system will also ⌐⌐⌐ y address their resolution. Finally, any additional new functions which may prove valuable for end-users and the business as a whole ought to be identified. Clearly if the system in development is not to replace an existing manual or computerized system, then specifications will need to be drawn up based upon likely end-user and business requirements.

Particularly in instances where new systems are to replace existing manual working arrangements, it becomes extremely important to use as many means as possible to determine how the existing system actually works. Manuals of job specifications and working procedures may be available in some companies, although they are unlikely to reveal the whole picture. Often companies are ignorant as to exactly what their staff are actually doing. Systems study data gathering techniques may therefore involve staff questionnaires and interviews, along with the workplace observation of daily routines. Only as a result of such detailed, practical analysis are the real strengths and drawbacks of existing provision (either manual or computerized) likely to be isolated.

Systems design

Whilst the systems study will appraise the business and end-user requirements of the new system —in other words *what* the new system must do — it is during the next phase of systems design that detailed specifications concerning exactly *how* the new system will operate will be determined. Such specifications will need to cover every detail of new IS technology and working arrangements, from the type of hardware and software to be employed, data file structures, storage media and back-up facilities, through to new job descriptions and employee and management responsibilities. Software display screens and user security access rights will need to be determined. Invoices, delivery notes, purchase orders and other forms of paperwork may also need to be (re)designed. It may even prove necessary to rearrange office layouts and/or to purchase new furniture. With the Health and Safety (Display Screen Equipment) Regulations 1992 now in force (implementing EC Directive 90/270), system design specifications must consider optimal work-place ergonomics in addition to process-specific hardware and software specifi-cation. Work surfaces will need to be non-reflective, desks and VDU screens positioned to avoid glare, chairs and screen supports fully adjustable, and so forth.

Technically and organizationally, systems design can prove very complex for all but the most basic IS developments. It is also the lifecycle stage wherein inputs from end-users can prove most critical in determining overall final implementation failure or success. If end-users are canvassed for their views when design specifi-cations are being drawn up, then they are likely to feel that they 'own' the resulting new system. Such system ownership can greatly impact upon employee perform-ance. As Senker and Senker report in Reading 7, involving secretaries in the selection of their computer equipment yields considerable benefits, including secretaries more committed to their jobs and more competent to produce better standards of work.

System development

Once the systems design phase has been completed, with the most effective final system specification decided upon, systems development can begin. Finally, hardware will be purchased and software coded from scratch, or installed, amended and customized to requirements. Perhaps hardly surprisingly, systems development is therefore largely a technical phase involving programmers and technicians. This said, it is important that any new system is rigorously tested before development is curtailed, and in this end-users and management may have an important role to play. Whereas programmers and systems analysts will be able to determine whether the new system is operating logically according to specification, if is quite likely that only managers and other end-users will be able to spot whether outputs are meaningful or not. Inevitably, mistakes will have been made during systems design and systems development, and it is therefore vital that end-users are involved in testing before any system becomes the one upon which they will depend.

IMPLEMENTATION

Once a reliable new system has been created, the nail-biting phase of implementation can begin. From a technical point of view, implementation involves hardware installation and a suitable preparation of the workplace, together with the conversion of data from the old to the new system. In the case of the former, the installation of new electrical supply and network cabling is likely to be necessary in addition to actual computer workstations and any new office furniture. With regard to data conversion, it is sometimes possible to export data from an old computer system for direct use within a new one. More commonly, however, new system data (client information, personnel records, accounts and stock codes, etc), will have to be typed into the new system from scratch.

Even when upgrading from one computerized system to another, manual data rekeying is still the norm. Surprisingly, such critical data entry is often allocated to temporary staff who cannot reasonably be expected to foster a great deal of commitment to the new system or the accuracy of the data held within it. If temporary staff are used to input initial data into a new system, then at the very least rigorous checking procedures should be coordinated by a senior member of staff (Barnatt, 1994: 126). It indeed remains a mystery why companies who are willing to invest so heavily in a new computer system also have a desire to rush through data conversion as quickly and as cheaply as possible.

One of the key decisions that management needs to take regarding implementation concerns the choice of changeover strategy. At one end of the scale, a policy of direct cut-over may be adopted. Under this scenario, the company simply ceases to use the old system one day and starts to use the new system the next. Such a strategy is cheap but risky, as it assumes that the new system will work perfectly from the word 'go'. Some companies therefore choose to adopt a strategy of 'parallel running', where both the new and the old system are run side-by-side for a few days, weeks or even months to ensure that the new system is performing at least as well as the old before it comes to be relied upon.

Whilst far less risky than direct cut-over, parallel running is also not without its problems. Most obviously these involve the expense and practicality of running two different systems side by side. There can also be problems when the parallel running period is due to end. Often, with staff having got used to the 'security' of running two systems in tandem, they become loathe to 'let go' and to rely on just one system again. Fortunately, hybrid changeover strategy alternatives located somewhere between direct cut-over and parallel running also exist. One such option is pilot running, where a direct cut-over occurs within just one section of an organization in advance of a direct cut-over across the board. For example, the personnel department may adopt a new system two weeks before all other business functions in order to highlight any teething troubles. However, whilst potentially an attractive option, the pilot running approach is becoming harder and harder to adopt due to the increased connectivity of interdependent interdepartmental systems.

A second hybrid changeover option is termed phased conversion. Here, different sections of a system are brought into operation across the organization one at a time — with the new system effectively introduced in stages. Such an approach is particularly suited to changeovers from mainframe or minicomputer to PC-based systems, where PCs can first be introduced as mainframe terminals before running the new downsized system software. The development of the Probe OLTP application at Richmond Savings Credit Union (Chapter 4, p.47) serves as a good case in point.

As well as selecting an appropriate changeover strategy to balance risk, cost and practicality, management also has a key implementation role in making sure that appropriate end-user training is provided. Unfortunately, it is not uncommon for top managers to expect good results from new computer applications, but not to be prepared to allocate sufficient training resources. In the case of computer numerically controlled machine tool systems, for example, some firms have given their supervisors no training, excluded them from decisions about its introduction, and have then expected them to manage the new system (Burnes, 1988). Further discussion of the role of training in ensuring an implementation success takes place within Reading 7.

Maintenance and review

Just because a new system has come to be implemented does not mean that system development will cease. Just as the painters of the Forth Bridge must start all over again whenever they 'complete' their labouring brushwork, so the systems development lifecycle model inwardly returns to self-assessment and review in its final phase. After several months or even years in development, there will be lessons to be learned from all major systems development projects. There are also likely to be new user demands and innovative emerging technologies to incorporate.

Making minor functional changes, fine-tuning software to suit final user requirements, and correcting errors, bugs and early hardware failures, are all tasks coming under the general heading of 'maintenance' (Martin and Powell, 1992: 224). Such 'systems development' is likely to be ongoing, with regular schedules and procedures needing to be established in most instances. If they are to remain germane to competitively-focused business needs, then all good information systems must adapt over time. In this sense the systems development lifecycle should therefore be viewed as a circular model, with the maintenance and review phase feeding back to the feasibility study for the system's next generation.

PROTOTYPING AND RAPID DEVELOPMENT

The lifecycle model, together with other similar traditional structured methodologies, inevitably involves a fairly lengthy systems development and implementation timescale. With computer information systems increasingly having to be tailored quickly to new business needs, various 'rapid development' approaches have therefore also emerged. Prototyping is one such method, and involves the development of a new system incrementally until it becomes fully functional. Rather than progressing through the detailed stages of an initial systems study and systems design, a prototype system with some facets of basic functionality is coded as quickly as possible. End-users are then allowed to experiment with the prototype in order to elicit feedbacks for improvements and bug fixes. Further development then ensues before the system is returned for a second round of end-user evaluation. Such review/development iterations continue until a satisfactory working system results.

Prototyping may be particularly beneficial in situations where exact system requirements are hard to identify from the outset, or where business needs are constantly changing. The involvement of end-users during iterative systems development also heightens employee commitment to a final implementation success. This said, even prototyped systems development takes time, and hence even more rapid methodologies are always being sought. Arguably the most rapid option is to purchase packaged software to be customized to the needs of the business.

PACKAGED SOFTWARE SOLUTIONS

With the increasing adoption of open, downsized systems, the possibilities for companies to invest in off-the-shelf rather than custom-programmed systems are increasing. In theory at least, packaged software solutions ought to allow for extremely rapid and cost-effective applications development, as costs are spread across the hundreds or thousands of purchasers of the package concerned. Unfortunately in practice, by the time an off-the-shelf package has been tailored to specific company requirements and is actually installed and running, many of the anticipated cost and time savings have been lost. Indeed, final development and implementation costs ten times greater than the packaged software selling price are not unheard of (Hofman and Rockart, 1994: 51).

It should also be noted that the use of packaged software does not eliminate the need for a managed systems development process. Business and end-user needs will still need to be appraised even if standard packages can be used straight out of their shrink-wrap. Similarly, the workplace will still need to be prepared for implementation, data converted, a changeover strategy decided, and end-users provided with adequate training and management support (Martin and Powell, 1992: 233).

THE TEMPLATE OPTION

A third and increasingly popular rapid development option, and one which attempts to combine the best of both 'build' and 'buy' approaches, involves the use of IT system 'templates'. Templates are existing systems, built using advanced computer-aided software engineering (CASE) tools, which companies purchase and customize to their own requirements. CASE tools remove the drudgerous stage of manual programming or reprogramming from system development, hence enabling rapid template customization. As explained by Hofman and Rockart, CASE tools:

> . . . assist developers in producing a computer-based design of the new system, expressed in diagrams and/or text. The design outlines the data relationships, the process flows, the screens, and the programs. The diagrammatic and textual representations are referred to as models. Many CASE tools also provide the ability to convert the design automatically into code. Minimal, if any, code handling is necessary, thus eliminating a major step. Maintenance is also greatly simplified. Rather than changing the *code* to mirror changes in the business, the change can be made at the *design* (model) level and the code can be automatically regenerated. (Hofman and Rockart, 1994: 50).

By adopting a template from a similar system and tailoring it to its own business requirements, organizations may benefit from the time invested in systems appraisal and development by other organizations. In effect, basic functionality is cloned, meaning that a CASE template adopter does not have to begin systems development from scratch. For example, in the mid-1980s Canadian Airlines purchased TWA's frequent flyer system, built using a Texas Instruments CASE tool. The system was then extensively redesigned and regenerated to Canadian's requirements in a period of only 10 months. In contrast, a totally custom-designed software solution would have taken around 18 months to develop. System maintenance also proves far easier than if a traditional custom system had been developed, as the design is modular and based upon CASE code which can be automatically regenerated to incorporate new developments (Hofman and Rockart, 1994: 53).

END-USER COMPUTING

Whilst many computer applications will continue to be developed and implemented by IS personnel, the widespread adoption of distributed PCs means that many end-users now also have the potential to engage in their own systems development activities. A finance manager, for example, may develop their own financial models within a spreadsheet, whilst marketing personnel might create their own database applications.

Most end-user systems are likely to be created using spreadsheets, databases, project management packages, or a conglomeration thereof. This said, there are an increasing number of 'object-orientated' applications development tools entering the PC marketplace. These allow programming 'objects' to be used as building bricks from which an end-user's application may be crafted. Visual BASIC is one such example of the genre. Another more specialist package — Authorware™ — allows interactive multimedia applications to be created by manipulating graphical icons upon a program 'flow line'. Using such graphical, object-orientated programming tools, end-users with fairly rudimentary computer skills may quickly learn to develop extremely professional customized applications.

When end-users do create their own applications, it is still important that some form of structured methodology is brought to bear upon the process. In particular, it is critical to appraise the true cost-effectiveness of creating an end-user application, as many end-users tend to forget that their own time is extremely valuable, and hence that they cannot simply create new applications 'for nothing'. It is also important for end-users to document all applications they create so that in future others may understand their operation. Testing of end-user created applications is also vital. Many companies base critical decisions upon the outputs of end-user created spreadsheet models, yet a great many contain errors. Amazingly, a survey by Coopers and Lybrand in 1992 reported that 90% of spreadsheets used for decision analysis in a range of blue chip companies contained at least one significant error such that results were wrong by more than 5% (Strategic Planning Society, 1992: 1).

EMPLOYEE CONCERNS AND TRANSFORMATIONAL LEADERSHIP

Whatever methodology comes to be employed to manage the systems development process, it is increasingly recognized that the relative success or failure of any new IS initiative depends upon the degree to which it gains support across an organization. No computer system ever objected to a human being. Many human beings, however, are opposed to — or even afraid of — computers. Even those who are happy with the use of IT frequently feel uneasy when new systems are being implemented. New IT systems inevitably transform the fabric of their operatives' working lives and are likely to be opposed to some degree as a result. Some workers may fear a loss of status, deskilling or redundancy when computers are introduced into their place of work. Others may fear embarrassment due to an ignorance of IT, and/or may be worried that they will not be able to cope with the new technology. All such fears are natural and are very real, and it is up to managers to reassure and to educate employees as to the benefits of IS changes.

The implementation of a new computer system will not only promote employee fears and anxieties. Just as significantly, managerial uncertainty is also likely to abound concerning how best to manage the complexities of the implementation process. As Brown suggests, one option may be for managers to adopt a 'transformational' leadership style in order to psychologically mould the attitudes of employees over the development and implementation period (1994: 1-2). Such transformational leadership will require managers to focus as much upon the values, beliefs and assumptions of their employees regarding the new IT system, as upon the new system's rational and technical requirements and specifications. Social situations will need to be created during which 'significant messages' may be communicated. Transformational leadership involves the subtle management of perceptions and an unlocking of the mental rigidities that make all of us resistant to change.

CHANGE MANAGEMENT

A common model of change management involves progression through three clear stages. Firstly, entrenched beliefs concerning the continued viability of the status quo will need to be *unfrozen*. Secondly, *movement* will need to occur in order that new ways of working come to be accepted. Finally, there will need to be a *refreezing* processes, with a lasting commitment to the new system propagated across the organization.

In order to achieve the above, support for any new IT initiative will need to be won from a wide variety of interest groups. As Adriaans notes in Reading 8, assembling a broad-based implementation team representing a range of interests is therefore likely to be vital. Above all else, gaining grass-roots end-user support is paramount for any new IT implementations success. Or as Davenport so succinctly puts it 'grand IT schemes that don't match what rank-and-file users want simply won't work' (1994: 131).

NICHE MARKETING AND IS LEGITIMACY

Within Reading 10, Andrew D. Brown details the means by which support for a new hospital information support system (HISS) was sought by seeking to legitimize its benefits to different employee groups. Rather than concentrating upon the technical aspects of the multi-million pound IS development, Brown focuses upon the political struggles that ensued in order to reap vital grass-roots support for the system's eventual success. With managers, doctors and other groups within the hospital having very different views as to the likely benefits and drawbacks of increased computer application, those responsible for implementation chose to be selective in the information they communicated. As a result, rather than attempting to share one 'all-embracing vision':

> . . . the implementation team were careful to tailor the messages they transmitted to the audience in hand. In practice, what this meant was that they engaged in a concerted niche marketing campaign which crucially involved the withholding, slanting and emphasising of selected information in a sophisticated micropolitical process (Brown, 1995 — Reading 10, p.143).

Clearly the above indicates the degree to which IS development and implementation initiatives tend to become as much managerial as technical. In a sense, the concept of the business/IT disconnect rears its head again in this context. Human nature, good and bad, can wreck the best-laid IT plans, yet technocrats are still constantly surprised when their technologically-empowered visions are perverted by the 'totally irrational behaviour' of end-users (Davenport, 1994: 119).

OVERVIEW

Undoubtedly, there is a disconnect to be healed when it comes to systems development and implementation as much as there is a strategic business/IS rift to be mended. As explored in the next chapter, IT-enabled reengineering initiatives redetermining the nature of work and organization are now unstoppable, yet this does by no means imply that all employees will embrace such changes with open arms. The new management challenge is not just to determine how to best utilize IT in order to reap competitive advantage. Additionally, it is to better understand how to manage the process of systems development in order that flexible systems that the majority will support come to be implemented on time and within budget.

REVIEW AND DISCUSSION QUESTIONS

1. Detail the advantages and the drawbacks of adopting the traditional lifecycle methodology for systems development.

2. Distinguish between prototyping, template customization, packaged software application, and end-user systems development, identifying the strengths and weaknesses of each approach.

3. Make a list of all the likely sources of resistance to the implementation of computer technology that may be exhibited within organizations today, together with an accompanying range of strategies that management may adopt in order to cope with such resistance.

REFERENCES

Barnatt, C. (1994) *The Computers in Business Blueprint*, Oxford: Blackwell Business.

Brown, A.D. (1994) 'Transformational Leadership in Tackling Technical Change', *Journal of General Management*, 19(4).

Burnes, B. (1988) 'New Technology and Job Design: The Case of CNC', *New Technology, Work and Employment*, 3(2).

Daniels, N.C. (1994) *Information Technology: The Management Challenge*, Wokingham: Addison-Wesley.

Davenport, T.H. (1994) 'Saving IT's Soul: Human Centered Information Management', *Harvard Business Review*, (March-April).

Eilon, S. (1993) 'Measuring Quality in Information Systems', *Omega: The International Journal of Management Science*, 21(2).

Hofman, J.D. and Rockart, J.F. (1994) 'Application Templates: Faster, Better, and Cheaper Systems', *Sloan Management Review* (Fall).

Martin, C. and Powell, P. (1992) *Information Systems: A Management Perspective*, London: McGraw-Hill.

Strategic Planning Society (1992) 'Spreadsheets can't be Trusted', *Strategic Planning Society News*, (October).

Taylor, P. (1995) 'New moves to Reduce the Cost of Ownership', *Financial Times Review: Information Technology*, 7th June.

6 REENGINEERING WORK AND ORGANIZATION

KEY CONCEPTS INTRODUCED

Business process reengineering and business process redesign ■ IT as an enabler of BPR ■ The Internet as a new business medium ■ Advertising and e-tail on the world-wide web ■ Management by wire ■ Data warehousing ■ Software agents ■ Telecommuting ■ Hot-desking and hotelling ■ Virtual teams and virtual organization.

Like it or not, innovative computer applications are changing the world. As already noted in the first chapter, computers are now used just as widely for communications purposes as they are for the effective processing and storage of information. Indeed, veteran cultural philosopher Timothy Leary has suggested that we should no longer talk of PCs, but instead think of our keyboard-equipped desktop companions as *interpersonal* computers (1994: 7). Certainly, increased CMC application is one of the greatest forces now decimating previously distinct departmental and disciplinary boundaries both within and between all forms of organization.

This final chapter before the readings explores some of managerial challenges associated with cutting-edge IT applications that are enabling the redesign of age-old methods of work and organization. Initially, discussion concerns the increasing focus upon business *processes* rather than *structures,* together with the pivotal role that IT has to play in so-termed business process reengineering (BPR). Attention is then directed toward the problems and opportunities to be experienced when managing in a 'wired world'. Finally, 'telecommuting' and other innovative working practices which may permit the emergence of new 'virtual' forms of organization come in for some scrutiny.

Each of the key concepts of BPR, 'wired management' and 'virtual organization' introduced within the following sections, are detailed in depth and application within Readings 11, 12 and 13 respectively. The goal of this chapter is therefore to overview some of the broad themes linking these three areas of related development. Chief amongst such themes is the need for managers to adopt a new way of *thinking* in order to benefit from (or even just to cope with) the impact of developments in areas such as EDI, CMC, electronic retailing, and even virtual reality, upon the business world. The customers and markets of tomorrow are likely to have very different demands from those of today, with effective IT application a prerequisite for success. 'BPR' and 'virtual organization' may already be terms overused and abused as sexy, blanket icons of a still-to-mature 'new age', yet this does not diminish their importance and in particular their *meaning*. Indeed, as noted in the recent book *Cyber Business*:

> Across entire industries and economies, the way in which organizations interact to do business has already started to alter. Electronic communications media have already negated the restrictions of time and distance across many multinationals and between countless other organizations. EDI now permits information and resource transactions to take place without the need to relocate physical goods or pieces of paper. Money has for years been a virtual commodity, and as the world goes digital, more and more information products and services will be traded solely across the webs of cyberspace (Barnatt, 1995: 184).

REINVENTING ORGANIZATION

Pressures for companies to become more lean, more flexible — more *effective* — are continually increasing. No longer can firms adopt Henry Ford's mass-production philosophy and produce a few standardized products in any colour so long as they are black. Back at the beginning of the century, mass production was an innovation. But it is no longer so today. Heightened customer demands for higher quality customized products, increased competition, not to mention technological advances in production and administration, now mean that organizations across the industrialized world are having to 'reinvent' themselves in order to survive.

The term BPR involves focusing upon the *processes* inherent in company operations — rather than the *structures* through which they are conducted — and rethinking them in the light of the industrial and technological revolutions of the late twentieth century. Processes, or sets of logically related productive tasks, may be recognized as having discrete customer outputs (either externally or internally to the organization). Processes also tend to cross internal and external organizational boundaries, involving relationships between purchasers and suppliers, research and development and production, marketing and distribution, and so forth.

There is still some confusion in the literature as to whether BPR stands for business process *reengineering* or business process *redesign*. Thankfully in practice, the exact wording behind the BPR acronym proves largely unimportant, as 'BPR' in almost all contexts seems to imply the same thing. When a distinction is made, business process redesign is said to be concerned with redesigning any business process at the micro level, whilst business process reengineering is more macro and focuses upon identifying the overall processes upon which an organization needs to concentrate in order to achieve its strategic goals (Edwards and Peppard, 1994: 254). Within the following, however, such subtle distinctions between business process redesign or business process reengineering are ignored. After all, as Edwards and Peppard also state, 'BPR is difficult to define yet somewhat easier to recognise' (1994: 252).

Whatever the 'R' stands for, BPR is about 'starting over' to do things far better, or, as two of its key-proponents more formally define the term, BPR:

> . . . is the fundamental rethinking and radical redesign of business processes to achieve dramatic improvements in critical contemporary measures of performance, such as cost, quality, service, and speed (Hammer and Champy, 1993: 32).

BPR is fundamental and radical in that it requires finding new solutions to the most basic of questions. It begins with no assumptions and demands more than superficial changes in order that customers become the primary focus of business operations. Customers, after all, don't care about how organizations achieve their outputs, who is involved, or within what structure they labour. All customers care about are the final products and services that an organization delivers. Yet for many organizations, rethinking their business processes — their value chains — so that they are totally customer driven can be painful and dramatic. As Hammer and Champy note, 'reengineering is about business *reinvention* — not business improvement, business enhancement, or business modification' (1993: 33).

THE ROLE OF IT

Traditionally, the application of information technology within business has been rather conservative, and has mainly involved the automation of existing processes within specific departments. Such an approach, whilst leading to efficiency gains in many instances, assumes from the outset that the original processes that came to be automated were satisfactory in the first place (Fiedler et al, 1994: 267). BPR challenges such an assumption, espousing the creation of new, more *effective* business processes. Often, IT plays a crucial role in redefining the means by which business activities may be undertaken, together with the interface which may mediate the relationship between customer and organization. As Hammer and Champy argue, IT is an 'essential enabler' of BPR, as it is through IT that companies come to reengineer their key processes (1993: 83). This said, it has to be appreciated that simply computerizing *existing* processes does not constitute reengineering. It is the process itself — and not the technology used within its accomplishment — that needs to be rethought from the ground up, to be *supported* by novel IT application. As Davenport and Short discuss in Reading 11, 'information technology should be viewed as more than an automating or mechanizing force; it can fundamentally reshape the way business is done' (Reading 11 p.160).

What's more, IT serves not just as a tool but as a recursive force within BPR — with computer application enabling the adoption of new processes which in turn enable the adoption of new forms of IT.

Key to Davenport and Short's analysis is the notion that 'IT levers' need to be considered before rather than after a business process is designed or redesigned. In other words, an awareness of IT capabilities should influence the development of all business processes. For example, if it is appreciated from the outset that project teams will be able to communicate widely via CMC, then the organization and structure of such teams both administratively and geographically may be very different than would be the case if no CMC links were to be available. More concrete examples of using IT to enable new working patterns are provided in later sections of this chapter. A far more detailed exploration of the relationship between IT and BPR is also entered into by Davenport and Short in Reading 11.

THE RANGE OF DEVELOPMENTS

Now that the fundamental concept of BPR has been introduced, we may proceed to investigate some of the more specific instances of novel IT application in business. Whilst the range of developments that could be included is extremely diverse, it is possible to group instances of IT-enabled reengineering under the following three basic topic areas:

- Developments opening up new mediums for customer advertising, liaison, sale and distribution.
- Developments permitting new and/or more effective means of management and organizational control ('management by wire').
- Developments empowering new working practices and hence new 'virtual' organizational forms.

Each of the above areas of novel IT application will now be detailed in turn.

A NEW BUSINESS MEDIUM

In little more than two years, the 'Internet' has emerged from obscurity to become the single greatest icon of the 'new age' of computer-mediated communications. Whilst the promise of a high-speed, interactive information 'superhighway' linking all homes and businesses may still be many years away, the Internet is a very real phenomena that is already allowing business to be conducted in the computer domain of 'cyberspace'. Hundreds of books have already been written detailing how to get 'wired' or 'on-line'. We are also witness to a multitude of magazines dedicated to 'the Net', several Internet-specific radio and television programmes, not to mention seemingly endless newsprint columns detailing the latest 'amazing advances'. Yet just what *exactly* is the Internet, and what are its real business implications?

The Internet — or the *Inter*national *network* — is a loose conglomeration of interconnected computer systems which share common communications standards (or 'protocols') so that data and messages can travel freely between them. The basis of the Internet's infrastructure grew up out of early military and academic networks, most notably the US military's advanced research projects agency network (ARPANET), and the US national science foundation's NSFNET. In the UK, the Internet's backbone infrastructure is based upon that provided by the joint academic network (JANET), and by its recent high-speed derivative Super JANET.

Around 2.5 million 'host' computers now enjoy a permanent Internet connection. However, computers that do not possess a direct link can still gain access by using a 'modem' to connect to an Internet host via a standard telephone line. At the time of writing, the Internet had approaching 50 million users around the globe, most of whom were accessing the system via PC-modem connections. Such dial-in users were typically paying a monthly subscription of around £10 to an Internet service provider to whom they were connecting at local telephone charge rates.

INTERNET FACILITIES

Computer users with an Internet connection have access to four key on-line facilities. The first is electronic mail (e-mail), whereby electronic messages and/or data files can be 'posted' to any other user with an Internet connection. E-mail can also be used to access 'mailbases' — open Internet 'conferences', organized by subject topic — within which subscribers may engage in information sharing and discussion. In addition to e-mail, an Internet connection permits the use of facilities known as FTP (the file transfer protocol) and IRC (Internet relay chat). Via FTP, Internet subscribers may copy (or 'download') programs and data files from remote computers. Via IRC, they may engage in interactive text-based communications, with two or more users sharing an IRC 'channel' over which they may conduct on-line conversations.

Whilst e-mail, FTP and IRC facilities have proved popular, the recent boom in the Internet's popularity was sparked by the emergence of the so-called 'world-wide web'. The Web makes the Internet easy to use — or 'browse' — by using a Windows-style interface based upon graphical icons and hypertext links. Via the use of hypertext, any Web 'page' or 'site' can 'point' to any other. All the user has to do to move between Web pages is to click with their mouse pointer upon highlighted words or graphic images which then move them on through the system. Web pages may contain not only text, but also graphics, animations, moving video, and even virtual reality simulations. What's more, anybody can learn to use the Web in minutes. It is therefore no surprise that many companies are now recognizing the Web's potential for attracting and for trading with their customers — especially as they can set up shop on the Web at very low cost. In short, the Web opens up cyberspace to anybody who wants to publish information and/or to establish a direct link to their customers, from the largest corporate organization right down to the lowliest entrepreneur (Kirkpatrick, 1995: 64).

ADVERTISING AND E-TAIL ON THE WORLD-WIDE WEB

The world-wide web has now established itself as a new, if still to mature, medium for advertising and electronic retailing (or 'e-tail'). Already, thousands of commercial organizations and educational institutions have their own 'home pages' on the Web. By mid 1995, there were over 35,000 individual Web sites and several on-line shopping malls had been set up. These included the Internet Shopping Network, Cybershop, the London Mall, SMART STORE Virtual and BarclaySquare. The latter includes 'virtual shop fronts' for the likes of Sainsbury's, Argos, Eurostar and Barclay's Bank. Other web shopping facilities include the Internet Bookshop — whose searchable archive contains details of 780,000 books currently in print — and even virtual estate agents. Rather than trawl highstreet windows, homebuyers can instead specify a location and a price range within an on-screen dialogue box in order to be presented with text and pictures detailing their potential ideal property.

Although the take-off of the world-wide web has permitted interactive cyberspace shopping to be made available long before the best guestimates of even the most hopeful futurologists, the system is not without its problems. Most notably the Internet (and hence the Web) can be painfully slow at peak times. There are also a great many concerns regarding the security of on-line financial transactions. However, such teething-troubles are being continuously addressed. Sceptics may argue that the Internet 'stinks as a place to do business' — noting in their *defence* that only $250 million of on-line sales were made in 1994 (Nulty, 1995) — yet the tide of on-line demand seems to be as much against them as more watery waves were against King Canute. Certainly, on-line adverts, shops, banks and consumer support services won't *replace* more conventional provision. What they will do is to *complement* them, providing new channels of customer liaison which many firms are already beginning to substantiate in order to reap fresh competitive advantages.

TOWARDS MANAGEMENT BY WIRE

Whilst the evolution of the Internet and the world-wide web have undoubtedly received the greatest public exposure, many equally radical business IT developments are starting to accrue more quietly behind the scenes. One such development concerns what Haeckel and Nolan in Reading 12 refer to as 'management by wire'. According to the latter's definition, management by wire is exemplified by the 'ability to run a business by managing its information representation'. In other words, the management by wire concept is based upon building a model of a business in software, and then controlling business operations by manipulating that software model. Or as David Gelernter contends, 'mirror worlds' will soon emerge, with software models upon computer screens not only showing us a representation of reality, but also allowing us to change reality by changing the software model (Gelernter, 1992). Click upon an on-screen icon within a management by wire model and stock will be moved between warehouses, lorries dispatched, production levels increased, overtime booked, or even 'surplus' employees made redundant.

At first, the management by wire concept seems like pure science fiction of the kind sculpted by Arthur C. Clarke when he wrote of the future city of Diaspar that could be redesigned via manipulation of its virtual representation (Clarke, 1956). However, we no longer have to hypothesize fictions millennia hence to find examples of interactive business software models. Granted, encoding an informational representation of a company into a robust software pattern may be complex, yet as Haeckel and Nolan contend, many firms have been hardwiring and interlinking their functions with IT for decades. At Mrs. Fields Cookies, for example, an enterprise model called ROI (retail operations intelligence system) is in use in more than 800 stores. This allows all managers access to an information representation of company founder Debbi Fields, whose *knowledge* of what products to mix, to discount, to promote and to sell becomes constantly available. Mrs. Fields Cookies thereby achieves its goal of providing a consistent product and service across its wide range of outlets.

Another management by wire example from Haeckel and Nolan concerns an alliance between US retail giant Wal-Mart and jeans manufacturer Wrangler. These two companies share both sales data and analytical software so that sales patterns may be learned over time, hence enabling their combined 'corporate IQ' to be boosted. For more detail upon management by wire in application a careful study of Reading 12 is strongly recommended.

The greater the range of business functions and communications that become dependent upon IT systems, the greater the potential benefits for 'wired management' will become. Already, many organizations are investing in technologies for 'data warehousing', whereby vast corporate databases are maintained to store the mass of detailed sales and customer profile information that may now be derived from EPoS, EDI and other IT systems. Once such a 'metadata' store has been accumulated centrally, 'intelligent' neural network interfaces can interrogate it in order to establish trends which will aid in the development of future business strategies. Rather than having to be programmed with explicit rules, neural networks are instead designed to isolate patterns and subsequently to spot and predict their recurrence. Only with neural networks can the mass of customer information that is now being gathered by many large organizations ever hope to be optimally exploited. Neural network interfaces to corporate data warehouses will therefore form the heart of many future MIS, DSS and EIS applications. By trawling its data warehouse, US retailer Wal-Mart identified an obscure relationship between the sales of nappies and beer on Friday nights. It subsequently grouped these items closer to each other on the shelves in order to boost their joint sales further. In the UK, British Airways is just one of the firms investing heavily in data warehouse systems in an attempt to better understand its customers' needs in order that it may 'personalize' its travel provision (Gooding, 1995: 15).

AUTOPILOTS AND SOFTWARE AGENTS

By seamlessly integrating information systems across departmental boundaries, permitting widespread data access, linking their IT systems to those of their main customers and suppliers, and equipping managers with neural network interface systems, organizations will have the ability to learn and hence to become 'intelligent'. No longer can *any* human being hope to grasp the complexity of the functioning of a large modern business organization. As a result, managers will be increasingly forced to rely upon IT systems if they are to manage most effectively. As Haeckel and Nolan explain, management by wire enterprise models will become like 'autopilots' for organizations, taking mundane decisions to ensure that the company stays on course. An 'executive crew' will then fly the business, using controls in its 'information cockpit', with:

> . . . managers respond[ing] to the readouts appearing on the console, modifying the business plan based on changes in external conditions, monitoring the performance of delegated responsibilities, and sending directions to subsidiary units such as manufacturing and sales (Haeckel and Nolan, 1993 — Reading 12, p.188).

In addition to management by wire enterprise models, future managers are also likely to be assisted by a new breed of programs called 'software agents'. Sometimes known as intelligent agents, these are effectively electronic servants. As such, software agents will soon take on mundane tasks for their human masters, such as searching databases, making travel arrangements and managing stock levels. For example, rather than having to make a daily search through newspapers and on-line sources for information that may be of interest, soon a manager will be able to dispatch an agent into cyberspace to constantly conduct such searches on their behalf. What's more, the agent will only report back when it has something of interest to deliver. In order to function in such a manner, agents need to be both smart and autonomous. As John Hoberg explains:

> . . . agents are mobile entities. They literally travel around a network and can copy themselves onto other computers to do their work. [Agents are also] . . . autonomous entities. They can work on their own, and have the authority to make decisions for their owners. Experts say that we will soon trust software agents with our checkbooks and investment holdings, authorizing them to spend our money for goods and services they know we want to buy. Finally, agents will be intelligent enough to

observe us and learn our habits and preferences as well as our personal demographics to serve us better (Hoberg, 1995: 3-4).

As agents learn from their masters they will build up profiles of personal preferences and decision criteria based upon previous actions. A manager's agent will therefore know what sort of hotels and which airlines she prefers, and hence will book preferred choices automatically when travel arrangements are requested. In this sense, agents will become like personal assistants in cyberspace, masking the complexity of computer networks and database jungles from computer users.

Whilst agent development is still somewhat in its infancy, the market for agent software is expected to be worth several billion dollars per annum by the year 2000. Already Apple Computer have created an agent known as 'Eager' which monitors operations upon a PC desktop so that it may 'jump in' and offer assistance when repetitive activity appears to be occurring. Microsoft have a similar software servant called 'Bob', whilst Andersen Consulting offer world-wide web access to a 'BargainFinder' agent that will scan on-line shops such as SMART STORE Virtual for the best deals. AT&T have also launched an agent-based communications system entitled Personalink, and as the market projections indicate, these are still very early days. Not many years hence, software agents will almost certainly prove essential for the fluid functioning of commonplace global management by wire systems.

New working patterns

In addition to empowering new communications and sales media, and augmenting managerial roles, IT systems are also increasingly permitting the organization of work itself to be reengineered. Nowhere are changes happening so rapidly as within the office, which has been witness to nothing less than a revolution with the widespread introduction of computer workstations over the past decade and a half. With the recent advent of CMC media in the form of electronic mail, together with increasingly widespread and cost-effective PC-based video conferencing, the office revolution is rapidly entering its second generation. As highlighted in Reading 13, the following key areas of new IT-enabled working practice may now be clearly delineated:

- Teleworking
- The adoption of hot-desk environments
- Hotelling, and hence
- The creation of virtual teams.

The first of the above IT-enabled working practices — teleworking — involves employees working remotely from their organization using groupware IS links.

This frees workers from the constraints of having to travel to the office, normally during set hours, as well as from having to live close enough to be within a reasonable travelling distance. Whilst the majority of 'teleworkers' are likely to work from home, others may congregate daily at a neighbourhood 'telecottage'. Either way, teleworkers will be able to access their organization's information systems, as well as being able to communicate with co-workers via telephone, fax, e-mail, voice-mail and quite possibly video links. As discussed in Reading 13, the time may not be too far distant when teleworkers will even be able to 'virtucommute' by donning virtual reality (VR) clothing in order to be transported to a computer generated virtual workplace.

For organizations, teleworking offers many potential advantages, not least in terms of overheads saved by not having to provide costly office space for every individual upon the payroll. It has also been reported that employees become more productive as teleworkers (due to fewer interruptions and better concentration during the working day), and that teleworking makes skilled employees easier to retain (Kinsman, 1987). American Express has reported savings per employee of $30,000 a year due to teleworking adoption, whilst in the UK companies such as Burger King and British Telecom have also reaped major cost benefits. In 1995 the Institute of Management reported that around 400,000 people in the UK could be classed as teleworkers. There were also 120 telecottages in the UK at this time according to the Telecottage Association (Pancucci, 1995: 78-80).

For the teleworker in addition to their employer there can also be considerable advantages to be gained from teleworking. Most obviously these derive from time and cost savings reaped by not having to travel to work and back every day. Teleworking also allows individuals greater flexibility and independence, permitting improved family relationships, more time for hobbies and interests, and the ability to share parental responsibilities. Indeed, for young mothers and those with disabilities, teleworking may on occasions provide the only avenue out into the world of work. However, whilst the range of advantages open to individuals can prove powerful, there are also several notable drawbacks. Most significantly, becoming a teleworker can rapidly lead to a feeling of isolation. Even with video links to make interactions with remote colleagues appear more 'real', the nature of an employee's relationship with co-workers is inevitably changed. Many teleworkers also fear that their promotion prospects will be curtailed. For management there is also the potential problem of how teleworkers may be controlled. As Charles Handy notes, 'at its simplest level, the managerial dilemma comes down to the question "How do you manage people who you can not see?"' (1995: 41). Out of sight must not come to mean out of mind. Equally, home workers must not come to be treated as a 'lower breed' of employee when compared to those 'real, live flesh-empowered people' who actually work in the same building as their manager. After all:

... some future managers will undoubtably have employees working for them who they have never actually met, and whom they are unlikely ever to encounter in 'reality'. Treating such individuals with equity may well prove quite a challenge. We will therefore all have to be careful that the people whom we come to know through computer-mediated links are not perceived as a different kind of being — as a lower kind of lifeform — than those individuals we experience with a real physical proximity (Barnatt, 1995: 203).

HOT-DESKS, HOTELLING AND VIRTUAL TEAMS

A second new working arrangement concerns the redesign of office environments to incorporate 'hot-desks'. Under such a regime, no longer does every employee have their own desk, computer, telephone and associated personal space. Instead, common hot-desks equipped with telephone and networked PC workstation are provided to be used by any employee as and when required. Many organizations have reasoned that many of their employees are often out in the field, and hence that providing all of them with desks and IT equipment that is often not in use is simply not cost-effective. Hot-desking gets around this efficiency problem, with companies only providing workstations for the maximum number of employees likely to be within the office at one point in time. One famous example of hot-desk adoption exists with Digital Equipment Corporation's 'office of the future' in Stockholm, as detailed in Example 1.2 (p.11).

A desire to reduce office space costs and requirements for 'absent' workers is also driving the adoption of a relative of hot-desking entitled 'hotelling'. Under this working arrangement, employees such as accountants, auditors and consultants who spend the majority of their working lives away from base no longer have any space entitlement within their 'home' organization. Instead, they are required to use client facilities like a 'hotel', keeping in contact with colleagues via advanced e-mail and voice-mail links. If hotelling employees do need to 'visit' their own office, then they simply call in to book a room for the duration of their stay.

Also associated with teleworking, hot-desk and hotelling office reengineering is the concept of virtual team creation. With CMC links and groupware applications such as Lotus Notes™, no longer do the members of a project team or department need to share any common physical space. Instead, they can work strewn across a myriad of locations both nationally and internationally, staying in contact with each other purely through the IT world of cyberspace. Once working in such a manner the allegiance of any individual to a common office location will inevitably diminish, hence increasing the likelihood that they will take the 'teleworking option' if it becomes available. In the UK, Unilever is just one of the many companies that has reengineered its business processes with groupware in order to create virtual teams synergously drawing together people from different disciplines and departments internationally (Glyn-Jones, 1995: 86). Further discussion of new IT-enabled working practices is contained within Reading 13.

THE VIRTUAL ORGANIZATION AND THE FUTURE

As home working, virtual team creation and increased intra-business connectivity proceed apace, the concept of 'virtual organizations' existing solely as patterns of employee and purchaser–supplier relationship is being taken increasingly seriously. Although little coherence of definition has yet to emerge, the concept of virtual organization may be encapsulated in a desire to use IT '. . . to enable a relaxation of the traditional physical constraints upon organizational formation and adaptation' (Barnatt, 1995: 64). Inevitably, therefore, as Charles Handy ponders, we have to wonder whether in future companies will be anything more than just (electronic) 'boxes of contracts' (1995: 41).

As discussed in Reading 13, over the breadth of this century we have seen an evolution of organizational forms headed away from rigid hierarchies toward more 'organic' and inherently flexible loose production networks. Linking together their functions and trading patterns across the computer domain of cyberspace offers organizations the ultimate in flexible inter-relationships. Like it or not, clear boundaries between organizations — and the 'internal' departments and functions thereof — are becoming increasingly fuzzed as businesses metamorph into software patterns across an emerging global IT hardware platform. What's more, the IT-enabled business reengineering developments we have already witnessed may just constitute the tip of a great iceberg. As Alvin Toffler argued in 1980, we have now entered the transition to the super-industrial revolution or the 'Third Wave'. Old ways of thinking and old ideologies — however cherished — no longer fit the facts and need to be discarded as humanity faces the greatest upheaval and creative restructuring of all time (Toffler, 1980: 18-26).

OVERVIEW

Over this and the previous five chapters, many of the managerial and strategic implications relating to the increased and potential adoption of information technology 'advances' have been outlined. Key technological developments in areas such as computer-mediated communications, groupware application, and the increased prominence of open PC systems, have been discussed alongside more managerial concerns regarding strategy formation in IS outsourcing, systems development and IT implementation. There has also been a fairly detailed consideration of the business issues raised when attempting to use IT to lever increased competitive advantage, together with some discussion of the social, cultural and political forces that still define a very negative divide or 'disconnect' between many IT departments and the rest of the organization.

As stated in the Preface, nobody can hope to understand, let alone explain in one book, the complexities of the managerial and strategic issues surrounding computer application in modern business. However, what you — the reader — should now be familiar with are the broad areas of potential and concern that may be more fully explored. Within the journal article reprints that follow, many of the concepts raised within the six chapters of the text are taken further. Some of the Readings are at first complex, their scope ranging from detailed case study evaluations to rigorous, conceptual academic debate, yet perseverance will be rewarded from gaining a thorough understanding of all seven. In order to cope with the complexities of the future a new *mindset* is needed that embraces concepts and information from a wide range of perspectives. It is up to you to decide where the line needs to be drawn between useful computer application and IT adoption that only degrades our humanity. So above all adopt an open and questioning mind as you forge ahead in your own, personal investigation of *Management Strategy and Information Technology*.

REVIEW AND DISCUSSION QUESTIONS

1. Describe what is meant by business process engineering, and explain why the concept is usually associated with developments in IT application.

2. Discuss the potential benefits to commercial and non-commercial organizations of setting up a site upon the world-wide web.

3. How may so called 'management by wire' systems help to improve the quality of managerial decision making?

4. Discuss some of the advantages and disadvantages, for both organizations and their employees, of:

   • Telecommuting
   • Hot-desk working arrangements
   • Using CMC links to empower virtual teams

REFERENCES

Barnatt, C. (1995) *Cyber Business: Mindsets for a Wired Age*, Chichester: John Wiley & Sons.

Clarke, A.C. (1956) *The City and the Stars*, London: Frederick Muller.

Edwards. C. and Peppard, J.W. (1994) 'Business Process Redesign: Hype, Hope or Hypocrisy?', *Journal of Information Technology*, 9(4).

Fielder, K.D., Grover, V. and Teng, J.T.C. (1994) 'Information Technology-Enabled Change: The Risks and Rewards of Business Process Redesign and Automation', *Journal of Information Technology*, 9(4).

Gelernter, D. (1992) *Mirror Worlds: The Day Software puts the Universe in a Shoebox: How it will Happen and What it will Mean*, NY: Oxford University Press.

Glyn-Jones, F. (1995) 'The Groupware Grapevine', *Management Today* (April).

Gooding, C. (1995) 'Boosting Sales with the Information Warehouse', *Financial Times Review: Information Technology*, (1st March).

Hammer, M. and Champy, J. (1993) *Reengineering the Corporation: A Manifesto for Business Revolution*, London: Nicholas Brealey.

Handy, C. (1995) 'Trust and the Virtual Organization', *Harvard Business Review*, (May–June).

Hoberg, J. (1995) 'Talk to my Agent: Software Agents in Virtual Reality', *Computer-Mediated Communication Magazine*, 2(1) (February).

Kinsman, F. (1987) *The Telecommuters*, Chichester: John Wiley & Sons.

Kirkpatrick, D. (1995) 'As the Internet Sizzles, Online Services Battle for the Stakes', *Fortune* (1st May).

Leary, T. (1994) *Chaos and Cyberculture*, Berkley, CA: Ronin Publishing.

Nulty, P. (1995) 'Why You Can — and Should — Wait to Get on the Internet', *Fortune* (26th June).

Pancucci, D. (1995) 'Remote Control', *Management Today*, (April).

Toffler, A. (1980) *The Third Wave*, London: Collins.

7 GAINING COMPETITIVE ADVANTAGE FROM INFORMATION TECHNOLOGY

JACQUELINE SENKER AND PETER SENKER *

Many firms that have invested in IT systems have failed to reap the full benefits desired. Sometimes this has been because they have failed to gain a thorough understanding of the technology employed at all appropriate organizational levels. In other instances, the human resource management implications of IT adoption have not been carefully planned or understood. Within this paper, Jacqueline and Peter Senker explore the means by which companies may gain competitive advantage from IT via a review of IT adoption across a range of manufacturing and service sectors.

(There has been a rapid diffusion of Information Technology (IT) throughout the economy for more than a decade.) In the last five years, growth in the use of IT in financial and business services has been more rapid than in manufacturing, where applications are often more complicated. Both service and manufacturing firms experience similar problems in managing the introduction of IT[1], and many companies have been disappointed by their failure to achieve the benefits they sought from their investment.

Porter has suggested that firms should identify all the technologies in their value chain, and then determine which technologies and potential technological changes have the most significance for reinforcing competitive advantage. He noted that 'in choosing among technologies to invest in, a firm must base its decision on a thorough understanding of each important technology in its value chain . . .' [2]. But it takes time and effort for firms to understand new technologies and to accumulate technological expertise [3]. This in turn may require investment in new competencies, in training and retraining.

For example, as a result of their 'cumulative expertise' in electronics technology, electronics manufacturing firms have been in a better position to exploit

* SCIENCE POLICY RESEARCH UNIT, UNIVERSITY OF SUSSEX.
REPRINTED WITH PERMISSION FROM, JOURNAL OF GENERAL MANAGEMENT, VOL. 17, NO. 3, SPRING 1992, PP. 31–45, THE BRAYBROOKE PRESS LTD., HENLEY–ON–THAMES.

computer aided design (CAD) technology than mechanical engineering or vehicles firms. Electronics firms can learn to use CAD systems relatively quickly, as these systems are closely related to the core business in which the principal expertise of the firm is concentrated. In contrast, firms whose strength is based primarily on mechanical engineering expertise find it difficult to learn to use CAD which is based on a technology alien to them [4].

Porter's 'thorough understanding' of new technology seems to imply a need for technical expertise. This is, of course necessary, but there is evidence reviewed in this paper that it is inadequate by itself. An extensive body of research on both manufacturing and service sectors has demonstrated that the effective introduction of IT requires not only technical expertise, but managers who appreciate that successful IT implementation requires changes to the way in which work is organized and in workers' jobs. The changes needed are not determined exclusively by the nature of the technology, but also in the way that it is implemented. IT can be used to 'centralise or decentralise control . . . to deskill or enrich jobs; to improve services or depersonalise them . . .' [5].

After outlining recent technological developments in IT equipment and systems, this paper presents experience of firms' use of IT in manufacturing, retailing, financial services, hotels and catering, and also considers implications for some important office occupations and for management training. We conclude that there is a need for firms to integrate IT strategy into overall corporate strategy.

DEVELOPMENTS IN INFORMATION TECHNOLOGY

Milestones in the development of IT were first the big, expensive mainframe computers introduced by some large companies in the 1960s to handle large-scale operations such as payroll and stock, production and inventory control. They were situated in specialist, centralized data-processing departments. Some years later the development of integrated circuits led to the production of smaller, less costly but powerful minicomputers. Computers were connected with 'dumb' terminals ('dumb' because they had no computing power and were communication devices only) for inputting data, and various output devices, such as printers.

In the 1980s, the computing power available for a given price continued to increase rapidly as computer manufacturers took advantage of the availability of cheap microprocessors to produce microcomputers and personal computers (PCs). Some current PCs costing a few thousand pounds are more powerful in some respects than the multi-million pound mainframe computers of 25 years ago. PCs can run their own software programs or form part of a distributed system when connected to central computers and used as 'intelligent' terminals. Intelligent terminals can download data from a central computer, and manipulate it. The second half of the 1980s has seen the wide adoption of PCs throughout organizations. This is largely due to the low price of PCs and the development of a wide range of user-friendly software packages for word processing, database, graphics or spreadsheet applications. For instance, cheap PCs are now replacing computer-based dedicated word processors which cannot be reprogrammed for other applications. A wide range of sophisticated software is available which makes it possible to use PCs for many applications in addition to word processing. It is also relatively easy to interlink PCs for communications purposes, and their flexibility of use allows for standardization between the equipment used by executives and secretaries.

As PCs have spread throughout their organizations, companies have seen the advantages of connecting them through distribution and linking technologies. Computers and associated peripherals linked together for data and text transmission systems within a limited geographic area are known as local area networks (LANs). In addition, wide area networks (WANs) permit links between more remote systems. They are accessed through telephone lines, using a modem to connect the computer to the telephone line. Linkages through LANs and WANs are likely to increase dramatically in the 1990s.

Within this basic framework many specialist applications have been developed and applied in manufacturing and service sectors.

MANUFACTURING

IT is incorporated on a significant scale into the products of electrical, electronic, instrument and mechanical engineering, and into vehicles and aircraft. Applications of IT in design and production processes are more widespread, and there are many users in engineering, paper and printing, food and drink and chemicals and metals industries [6].

COMPUTER-AIDED DESIGN

In the 1960s computer systems were developed which were interactive and could display data in the form of graphics. It became possible for designers to use computers in place of drawing boards. Early CAD systems were based on mainframe computers, but technological advances allowed small powerful CAD systems to be based first on minicomputers and then on PCs. As with other IT systems, falling costs have made CAD available to small as well as large firms, although small firms tend to use CAD for simpler applications than large ones. CAD software is available for a variety of applications ranging from electronic engineering to mechanical engineering, mapping, architecture and construction. CAD also allows for integration with manufacturing, but direct computer links between design and manufacture are rare. Most companies use CAD for two-dimensional (2D) drawing and design automation, but use in 3D applications is found much less often. The communications of CAD-generated data between departments through on-line networks is still rare, and links are mainly paper-based. Knowledge and experience of CAD has been accumulated by relatively junior engineers and managers, but they are not in a position to realize the strategic potential of integrating CAD with other company functions. Integration between the functions of various previously separate company departments requires organizational change which can be initiated only by senior managers.

Currie undertook several case studies and found that the introduction of new technology was not generally initiated nor managed by senior management. The pattern of investment depended on a series of 'sub-strategies' not linked into any coherent overall strategy. Engineering managers devised various informal techniques to circumvent the rigidity imposed by centralized and bureaucratized resource allocation: managers entered into informal negotiations with managers of other departments to try to ensure that all the costs involved in introducing the technology effectively were included in somebody's budget.

There were severe problems in the relationship between accountancy and engineering management. Several engineering managers were critical of top management who expected good results from the applications of new technology, but were not prepared to allocate sufficient expenditure for the training necessary to achieve these goals [7].

The need to create information flows between departments on the basis of databases held on computer presents considerable problems. The problems involved were described particularly clearly at one company.

> Design management would have liked to see the various business, design and production elements linked, at least in terms of information flow. There were thought to be too many departmental barriers. Links with production were particularly convoluted. Both areas had equal status and there was a paucity of senior managerial experience to negotiate day-to-day compromises or to initiate more fundamental change.

> CAD was still isolated from the rest of the business. Engineering and design had continually offered to produce parts listings and other costing-related information, for central systems. This had never been taken up. Data was still input manually. This was also the case with parts lists and costings for component insertion and test. Many of the working procedures were felt to be too laborious, with lots of paper being passed between designers and engineers, with project managers signing everything, checking modifications and updates. Data management was 'a bit of a nightmare'.

> The poor links between the different departments and phases of the design to manufacture process, made it very difficult to manage such things as engineering changes. Changes were not immediately updated in the database, so the latest information on work and engineering changes was often not available [8].

Traditionally, manufacturing companies have operated on the basis of virtually independent departments: design, engineering, production, finance, marketing, production control, etc. Changes are needed in organizational behaviour to facilitate the flow of information between departments. Many difficulties arise largely as a result of senior managers' failure to undertake the necessary training, and to stimulate sufficient training amongst more junior managers and supervisors. Outside the electronics industry, senior managers tend to be relatively ignorant of CAD and its potential, and not very willing to go on training courses to enhance their knowledge, for fear that this would be taken as a sign of their inadequacy.

Knowledge of CAD and its potential accumulates in design departments which have had direct experience of it and have gained expertise in its use. In the case of new and rapidly developing technologies such as CAD, relatively junior engineers and managers are the principal repositories of companies' accumulated knowledge and experience. But this knowledge and experience does not include knowledge about the organizational and strategic implications of this technology, because relevant experience does not yet exist. Thus, the senior managers who are charged with dealing with strategic and organizational matters do not have relevant technical knowledge or experience to draw on. At the same time, junior managers and engineers possess more technical expertise, but lack their seniors' presumed experience of dealing with strategic issues.

Design departments have problems communicating with senior management because, as CAD is relatively new, most senior managers were initially completely ignorant of its potential. There has been a tendency for some senior managers to reject requests for investment in the long-term potential of CAD, whether, for example, through training programmes, in developing parametrics, putting data into databases, or establishing new links and relationships between functions and departments. There appears to have been insufficient communication between top managements and their juniors. Middle-level managers have been largely responsible for implementing CAD within design and drawing offices. When issues of communicating data between design and other functions within the company arise, design managers have insufficient power to ensure that issues of data compatibility are properly tackled: indeed, there is evidence in the case studies that their colleagues sometimes resent CAD, perceiving the extension of its use as a means by which design managers are seeking to enhance their power within the firm as a whole [9].

Experience of integrated systems is extremely limited, experimental and reflects only partial integration. Outside the electronics industry, there are few examples of fully integrated CAD/CAM systems. The lack of generally adopted software standards makes it difficult for manufacturing systems to communicate. More crucial to the achievement of manufacturing integration is ensuring that the necessary degree of organizational integration is available to support technological integration.

ADVANCED MANUFACTURING TECHNOLOGY (AMT)

The benefits sought from AMT include raising quality, accuracy, consistency, increased machine utilization, cost reduction, productivity increases and coping with shortages of skilled labour.

Hard-wired numerically controlled machine tools (NC) controlled by coded paper tapes date back to the late 1940s. Each operation was carried out by a single special purpose machine. The availability of minicomputers in the 1970s led to the development of computer numerically controlled (CNC) machine tools. Their built-in computers allow for the storage and editing of a wide variety of programs. CNC machine tools equipped with automatic tool changing can be used for a variety of functions.

Direct numerical control (DNC) describes a production cell where a master computer controls a set of multi-function machine tools. Flexible manufacturing systems (FMS) are more advanced than DNC systems. FMS also involves computer controls of the movement of workpieces between workstations by robots, conveyors or automatic guided vehicles (AGVs). Adoption of FMS is not yet widespread, but firms are thinking increasingly about its introduction [10].

Preparatory planning for FMS can highlight existing custom and practice which is detrimental to costs. Managerial and work-based organizational changes are thought to have contributed many of the benefits derived from robot and FMS installations [11]. The effective use of FMS requires multi-skilling, but adherence to traditional job classifications could discourage operators from working outside their prescribed areas and limit the flexibility of the systems. Operators need to learn about the system as a whole, including programming, inspection, scheduling, operation and maintenance of the machines, so they can be involved in all the tasks necessary to keep plant running [12]. This requires major changes to operators' skill patterns. Lack of broad-based skills and training could affect the ability of firms to achieve best practice performance with advanced manufacturing technology systems [13].

Integrated manufacturing systems such as CAD/CAM and FMS require design and production departments to work together more closely. The need for complex manipulations has to be eliminated in design to render products suitable for manufacture in highly automated facilities. AMT is most successfully introduced where supervisors have received appropriate training, but some firms automate with a minimum of planning. They give their supervisors no training for CNC, exclude them from decisions about its introduction and yet expect them to manage it [14].

In contrast to Japan, robotics assembly is used in the UK as a sophisticated form of special-purpose automation. As with other AMT applications, British firms assume that operators have few skills and are unable to carry out routine maintenance, clear blockages or amend programs. UK practice tends to be expensive, unreliable and inflexible. Japanese firms use less sophisticated robots but use them more flexibly, and place great emphasis on training workers. Operators play a 'fire-fighting' role as well as performing some assembly work and supplying components. These keep the robotic assembly systems running smoothly [15]. The progress of AMT in Britain has been inhibited by shortages of graduate engineers with broad skills and of managers who understand the wider implications of the technology. Graduate engineers are mainly employed in R&D

and design departments but not enough in manufacturing and production engineering.

SERVICE SECTORS

⌈Since the middle of the 1980s there has been an enormous increase in the use of IT throughout the service sector and great changes in its use. This is linked with the rise of the PC, the increasing use of computer networking and a convergence towards common standards.⌋

In banks and building societies ⌐a distributed network may link the Head Office computer, which holds records of all customers, with bank tellers' computers and with the hole-in-the-wall automatic telling machine (ATM), from which customers withdraw funds.⌋ The diffusion of IT in retailing is now gathering pace, after a slow start in the 1980s. Electronic Point of Sale (EPoS) is a development of the cash register which can capture extensive data about a transaction. Optical scanning of barcodes at point of sale, at goods receiving point and throughout warehousing and distribution is being used increasingly to enter data into users' computers on the movement of goods. The low price of PCs and the availability of software tailored to the needs of individual retail sectors has led to the wide diffusion of EPoS terminals in large multiples. The data recorded by EPoS can be used for straightforward accounting purposes, for stock control and for management information systems to aid decision-making.

The use of electronic trading — direct communication between firms' computers via a telephone network for enquiries, purchase orders, delivery notes and invoices — is likely to grow enormously in the 1990s. Direct exchange of electronic data, or EDI, is also used in freight transport, to transfer funds between clearing banks, exchange information between insurance companies and brokers or tour operators and travel agents and also for intra-firm transactions. Inter-firm computer communication is facilitated by companies which provide telematic services, i.e. they run third-party value-added networks and/or offer value-added services.

OFFICE MANAGEMENT

Secretarial work has followed a pattern of centralization followed by decentralization. Expensive, dedicated word processing equipment was first introduced as a central facility either to existing typing pools or to new word-processing pools based on typists who had formerly worked for an individual or small group on a range of tasks. There are many reports of a lack of job satisfaction for typists working under these conditions and managerial dissatisfaction with the quality of work produced [16].

The advent of cheap PCs with sophisticated word processing software is leading to the break-up of pools. PCs are replacing typewriters and word processor operators are located closer to the people they work for. Experience has shown that involving secretaries in the selection of equipment to be used for word processing yields considerable benefits, including better trained secretaries committed to the new technology and competent to produce professional standards of work. The standardization of word processing equipment throughout organizations facilitates training, and optimizes the use of peripherals and shared support staff [17].

Some managers with PCs use them to write reports, but few are prepared to use PCs themselves. Many managers put them on their secretaries' desks, delegating a wide range of other computer applications, including diary management, spreadsheet, database, accounts, and electronic mail to them. This phenomenon of senior managers relying on intermediaries to use IT on their behalf has been called 'chauffeured' use [18], and can be explained by the lack of management training accompanying the delivery of a PC [19]. Managers, however, often fail to provide adequate training for their 'IT chauffeurs'. PCs are also used for databases and spreadsheets, but few secretaries understand how to use them effectively [20]. Secretaries who acquire the skills to use these new applications may be able to take on many administrative tasks, acting as a personal assistant to their bosses. Too often however, secretaries are not given the necessary training to upgrade their skills. This is even true of word processing, where they have to learn a wide range of additional skills to those used by a traditional typist, for instance the requirement to organize the storage and indexing of computer disks and their files, and to take responsibility for their safety and security [21].

Employers who wish to maintain centralized data input or word processing as a function need to consider seriously whether this is in their companies' best interests. Employees using computer keyboards continuously are susceptible to repetitive strain injury (RSI) which has become a widespread industrial disease. Compensation awards for those affected by RSI are increasing [22]. Ergonomic design of office equipment and an appropriate organization of work can reduce the occurrence of RSI, and office managers need training in these matters.

FINANCIAL SERVICES

In the early days of computing, banks and insurance companies confined mainframe computers to Head Office in the Finance or Accountant's Department. Because computers were so expensive, they had to be used to the maximum. New types of clerical jobs grew up to serve these centralized computers, consisting of batches of narrow sub-tasks, for instance data preparation or data processing. Centralized computing facilities can now be used to hold a central database for distributed computing and communications networks. The new on-line systems allow direct entry and amendment of databases from decentralized intelligent terminals, and could enable branch managers to access information on which they could base local decisions. For instance marketing campaigns for new services can be offered to designated sub-sets of customers.

In practice, central control is very often maintained by headquarters staff, eroding the responsibility delegated to branch managers who have lost many of their day-to-day supervisory and training responsibilities and their autonomy over local decisions. Some bank branches are now controlled by senior clerks [23]. Whilst early computerization reduced clerical skills, decentralized 'on-line' inter-active systems could increase them. The outcome rests not on the technology, but on the way it is used. There are examples of decentralization where clerks continue to carry out deskilled routine, fragmented keyboarding tasks. Here again, managers should consider changing the organization of work [24].

The experience of Branch Network Reorganization (BNR) introduced by some banks to reduce operating costs shows that deskilling workers does not necessarily reduce costs. Under BNR, only the central 'Hub' branch provided a full range of specialist services and many fragmented data sorting and entry tasks were dele-gated to clerks relocated to a data processing office, which also served a series of satellite branches. Some clerks from satellite branches were also relocated to the data processing office. Reduced numbers of staff in satellite branches offered only a narrow range of services to personal customers. BNR was not cost-saving in practice. It increased the time devoted to management and co-ordination and did not reduce the number of clerical staff required. Morale was low among clerks engaged in routine, monotonous tasks at the data processing office. At the satellites overtime increased and there were difficulties in coping with staff sickness, holidays and absences for other reasons. Automation of branch accounting led to loss of customer knowledge by the manager [25].

Staff in specialized data processing offices are now being reabsorbed into branches, where they share diverse tasks with other clerks. Some bank clerks have been upgraded to become personal bankers, with IT giving them the ability to answer queries on financial services and grant straightforward loans [26]. Decentralization could return autonomy to branch managers, both in banking and insurance, but some analysts believe that organizational politics will act to maintain control at the centre [27].

There has been a great deal of 'hype' surrounding the application of expert systems to the financial services sector, but so far there have been only a few small-scale experimental developments [28]. Expert systems, for instance, could provide branch managers with information relevant to evaluating lending propo-sitions [29]. In one insurance company, an expert system has enabled unskilled clerks to do jobs formerly undertaken by scarce, overworked, expert underwriters [30].

In the Head Office, Decision Support Systems (DSS) for top management have not been greeted with much enthusiasm. DSS do not provide answers. They give information and insights on which managers can base decisions. One study found that these systems were rejected because of the time and effort required to learn how to use them. The second reason for rejection was that the systems were incorrectly oriented towards the nature of senior managerial work [31].

HOTELS AND CATERING

In hotels and catering IT is used mainly for bookkeeping, word processing, reservation and check-out facilities. Fast food chains are introducing EPoS. Some large hotel groups go beyond these routine applications and use LANs to provide their customers with a wide range of services, e.g. car hire, entertainment, etc. Training is required to equip clerks and receptionists with relevant computing skills.

Formal training programmes for staff are unusual, because of high levels of staff turnover in this sector. The burden of operator training tends to fall on supervisors. Few companies have adopted a policy of participation and consultation with unit managers and lower grade staff about the installation of new IT equipment. As a result there is a lack of commitment to new technology by unit managers and staff. Successful implementation and high levels of staff commitment are more often experienced in pilot sites where the experiment is supported by finance, training and expertise.

Systems are often implemented in a piecemeal way with insufficient attention being paid to the benefits which can be derived from integration, for instance, communication between marketing, reservations, food and beverage management and personnel functions [32]. One company developed a system to calculate daily staff requirements in a hotel chain. It was not used, however, because it was inaccurate, inaccessible to department managers and did not provide information in a user-friendly way [33]. A study of a more successful hotel system suggests that effective use requires managers to have three capabilities: knowledge of how the information system functions, ability to specify their information needs clearly, and judgement in using the information [34]. This suggests a need for hotel managers to acquire skills in acquiring and analysing information through the use of IT equipment which could assist in strategic planning and marketing [35].

RETAILING

The data captured by barcode scanners at retail EPoS checkouts can be a direct input into shops' accounting and inventory systems. In retailing, for instance, EPoS data about goods purchased can automatically provide shelf replenishment from a central warehouse [36]. The same data has been used by central management to determine staff rostering for each store [37]. Work is proceeding on systems to determine the location and amount of shelf space to be given to each product and detailed advice on store layout and merchandising [38]. These are all examples of Management Information Systems (MIS) which focus on producing answers to specific problems through the use of objective and quantifiable data. The responsibility of store managers is eroded as more central control is taken over staff rostering, purchase decisions, store layout and merchandising. Other sectors have already provided ample evidence that deskilling workers' jobs leads to less rather than more productivity.

One final example from warehousing is instructive as it illustrates how the way in which work is organized can have crucial effects on the success or failure of IT implementation. Software programs can be used to plan warehouse layout, vehicle loading and route planning. One system produced the list of goods to be collected from the shelves by warehousemen in the same order as they appeared in the warehouse. But this decreased the productivity of warehousemen rather than increasing it. While they no longer had to remember where individual items were located, lack of concentration made them forget which aisle they were in. When an item on their list could not be found on the shelves, warehousemen often assumed that an item was out of stock, when in fact their failure to find it was because they were in the wrong aisle [39].

CONCLUSION

The research evidence has shown that many firms in both manufacturing and service sectors often introduce new IT equipment and systems without the necessary 'thorough understanding' of the technology. The necessary knowledge is both technical and, perhaps more important, knowledge about implications for human resource management. As a result, companies often fail to secure the full potential of competitive advantage from their investments in IT. Many managers need to acquire the knowledge which will enable them to devise strategies for introducing new technologies, and to understand the necessity to reorganize work and to initiate appropriate training programmes. Shortages of people with the skills necessary to implement new technology effectively can be a major cause of failure to secure the quality, productivity and new product markets available to those companies which exploit IT properly.

Managers also need to understand that their companies may suffer if they maintain that decisions about the introduction of new technology should be the sole preserve of management. Participation in decision-making by those directly involved in using the technology can yield important benefits — to companies as well as to employees. Both workers and managers need to learn about the new technology and its implications for their work in order to participate effectively in decision-making. Problems can be solved more quickly and new equipment used better when users are involved in its selection.

The shift from centralized, corporate IT departments to decentralized and distributed systems integral to line organizations has far-reaching implications for management. The effective use of new technology now demands IT literacy throughout organizations, not just in computer services departments. It also requires changes in management attitudes and organizations. Firms need to integrate IT into overall business strategy, not merely use if for short-term profit motives. 'Hybrid' managers with skills in business management and IT could bring about significant change within organizations. They would have the ability to recognize IT opportunities and understand how to implement them [40].

As Porter suggests, firms need a thorough understanding of the technologies they choose to invest in. Managing new technology effectively depends on understanding the technology and on adopting training and recruitment policies which ensure that the necessary technological expertise is accumulated. It also requires changes in management attitudes and work organization, especially appreciation of the need to implement IT in ways which enhance workers' skills and experience. Managers with this type of thorough understanding can help their companies to gain competitive advantage from the use of IT.

ACKNOWLEDGEMENTS

We are grateful to the Training Agency for sponsoring the research which forms the basis for this paper. Except where otherwise attributed the opinions expressed are those of the authors alone and do not necessarily reflect the views or policies of the Employment Department.

REVIEW AND DISCUSSION QUESTIONS

1. Why do you think that so many companies have been disappointed by their IT investments?

2. What are the key factors that contribute towards successful IT implementation?

3. Explain the concept of interdepartmental integration, and the role it may have to play in reaping the full benefits from new IT systems.

4. Discuss the need for both management and workers to participate in systems development and implementation.

REFERENCES

[1] Senker, J. and Senker, P., *Technical Change in the 1990s. Implications for Skills, Training and Employment,* Science Policy Research Unit, University of Sussex, 1990.

[2] Porter, M., 'Technology and Competitive Advantage', *The Journal of Business Studies,* Winter, 1985, pp. 60-78.

[3] Senker, J., 'Technology and Competitive Strategy in Food Retailing', in Loveridge, R. and Pitt, M., eds, *Strategic Management of Technological Innovation,* Chichester: John Wiley & Sons, 1991.

[4] Senker, P. and Simmonds, P., 'Changing technology and design work in the British engineering industry 1981-1988', *New Technology, Work and Employment,* vol. 6, no. 2, Autumn 1991, pp.91-9.

[5] Whitaker, M., 'Overcoming the Barriers to Successful Implementation of Information Technology in the UK Hotel Industry', *International Journal of Hospitality Management,* vol. 6, no. 4, 1987, pp.229-35.

[6] Northcott, J. and Walling, A., *The Impact of Microelectronics. Diffusion, Benefits and Problems in British Industry,* London: Policy Studies Institute, 1988.

[7] Currie, W., *Managerial Strategy for New Technology,* Aldershot: Avebury, 1989.

[8] Senker and Simmonds, op cit.

[9] Ibid.

[10] Haywood, B., 'Organizational Aspects of FMS in the United Kingdom', in Wobbe, W., ed., *Flexible Manufacturing in Europe - State of the Art of Approaches and Diffusion Patterns,* FAST Occasional Paper No.155, Commission of the European Communities, 1987.

[11] Tidd, J., *Flexible Manufacturing Technologies and International Competitiveness,* London: Pinter Publishers, 1991. Bessant J. and Haywood B., *The Introduction of Flexible Manufacturing Systems as an Example of Computer Integrated Manufacturing,* Innovation Research Group, Department of Business Management, Brighton: Brighton Polytechnic, 1985.

[12] Jones, B. and Scott, P., 'Flexible Manufacturing Systems in Britain and the USA', *New Technology, Work and Employment,* vol. 2, no. 1, 1987, pp. 27-36.

[13] Bessant, J. and Haywood, B., 'Islands, Archipelagoes and Continents: Progress on the Road to Computer-integrated Manufacturing', *Research Policy,* vol. 17, no. 6, December 1988, pp. 349-62.

[14] Burnes, B., 'New Technology and Job Design: the Case of CNC', *New Technology, Work and Employment,* vol. 3, no. 2, 1988, pp. 100-11.

[15] Tidd, J., op cit.

[16] Long, R., *New Office Information. Technology, Human and Managerial Implications,* London: Croom Helm, 1987.

[17] Huggett, C., *Participation in Practice, A Case Study of the Introduction of New Technology,* EITB Research Report No. RC22, Watford, 1987. Thompson, L., *New Office Technology and the Changing Role of the Secretary,* Work Research Unit Occasional Paper 44, London, 1989.

[18] Martin, C., 'Management Computer Support: Analysing the Top Manager's Perspective on Interactive Systems', in *Knowledge Based Management Support Systems,* Chichester: Ellis Horwood, 1989. McCandless, H. and Duffy, L., 'Changing Roles in the High-Tech Office', *Practical Computing,* July 1989, pp. 39-46.

[19] Hall-Sheehy, J., 'Management Turn-On to Computers', *International Journal of Computing. Computers in Adult Eduction and Training* (UK), vol. 1, no. 2, Autumn 1988, pp. 15-20.

[20] Fenton, J.S., *Skills Shortage of Computer Scientists in Industry*. Paper presented to the Conference of Professors of Computer Science, University of Lancaster, 3-4 July 1989.

[21] Quintas, P., 'Information Technology and Employment in Local Government', *New Technology, Work and Employment,* vol. 1, no. 2, Autumn, 1986, pp. 172-84.

[22] Buckingham, L. and Beavis, S., 'New technology strains alarm insurers', *The Guardian,* 28 December 1989.

[23] Smith, S., 'Information Technology in Banks: Taylorization or Human-centered Systems?', *Science and Public Policy,* vol. 14, no. 3, June 1987. Storey, J., 'The Management of New Office Technology: Choice, Control and Social Structure in the Insurance Industry', *Journal of Management Studies,* vol. 24, no. 1, January 1987, pp. 43-62.

[24] Rolfe, H., 'Skill, deskilling and new technology in the non-manual labour process' *New Technology, Work and Employment,* vol. 1, no. 1, Spring 1986. Smith, S. and Wield, D., 'New Technology and Bank Work: Banking on IT as an 'Organizational Technology' in Harris, L. et al eds. *New Perspectives on the Financial System,* London: Croom Helm, 1988.

[25] Smith, 1987, op cit.

[26] Swann, J., *The Employment Effects of Microelectronics in the UK Services Sector,* London: Technical Change Centre, 1986.

[27] Storey, op cit.

[28] Stevenson, H., 'Expert Systems in the UK Financial Services Sector: A Symbolic Analysis of the Hype', in Doukidis, G., Land, F. and Miller, G., *Knowledge-Based Management Support Systems,* Chichester: John Wiley & Sons, 1989.

[29] Forsey, G. and Finlay, P., 'Information Technology Support for Corporate Bank Lending', *The Service Industries Journal,* vol. 9, no. 1, January 1989.

[30] Senker, P., Townsend, J. and Buckingham, J., 'Working with Expert Systems: Three Case Studies' *AI and Society,* no. 3, 1989, pp. 103-16.

[31] Martin, op cit.

[32] Whitaker, op cit.

[33] Guerrier, Y. and Lockwood, A.J., 'Managing Flexible Working in Hotels', *The Service Industries Journal,* vol. 9, no. 3, July 1989, pp.406-19.

[34] Buchanan, D. and McCalman, J., 'Confidence, Visibility and Pressure: the Effects of Shared Information in Computer Aided Hotel Management', *New Technology, Work and Employment,* vol. 3, no. 1, Spring 1988, pp. 38-46.

[35] Whitaker, op cit.

[36] Smith, S., 'How Much Change at the Store? The Impact of New Technologies and Labour Processes on Managers and Staffs in Retail Distribution', in Knights, D. and Wilmott, H., *New Technology and the Labour Process,* Macmillan, 1988.

[37] Graves, D., 'EPoS — Staff Scheduling — Customer Service', *EPoS/EFTPoS '89 Conference Papers,* RMDP, Brighton, 1989.

[38] Jones, G., 'EPoS and the Retailers' Information Needs', in McFadyen, E., ed, *The Changing Face of British Retailing,* London: Newman Books, 1987.

[39] Smith, 1988, op cit.

[40] Palmer, C., 'Using IT for Competitive Advantage at Thomson Holidays', *Long Range Planning,* vol. 21 (6), no. 112, December, 1988, pp. 26-9.

8 WINNING SUPPORT FOR YOUR INFORMATION STRATEGY

W. ADRIAANS *

Whilst increasingly important, strategic planning in IS is complicated and not does always have the desired effect. Often IS planning failures are due to a lack of involvement from key staff across all levels of the organization. This paper addresses these points in depth, and discusses a range of factors which may explain how managers can build support for an information strategy and hence secure its effective implementation.

In recent years, the drawing up of an information strategy has come to be seen as an activity which must precede system development.

Experience has shown that strategic planning for information systems is extremely complex. Methods have been developed to support information planners and they give directions on how to reach the desired result. These techniques appear to be useful but they are no guarantee of success because they concentrate primarily on achieving a tangible goal: the plan itself.

An equally important product of information systems planning is, an organization which is willing and able to get down to business and to implement the information strategy i.e to provide the organizational support.

The people in the organization must believe that the information strategy is feasible. Similarly, the various user groups must believe that the results of the plan will help them to accomplish the company's goals and their own goals.

This article examines the factors that are important for the production of a good information systems plan and for winning and maintaining the necessary organizational support. It also describes conditions which may have a critical impact on the completion of the plan.

* PARTNER OR MORET ERNST & YOUNG MANAGEMENT CONSULTANTS IN UTRECHT, THE NETHERLANDS AND MANAGER OF THE INFORMATION STRATEGY AND MANAGEMENT GROUP.
REPRINTED WITH PERMISSION FROM, LONG RANGE PLANNING, VOL.26, NO.1, SPRING 1993, PP.45–53, ELSEVIER SCIENCE LTD., PERGAMON IMPRINT, OXFORD, ENGLAND.

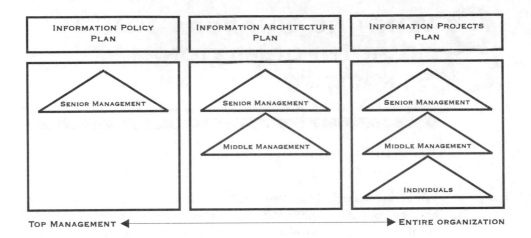

Figure 1 Developing support for the plan.

INFORMATION SYSTEM PLANNING

The term Information Systems Plan may be used to describe a wide range of products. We can distinguish between:

(1) *The information strategy*
This outlines the information strategy and the conditions for implementing it. It is a strategic plan and is in line with the company strategy and the business philosophy.

(2) *The information architecture plan*
This plan contains a general design of the information system and its subsystems, an outline of the information technology to be used, and an overall general plan for the organization of the information system. The design is aimed at producing an information system which is in line with the information systems strategy.

(3) *The information projects plan*
This plan describes the projects required to bridge the gap between the present and desired situation. It lists them in order of priority and implementation and within the time set. The emphasis is on implementation.

In large organizations, an information structure plan is sometimes prepared in addition to the information architecture plan. The structure plan describes the connection between the systems at a conceptual level.

In practice, the types of information plan described above are prepared separately and in coordination with each other. The information systems plan is a combination of these three plans.

THE SUPPORT REQUIRED

Depending on the type of plan, support will have to be generated at various levels in the organization (see Figure 1).

An information systems plan requires support at the highest level and has to be executed by middle management. The project plan has to be supported mainly at an operational level. This means that when preparing an information systems plan it will have to be supported at all levels of the organization.

THE PLANNING PROCESS

Figure 2 describes the information systems planning process. Although the diagram outlines a sequence of activities, the implementation process is iterative. The planning process has two main parts:

- creating a model for the real system and the information system;
- creating a plan for the information system.

CREATING A MODEL FOR THE REAL SYSTEM

The first step in information systems planning is to define the business strategy (the strategy model). This is followed by the definition of the business model and the control model.

The *strategy* model is based on the results of an analysis of the business environment and a SWOT analysis and sets out:

- the company's position in relation to its environment;
- the long-term objectives of the organization;
- the critical success factors;
- the policy assumptions for the information system and information technology.

The *business model* generally includes:

- the business processes (in this case, a combination of logically linked tasks aimed at a specific business goal);
- the organization (personnel, structure, location and equipment).

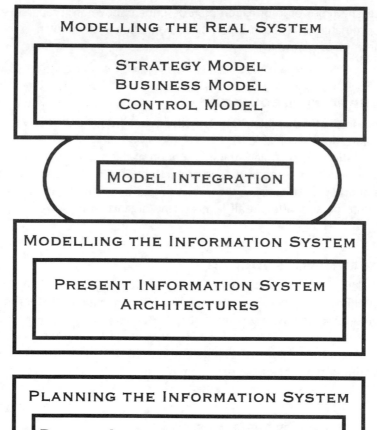

Figure 2 Planning for information systems.

The *control* model generally includes:

- the control variables,
- the control structure, and
- the control instruments.

The strategy model, the business model and the control model are all related to the real system.

CREATING A MODEL FOR THE INFORMATION SYSTEM

Creating a model for the information system means:

- defining the present information system and the information technology applied, including bottlenecks and information requirements;
- determining the extent to which the present information system meets the requirements set by the future system;
- designing the:

  - system architecture (process model, data model and information systems models);
  - information technology infrastructure;
  - information systems organization.

MODEL INTEGRATION

This modelling process in not implemented in separate steps. At the model stage, it is important to bear in mind the possibilities offered by information technology to improve the efficiency and the effectiveness of business processes. It is not so much a question of using information technology to obtain information *about* the process, but rather using information technology as part of the process — a form of instrumentation. This approach will result in *business process redesign*. Business process redesign can be used particularly in those situations in which the system consists chiefly of data processing, as in the case of banks and insurance companies.

Business process redesign can have far-reaching effects on an organization, so that the information systems planning procedure becomes a process of organizational change.

CREATING A PLAN OF THE INFORMATION SYSTEM

The information plan involves:

- establishing the policy assumptions for the information system and the applications of information technology;
- determining the migration path of the current system to the future system, expressed in terms of the *project calendar*.

The projects could be related to:

- organization and management,
- information technology, and
- system development.

DEFINING THE TARGET ORGANIZATION

THE OBJECTIVE OF AN INFORMATION SYSTEMS PLAN

The objectives of an information systems plan are:

- matching the information system to the objectives of the organization;
- outlining the planning and management of the information supply;
- organizing the data processing processes into a logically linked information system and dividing it into subsystems.

The data processing subsystems maintain a collection of logically linked data (the company data bank) which cover all the company's operations. The information systems plan contributes to the ultimate goal of information supply, namely the provision of the transformation, the support and the business processes for up-to-date, correct and complete data. A good information system is structured in such a way that all sections and levels of the organization can be supplied with adequate information. A company data bank is therefore indispensable.

As the top management of an organization must be provided with concise 'company-wide' information, an information system plan should be compiled for the entire company. In principle, the entire company is the target organization.

ORGANIZATION UNITS

The information system described earlier assumes that the organization to which the system is designed is a total unit entity. From this point of view, one organization has one information system and one logical collection of data in one information systems plan.

An organization of any size involves delegation, divisions, and departments. In addition to centralized organization, nowadays sub-units are frequently given a degree of independence. The sections in the organization have, within certain limits, their own objectives and associated organization and information systems. The level of managerial decentralization, the diversity of the primary processes, the size of the organization and the extent of geographical spread, are dimensions which indicate the level of organizational decentralization.

The decentralized organization units shown in Figure 3 are relatively autonomous units. It is assumed that by delegating business decisions to the units, that overall performance is higher than in a centralized organization.

In practice, there are examples of decentralized organizations which are well-managed. However, there are also organizations where decentralization has been introduced in a less controlled manner. In these organizations, the organization units are too autonomous and operate too independently.

Given the structure of organizations, it is clear that the assumption: one organization, one information system, one information strategy plan must be seen in its proper perspective, since what may look like one organization often is not.

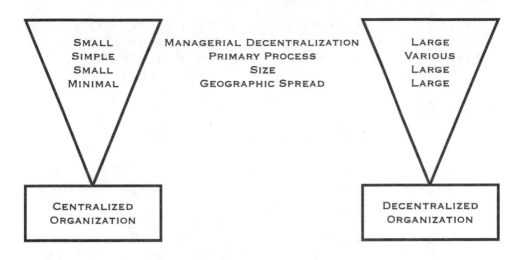

Figure 3 Centralized and decentralized organizations.

THE TARGET ORGANIZATION FOR AN INFORMATION SYSTEMS PLAN

The Organization Structure. The problems outlined above will prompt information planners to reflect whether one organization can be used as a target organization for the information systems plan. Can one overall information systems plan be produced?

The correct choice of the target organization is a decisive factor for the acceptance of the plan. In practice, a concentrated organization will have less trouble in drawing up and implementing an information system plan than a decentralized organization.

Before we can begin to prepare an information systems plan it is necessary to determine the type of plan, and to what extent the target organization is centralized or decentralized.

When determining the target organization for a decentralized organization, it is advisable to view it as a federal structure. Separate information plans have to be prepared for each of the units. Preparing an information structure plan for the overall organization can help with the integration of these plans.

However, even in a decentralized organization, many processes such as finance and personnel, are managed from a central point. It may therefore be necessary to draw up an information plan for the group, aimed primarily at these processes prior to the plans at the unit-level.

The objective is to integrate the individual plans into the overall information systems plan. Without this integration, which provides for the necessary links between systems, it is difficult to provide up-to-date, correct and complete managerial information at group level. In many organizations, there are still shortcomings in the managerial information supply at group level.

Companies often fail, not because their primary processes have been badly executed, but because of a lack of information on the current state of the company's affairs, which causes them to run into financial difficulties.

BUILDING SUPPORT

An information systems plan must result in two end products:

- the plan itself (including the underlying project documentation),
- an organization which is willing and able to implement the information systems plan.

In most planning processes, attention is invariably focused on the plan itself and the documentation. Techniques drive out thinking. They invariably lead to an acceptable pile of paper and a well-structured plan can be designed even though some essential activities may have been omitted or only half-heartedly executed. Problems are simply ignored or brushed aside. Of course, these problems appear as soon as an attempt is made to implement the plan. At this point, the plan is judged unsuitable and added to the pile of impracticable plans.

A number of activities essential for supplying a good plan are examined in more detail in relation to opportunities and threats. The chances of an information systems planning process succeeding are also assessed.

The following aspects will be discussed:

- the condition of the target organization;
- the approach to the planning project;
- the implementation of the project;
- the organization of the plan's implementation.

THE CONDITION OF THE ORGANIZATION

Before designing an information systems plan, the following questions should be answered.

Is an Information Systems Plan necessary? Improvements in the information system of an organization may be less urgent than improvements in the business operations. If the organization is in a crisis this may not be the right time to review the information system.

Is the organization ready for an Information Systems Plan? An important condition for success is that the organization must be 'ready' for an information strategy plan. Management should feel that the development of the system and the procurement of new equipment is not possible without a basic review of the architecture. Also management must be willing to put time and effort into the planning operation.

Preferably the organization should be stable, so that the information systems planning will have a reasonable chance of success.

Developing an information strategy in an organization which is being reorganized and restructured involves considerable complications. It is difficult to win support under these conditions because the organization structure is changing and the staff are uncertain what jobs they will have in the future.

Nevertheless, it is useful to work on an information strategy during a reorganization, because the information strategy can be developed alongside the business strategy. Also there is an opportunity to redesign the business process making the best use of information technology.

Is management ready? An important consideration is whether management sees any benefit in a planned approach to information systems and automation. If management is satisfied with the existing information system and it does not see the use of new information technology applications, it will not be willing to invest the time and money in an information systems plan.

APPROACH

The approach taken to an information planning project plays a crucial role in its success.

Defining the target organization. We have already emphasized the importance of defining the target organization. This sometimes results in an overall plan which is made up of subplans which may prevent the development of a coherent information system and data collection.

WORKING METHOD

A consistent approach. The methods and techniques which are used for preparing an information plan should match as closely as possible the methods and techniques used for system development. Case tools today sometimes include the strategic planning stage, so this can be used. Partly because of the differences in the work of information planners and system developers, there are 'cultural differences' between the two and this leads to difficulties in matching the information plan with the systems development. Systems developers tend to equate the generality of the information system plan as inexactitude and incorrectness. In view of the detail on which they need to base their analysis, design and implementation, the system developers naturally require changes in the system architecture. This is not a bad thing, on the contrary, the architecture benefits.

Turnaround time. The time taken to produce an information systems plan is approximately four to six months. It is almost impossible to develop a strategic information plan in a shorter period. When the timetable exceeds six months the organization's interest in the preparation of an information plan will wane. The question then is whether the plan will ever be completed, or if it is completed, whether it will be accepted. If an organization is preparing a strategic information plan for the first time, management should not expect total success at the first attempt. It is better to settle for less than optimum quality, say 80%, than to be stopped at the development stage through striving for 100% quality. The plan's beauty will be its death knell.

The turnaround time is influenced to a large extent by the quality of the information planners and by the ability of management to decide that once certain steps have been taken in the information planning, strategic decisions will have to be made.

Estimate of time and costs. One of the most difficult aspects of information systems planning is estimating the time and the cost of implementing the planned projects. Given the relatively high level of abstraction in an information plan, it is not realistic to expect precise estimates. There are many estimation techniques available and comparable projects can be used as a guide. However the future is not in the hands of information planners and events will invariably crop up which have not been anticipated. Therefore the information planner should make it clear to the management that the estimates they give are only an indication. This will avoid disappointment, which could result in a loss of confidence during the implementation phase of the plan.

ORIENTATION

Vision. The information systems plan must take account of future developments. The future environment, expected changes in the organization structure, management, markets, and future information technology need to be anticipated. Looking ahead requires vision. All important is the general management's vision of their information systems and the use of information technology. Without this vision, an information plan will have little impact and a short lifetime.

Projections. The need for prediction, when preparing an information systems plan can vary considerably according to the type of organization. In a stable organization, it may be possible to look five or more years ahead. There are also many organizations which operate in the turbulent environment and for them it is more realistic to make projections of less than five years.

Matching specific problems. An information systems plan is a tailor-made plan that must take account of the specific characteristics and the situation of a specific organization. An information plan that ignores the specific characteristics of the organization will lack credibility and will therefore not be accepted. Following a particular technique to the letter is also fatal. This will often result in models which are technically sound but which do not correspond with the actual situation.

No details. When drawing up an information systems plan, there is often an urge to investigate and analyse in great detail. Details distort the overall picture and unearthing them will prolong the process.

IMPACT ON THE ORGANIZATION

Staffing. To guarantee the quality of the plan, it is essential that the team responsible for producing it is well-balanced. In building the team, management should look for the following qualities: expertise, maturity, authority, leadership and determination.

In addition to information planning experts, the organization's line managers should be included in the team.

Interaction. At the preparation stage of the information systems plan, measures should be taken to encourage the organization to become involved. This is the best way to obtain support for the project results. If support is lacking, it will not matter whether a good or a bad information systems plan is produced; the organization will not accept it.

The participants in the information planning process, namely the planners, the information providers, consultants, and the 'maintenance crew' (experts–supporters), all need to support the objectives of the organization, and the objectives of the information systems plan.

The organization can be involved in the plan in several ways. First of all, line managers can work on the project direct as members of the project team. Various senior staff from the organization should be consulted by means of interviews, meetings, questionnaires, etc. The interim and final results should be agreed with or reviewed by these individual and groups.

The primary rule is that the information planning team is 'open' and willing at all times to explain what it is doing not just by providing information, but also by discussing its approach. In addition, it is necessary to provide information, orally and in writing, on results and progress.

The way the project team presents its material is crucial. Although the team uses specialized techniques they should explain clearly how they have produced their plans.

IMPLEMENTATION

Creating a model of the real system. Once a decision has been taken to draw up an information systems plan and the target organization has been defined, a number of activities will need to be carried out. These include mapping out the strategy model, the control model and the business model.

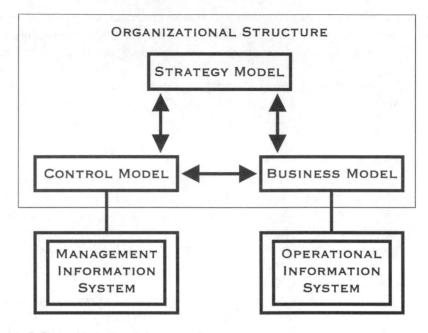

Figure 4 Creating a model.

Figure 4 shows how the strategy of an organization determines the business processes and the way in which they are managed (the control model). This 'translation' from strategy to the business process and the control model is the job of the managers.

The control model is used by management to specify the information they require. The business processes determine the operational information requirements for the organization to function. The business model and the control model are also designed for a specific organization structure.

Objectives. The future information system is derived from the longterm objectives of the organization. In many organizations, these objectives are implicit but have not been precisely defined and communicated to the organization.

Members of management teams sometimes keep their own set of objectives, which may overlap or be in conflict. In only a few cases is there a set of well-defined objectives which have been communicated to all personnel and which has been 'adopted' by them.

When drawing up an information systems plan, the objectives of the organization will need to be made explicit, no matter what; if there are no formulated objectives therefore, they will have to be determined in more detail for the purpose of the information systems plan. To bring these objectives to the surface with the help of top management and to formulate and quantify them requires the information planners to have a knowledge of business, considerable experience and sufficient seniority.

Even if the team is successful in formulating a set of objectives that sufficiently meet their requirements, it is an almost impossible task to convey these objectives to the lower levels of the organization, in the time available for information planning.

Nevertheless, the information planning process can be continued on condition that attention is paid to conveying objectives during and after the process. If it is not possible to formulate a useful set of objectives, it means that the organization is not yet ready to draw up an information systems plan. The information planning process should then be put on hold until the objectives have been clarified.

Sometimes, management is not willing to take such a decision. After all, if it was not in a position to formulate its objectives it will be the last to want to make this public by halting the information systems planning project.

In organizations with a stable mission, an information systems plan can also be drawn up on the basis of that mission alone. For example, a water board has a clear mission, even for outsiders. This means that there are a number of traditional, implicit objectives which are known throughout the organization. On the basis of the traditional mission, a traditional (non innovative) information systems plan will evolve. At the very least, one may ask whether such a plan takes sufficient account of developments (in this example, economics of scale, mergers, acquisitions, and environmental problems) from which even a water board is not exempt nowadays.

The impact of information technology on management. During the information systems planning process, information technologies are listed and their applicability assessed. Their impact on company objectives and business processes is also examined. In certain cases, by applying information technology, it is possible to achieve an advantage over the competition. In other cases, the application of information technology can lead to a totally different business process design which is more efficient.

The possibility of achieving a competitive advantage by applying information technology should be seen in perspective. Competitors can often install the same application quickly. It is important, however, to keep abreast of new developments, so that it would be better to regard a new development as a 'strategic necessity'.

The impact of information technology on objectives and business processes is a complicating factor when designing the business model. If innovation is possible, it will result in a process of change, and this process could lead to a changed organization, in which it is even more difficult to bring the information systems planning process to a successful conclusion. Obviously it is only worthwhile looking at an innovative application of information technology if the company has a good set of objectives.

Control variables. Control variables can be derived from the objectives, the critical success factors and the nature of the business processes. To determine control variables in outline offers a good opportunity to interest management in the information systems plan. They should be especially interested in the provision of management information.

Sometimes very little attention is paid to the compilation of management information systems plans. It is assumed that it takes a long time before the basic systems are in place to supply the necessary data.

However, in many cases it is possible to prepare management information entirely or partly 'by hand', if this information is only needed occasionally and the system development costs are small. Failure to provide management information, even in outline, means a missed opportunity to interact with management and to build their support for the information plan.

CREATING A MODEL OF THE INFORMATION SYSTEM

Mapping out the present situation. Mapping out the information currently supplied requires expertise and social skills. In addition to written questionnaires, this phase will involve personal contact between the planners and a wide range of representatives from the organization.

These representatives have expectations about the direction and content of the information systems plan through their contact with the information planners. If their experience with the planners is negative, the chances of implementing the information systems plan will already have been damaged. If their experience is positive, however, there is the danger that their expectations will be too high and that those expectations will not be able to be fulfilled. It is no easy task for the information planners to keep the balance. The organization and staffing of the project are crucial in this phase.

Architecture. This stage involves the design of the information systems infrastructure, systems and technology. It is vital for the team to have professional skills in these areas, so that architectures can be designed which are in touch with present realities and future requirements.

In the development stage, a detailed review of the architecture is carried out for each project and shortcomings can be corrected.

CREATING A PLAN FOR THE INFORMATION SYSTEM

Basic policy assumptions and migration path. Policy assumptions for information systems and the migration path are both derived directly from the objectives. The involvement of users in this phase is also indispensable to ensure acceptance. In information systems planning, the users are involved in determining the sequence of the implementation of the various system development projects. Failure to prioritize at this stage will mean losing an important chance to obtain the required support.

ORGANIZATION OF THE PLAN'S IMPLEMENTATION

Continuity. A large number of people will be involved in preparing the plan: the planners and those who provided information or reviewed certain aspects of the plan. It is advisable to involve ex-members of the planning team at the implementation stage. This will encourage consistency between planning and implementation, while at the same time good use can be made of their know-how and experience. It is also conducive to a smooth implementation of the plan if line managers continue to occupy the same positions in the organization during the implementation period.

In a dynamic organization, this will not be the case. Changes take place in management positions, and the new managers often have completely different ideas on information systems from their predecessors. As a result, an information systems plan may need to be revised before it has been implemented. An information systems plan must be flexible enough to support these changes in the real system.

It is not sufficient to win the support of just a few managers. The plan must be supported by the entire organization. Also, continuity in the organization is vital for successful implementation.

Maintenance of the plan. An organization must continuously adapt to a changing environment and to the changing views of management. The information systems plan must keep up with these changes and must be updated accordingly.

It is advisable to set up a maintenance team, preferably consisting of ex-members of the planning team. This will encourage a consistent approach to successive versions of the plan. Inconsistency tends to undermine users' confidence in the planning process.

Management involvement. Management involvement in the sense that managers are willing to support the implementation and use of the plan as a basis for further development is another indispensable element in information systems planning. Management commitment begins with the formulation of objectives. However, involvement alone is not enough. The management involvement must leave its mark on the organization. Weak management produces poor information plans.

CONCLUSIONS

The preparation of an information systems plan is fraught with difficulty from start to finish. The choice of the area of the information systems plan, the quality of the objectives (and the extent to which they can be successfully introduced into the organization) and the leadership qualities of the management will largely determine the quality of the information systems plan and the chances of implementing it successfully.

However, the approach to the project, the staffing and their way of dealing with the organization are also important. It is not surprising that many plans fail on the path from preparation to implementation. On the other hand, experience has shown that if these aspects are handled with care, there is a better than even chance of achieving success.

Review and discussion questions

1. Explain why information systems planning is extremely complex, and how the formation of an information strategy, an information architecture plan, and an information projects plan, may aid in the management of the involved process.

2. Explain why, ideally, every 'target' organization will have just one information systems plan.

3. Discuss how and why information systems plans need to be supported at every level of organization.

References

A.L. Lederer and V. Sethi, The implementation of strategic information systems planning methodologies, *MIS Quarterly*, September (1988).

T.H. Davenport and J.E. Short, The new industrial engineering: information technology and business process redesign, *Sloan Management Review*, 31 (4), (1990) [Reading 11].

W.D. Giles, Making strategy work, *Long Range Planning*, 24 (5), (1991).

N. Goldsmith, Linking IT planning to business strategy, *Long Range Planning*, 24 (6), (1991).

9 HOW TO MANAGE AN IT OUTSOURCING ALLIANCE

F. WARREN MCFARLAN AND *
RICHARD L. NOLAN **

With increasing concerns regarding cost and quality, the popularity of outsourcing a company's IT provision to an external marketplace supplier is increasing. However, there are many potential hurdles to be overcome, not least due to the long timescales associated with outsourcing contracts. Within this paper, Warren McFarlan and Richard Nolan offer their suggestions for the structuring and management of an IT outsourcing agreement. In particular, they contend that such agreements must come to be viewed as strategic alliances in order for outsourcing to be most successful.

Long-term sustained management of a strategic alliance is turning out to be the dominant challenge of effective IT outsourcing. From a relatively unusual entrepreneurial activity, IT outsourcing has recently exploded across the global corporate landscape.[1] Xerox, Delta Airlines, AMP Insurance (Australia), British Aerospace, and the Inland Revenue Service are the latest of these mega-alliances. Several years ago, Shell Oil outsourced its Brazilian IT activities. Like marriage, however, these arrangements are much easier to enter than to sustain or dissolve. The special economic technology issues surrounding outsourcing agreements necessarily make them more complex and fluid than an ordinary contract. Both parties need to make special efforts for outsourcing to be successful. In addition to clear successes, we have identified troublesome relationships and several that had to be terminated.

Our purpose in this article is to provide a concrete framework to help senior managers think about IT outsourcing and focus on how to manage the alliance to ensure its success.

* ROSS GRAHAM WALKER PROFESSOR OF BUSINESS ADMINISTRATION, HARVARD BUSINESS SCHOOL.
** CLASS OF 1942 PROFESSOR OF BUSINESS ADMINISTRATION, HARVARD BUSINESS SCHOOL.
REPRINTED FROM SLOAN MANAGEMENT REVIEW, 36(2) WINTER 1995, PP. 9–23, BY PERMISSION OF PUBLISHER.

WHY OUTSOURCING ALLIANCES ARE DIFFICULT

Outsourcing contracts are structured for very long periods of time in a world of fast-moving technical and business change. Ten years is the normal length of a contract in an environment in which computer chip performance is shifting by 20 percent to 30 percent per year. (This standard contract length has emerged to deal with switching cost issues and to make the economics work for the outsourcer.) Consequently, a rigid deal that made sense at the beginning may make less economic sense three years later and require adjustments to function effectively.

Exacerbating the situation is the timing of benefits. For the customer, the first-year benefits are clear; usually the customer receives a one-time capital payment. Next, the customer feels relieved to shift its problems and issues to another organization. Finally, the tangible payments in the first year occur in an environment in which the outputs most closely resemble those anticipated in the contract. In each subsequent year, the contract payment stream becomes less and less tied to the initial set of planned outputs (as the world changes) and, thus, more subject to negotiation and misunderstanding.

The situation from the outsourcer's perspective is just the reverse. During the first years, there is a heavy capital payment followed by the extraordinary costs for switching responsibility and executing the appropriate cost-reduction initiatives. All this is done in anticipation of a back-loaded profit flow. At precisely the time the outsourcer is finally moving into its earnings stream, the customer, which may feel the need for new services, is chafing under monthly charges and anxious to move to new IT architectures. If the customer has not had experience in partnering activities before, extraordinary tensions in the relationship can develop.

A further complication is the fact that only a few outsourcers have the critical mass and access to capital markets to undertake large contracts. Electronic Data Systems (EDS), Computer Sciences Corporation (CSC), IBM, and AT&T make up the largest part of the current market. A much larger group of firms specializes in certain niches in the outsourcing market, fulfilling either small contracts or specific subfunctions such as network operations. If an alliance is not working out, a company has limited options for resolving the situation, particularly because outsourcing is relatively easy, but insourcing again is very difficult. One international oil company transferred the relationship to another outsourcer.

Finally, the evolution of technologies often changes the strategic relevance of IT service to a firm. From the customer's viewpoint, assigning a commodity service to an outsider is very attractive if the price is right. Delegating a firm's service differentiator, however, is another matter. The customer that made the original decision based on efficiency will judge it differently if using effectiveness criteria later.

OUTSOURCING IN RETROSPECT

IT outsourcing has been around for a long time. In the mid-1960s, for example, computer services bureaus ran a variety of programs. These applications were focused heavily in the financial and operations support areas (general ledger, payroll, inventory control, and so on). The programs were both customized and general purpose, in which the individual firm had to accommodate its operations to the standard options in the package. The customers of the service bureaus were mostly small and medium-size firms, although some large firms used them for specialized needs or highly confidential items like executive payroll.

A good example of a provider in this industry then and now is AD. AD, which began as a small punchcard payroll company in 1949, grew to a $3 billion organization by specializing in large-volume, standard transaction-type activities, such as payroll and handling proxy solicitations (almost 100 percent of the industry). Software contracting companies like Andersen Consulting in the private sector and CSC in the public sector developed large turnkey applications for firms that required either specialized staff or a large number of staff people, which the firm found was inconvenient, imprudent, or impossible to retain. EDS, in the state and local government sector, provided full outsourcing for organizations whose cultures and salary scales made it impossible to attract people with the necessary skills in a competitive job market. These were the exceptions, however, to the general trend of developing IT in-house. Until 1990, the major drivers for outsourcing were primary:

- Cost-effective access to specialized or occasionally needed computing power or systems development skills.
- Avoidance of building in-house IT skills and skill sets, primarily an issue for small and very low-technology organizations.
- Access to special functional capabilities.

Outsourcing during this period was important, but in retrospect, largely peripheral to the main IT activities that took place in midsize and large organizations.

Kodak's decision in 1989 to outsource IT was the first real wake-up call for complacent IS (information systems) managers, now more commonly called CIOs (chief information officers).[2] Kodak's then CIO, who had been a general manager rather than a computer professional, took an aggressive position in outsourcing mainframes, telecommunications, and PCs. Until then, outsourcing for medium-size to large companies had been mostly a sideshow, and outsourcing was generally something reserved for small and medium-size companies with problematic, grossly mismanaged IS departments. After Kodak's decision, there was a flurry of over-subscribed IS conferences on outsourcing at which the Kodak CIO was often the featured speaker. We both attended a number of these conferences and independently witnessed the hostility from many CIO participants (who perceived outsourcing as a terrifying threat to their status quo) towards the Kodak CIO as she explained her rationale.[3] Even today, many of those very same CIOs who attended the conferences quickly point out with some relief that only one of the three original Kodak outsourcing contracts was totally problem free — albeit the far largest one (although all three contracts are still in place).

OUTSOURCING IN THE 1990s

We have conducted more than four years of case research on the Kodak, General Dynamics, and over a dozen other outsourcing situations and have concluded that IT outsourcing is not a "flash in the pan" management fad.[4] IT outsourcing is a harbinger to the transformation of traditional IT departments and provides a glimpse at the emerging organizational structures of the information economy. Our research indicates that more than half of midsize to large firms have outsourced or are considering some type of outsourcing of their IT activities. This phenomenon has not occurred only in the United States; for example, in 1993, AMP Insurance Company (the largest insurance company in Australia), British Aerospace, and the UK Inland Revenue Service all outsourced substantial parts of their IT activities.

Two factors have affected the growth of IT outsourcing — the recognition of strategic alliances and the changes in the technological environment.

• **Acceptance of Strategic Alliances.** The value of strategic alliances has been widely recognized.[5] Inter-related forces underlie the creation of alliances. On one level, finding a strong partner to complement an area of weakness gives an organization an island of stability in a turbulent world. It is difficult to fight simultaneously on all fronts, and alliances allow a company to simplify its management agenda safely. Alternatively, alliances allow a firm to leverage a key part of the value chain by bringing in a strong partner that complements its skills.[6] Such a partner may create an opportunity to innovate synergistically, in which the whole is greater than the sum of the parts. Also, successful early experiences with alliances increase a firm's confidence in undertaking new alliances in other parts of the value chain as a profitable way to do business. This experience gives the firm insight into how to increase the likelihood of a successful alliance.

It is worth noting that, for an alliance to be successful and endure for the long term, both firms must believe that they are winners. Because of the synergistic potential of the relationships and the opportunity to specialize, both firms should legitimately feel that they are benefiting from the alliance. This is not a zero-sum game.

• **IT's Changing Environment.** The stages theory of computer growth describes how companies have assimilated computers over extended organizational learning periods (fifteen to twenty years).[7] Each period has a target market focus in the firm and a particular model for application (see Table 1). The DP era (1960-1980) focused on transaction processing systems by automating the existing manual systems. The micro era (1980-1995) focused on leveraging professional workers (eg, engineers, financial analysts, and managers) by using the computer to do analytic computations, access data, and print various renditions of drawings or graphics. During both of these eras, the use of the computer was primarily within the company.

Table 1 IT markets

Location	Physical Aspects	Information
Internal	Automating: Computerizing physical and clerical processes. DP era (1960-1980) ● Dominant use of mainframe and minicomputers. ● Operational level systems automated primarily with COBOL. ● Process controls automated primarily with machine language. ● Standard packages for payroll and general ledger. ● Applications portfolio consists of millions of lines of code with 50% typically purchased from outside.	Informating: Leveraging knowledge workers with computers. Micro era (1980-1995) ● User tasks leverages through direct use of microcomputers enabled by graphical user interfaces (GUI) and purchased software such as word processing, spreadsheet, graphics, and CAD/CAM. ● Local area networks (LANs) - user-orientated software for e-mail, database sharing, file transfer, and groupware for work teams. ● Microcomputer software consists of millions of lines of code - almost 100% purchased from other companies.
External	Embedding: integrating computers into products and services. Micro era (1980-1995) ● Specialized code embedded into products and services to enhance function. ● Microcomputers in physical products such as automobiles and "smart cards" in services. ● Thousands of lines of code developed by both specialized internal programmers and outside contract programmers.	Networking: "The Information Highway" Network era (1990-?) ● Wide area networks (WANs) networking workers, suppliers and customers. ● Internet for commercial use. ● Millions of lines of code; almost 100% purchased and maintained from outside software firms.

Overlapping the micro era is an emerging external market where the computer is embedded into products (eg automobiles) and services (smart cards). By and large, outsourcing is not having an impact on this market; when General Dynamics outsourced its IT activities, it retained the 800 systems people doing this type of work.

The network era (1990-?), currently overlapping the micro era, has emerged from the fusion of computers and telecommunications technologies.[8] In this era, firms are integrating both internal and external computers so they can change their structure to more efficient forms for competing flexibly in the global marketplace. We call this the IT-enabled network firm. This integration is putting extraordinary pressure on firms that are trying to keep the old services running while developing the interconnections and services demanded by the new environment. Thus outsourcing has become a viable alternative for those firms to get access to appropriate skills and to speed up the transition reliably and cost effectively.

We should note that, as shown in Table 1, the development of most of the code that companies now use has already been outsourced. A distinct minority of the code in operating systems, e-mail systems, word processing packages, and spreadsheet software was actually developed within the firm (with a much smaller percentage expected in the future). This trend, which occurred for the obvious reasons of economies of scale and scarcity of competent staff, will only continue. Currently, Computer Associates, Lotus, IBM, Borland, and Microsoft are the de facto software providers to most companies. The internal IT organization is already a selector of code rather than a developer.

At the same time, many firms have a residue of fifteen- to thirty-year-old systems primarily written in COBOL and PL/1. Although this problem is particularly acute in the financial services industry and manufacturing, it is not confined to it. The cost-effective transformation of these systems to the client/server model (a key technology of the network era that separates the management of files and their integrity onto one machine, the server, from devices accessing these files, the clients) is an enormous challenge. On the one hand, firms are looking for low-cost maintenance of the old systems to ensure they operate reliably, while gaining access to the new skills to permit their transformation to the new model. This shift is as significant today as the move from tabulating equipment thirty-five years ago in terms of providing new capabilities to the firm. A number of organizations see outsourcing as a way of bringing the appropriate specialized skills to this task.

WHAT DRIVES OUTSOURCING?

The mix of factors that raise the possibility of outsourcing varies widely from one company to another.[9] In our research, we have uncovered a series of themes that, in aggregate, explain most of the pressures to outsource.

- **General Managers' Concerns about Costs and Quality.** The same questions about IT costs and response times came up repeatedly when we talked to managers: Can we get our existing services for a reduced price at acceptable quality standards? Can we get new systems developed faster? We have uncovered the following ways an outsourcer can save money for a customer:
- Tighter overhead cost control of fringe benefits. On balance, the outsourcers run much leaner overhead structures than many of their customers.
- More aggressive use of low-cost labour pools by creatively using geography. Frequently, the outsourcer moves data centers to low-cost areas (modern telecommunications make this possible).
- Tough world-class standards applied to the company's existing staff, all of whom have to requalify for appointment at the time of outsourcing. Frequently, employees may have become lazy or are unskilled in leading-edge IT management practices.

- More effective bulk purchasing and leasing arrangements for all aspects of the hardware/software configuration, through discounts and better use of capacity.
- Better management of excess hardware capacity. The outsourcer can sell or utilize underused hardware that would otherwise be idle by combining many firms' work in the same operations center. One small firm's on-line operations (a $27 million ten-year contract) was transferred to a larger data center at no extra cost to the outsourcer. Capacity was simply better used.
- Better control over software licenses, through both negotiation and realistic examination.
- More aggressive management of service and response time to meet, but not wildly exceed, corporate standards. Tighter control over inventories of paper and other supplies.
- Simply hustling. Outsourcers are professionals; this is their only business, and their success is measured by satisfied customers who recommend them to others, by bottom-line profitability, and by stock market performance.
- The ability to run with a leaner management structure because of increased competence and critical mass volumes of work.
- Creative and more realistic structuring of leases.

While the cumulative impact of these items can be very significant, we issue a few cautionary notes. Until several knowledgeable bidders have closely analyzed your existing operation to propose an alliance, you don't have a true picture. An IT efficiency study funded by the IT department and done by a consulting company hoping to get future business is simply inadequate. And equally important is assessing whether the outsourcer can rapidly mobilize its staff for the quick-response development jobs needed to get products and services to market much faster.

- **Breakdown in IT Performance.** Failure to meet service standards can force general management to find other ways of achieving reliability. As we reflect on the past thirty years of computer growth in most companies, it is not atypical to find a company in which cumulative IT management neglect eventually culminated in an out-of-control situation from which the current IT department could not recover. For example, Massachusetts Blue Cross and Blue Shield's decision to outsource to EDS was triggered by the failure of three major systems development projects (and losses in their tens of millions of dollars). It saw outsourcing as a way to fix a broken department. Similarly, a midsize bank's interest in outsourcing came after a one-day total collapse of its ATM network, caused by faulty, internally designed software patches.

An additional driving factor is the need to rapidly retool a backward IT structure to maintain its competitiveness. In one firm, general managers thought (correctly in judgment) the internal IT culture was both frozen and backward; it needed to leap forward in performance. The general managers, who lacked both the time and the inclination to personally undertake the task, found outsourcing a good choice for making the transition from the DP era to the network era.

- **Intense Supplier Pressures.** Kodak's decision to outsource its data center and telecommunications to IBM, DEC and Businessland was a flash point. Suddenly, all general managers saw outsourcing as a highly visible, if often misunderstood, alternative. At the same time, IBM and DEC were looking for new value-added services to reach their customer bases and compensate for declining hardware margins and sales. They moved aggressively into the field with expanded and highly energetic salesforces. EDS, the largest firm in the field, used its General Motors operations center to demonstrate its expertise. CSC, strong in the federal sector, built a bridge to the commercial sector with its General Dynamics contract. The visibility of these and other arrangements, combined with the suppliers' aggressive salesforces, enabled them to approach general managers with compelling reasons to outsource.

- **Simplified General Management Agenda.** A firm under intense cost or competitive pressures, which does not see IT as its core competence, may find that outsourcing is a way to delegate time-consuming, messy problems so it can focus scarce management time and energy on other differentiators. If the managers perceive the outsourcer as competent and are able to transfer a noncore function to reliable hands, they will not hesitate to choose outsourcing. These activities must be done respectably, but long-term upside competitive differentiation does not come from executing them in an outstanding fashion.

- **Financial Factors.** Several financial issues can make outsourcing appealing. One is the opportunity to liquify the firm's intangible IT asset, thus strengthening the firm's balance sheet and avoiding a stream of sporadic capital investments in the future. An important part of many of the arrangements struck in the past two years has been the significant upfront capital paid for both the real value of the hardware/software assets and the intangible value of the IT systems. General Dynamics, for example, received $200 million for its IT asset. Publicly held outsourcers that have access to the capital markets have pushed this; partnerships like Andersen Consulting do not have such access.

    Outsourcing can turn a largely fixed-cost business into one with variable costs; this is particularly important for firms whose activities vary widely in volume from one year to another, or which face significant downsizing. The outsourcer can make this change much less painfully than the firm, broker the slack more effectively, and potentially provide greater employment stability for the company's IT employees who are there because of their ability to handle multiple operations. In fact, outsourcing has been very positively received by the staffs at several of the firms we studied. They saw themselves leaving a cost-constrained environment with limited potential for promotion and entering a growth company where IT was the firm's only business. In variable cost arrangements, price deescalation clauses should be negotiated in the sections of the contract that deal with IT hardware costs, rather than inflation protection clauses, because of the dramatic downward changes in the technology costs.

Finally, a third-party relationship brings an entirely different set of dynamics to a firm's view of IT expenditures. It is now dealing with a hard-dollar expenditure that all users must take seriously (it is no longer soft-dollar allocation). There is a sense of discipline and tough-mindedness that an arm's-length, fully-charged-out internal cost center has trouble achieving. Further, firms that do not see IT as a high leverage function may perceive outside professionals as adding special value and, hence, as quite influential.

For a firm considering divestiture or outright sale of one or more of its divisions, outsourcing has special advantages. It liquifies and gets value for an asset that is unlikely to be recognized in the divestiture. It gives the acquirer fewer problems to deal with in assimilating the firm. And the outsourcing contract may provide the acquirer a very nice dowry, particularly if the firm is small in relation to the acquirer. The contract can be phased out neatly, and the IT transaction volume can be added to the firm's internal IT activities with little or no additional expense. In several midsize banks we studied, this was the guiding rationale for outsourcing. It gave them access to reliable IT support, while making their eventual sale (which they saw as inevitable) more attractive from the acquirers' viewpoint.

- **Corporate Culture.** The company's values can make it very hard for managers to do the right thing. For one firm we studied that had several internal data centers, there were obvious and compelling advantages to consolidating them. The internal IT department, however, simply lacked the clout to pull off the centralized strategy in what was a highly decentralized firm, built up over the years by acquisitions. The firm saw the decentralized culture as a major strength, not subject to reconsideration. Outsourcing, driven by very senior management, provided the fulcrum for overcoming this impasse since it was not directly associated with any division or corporate staff. Similarly, an internal IT organization may fall behind the state of the art without being immediately attacked, while an outsourcer is forced to keep up with the latest technology to be successful.

- **Elimination of an Internal Irritant.** No matter how competent and adaptive existing IT management and staff are (and usually they are very good), there is usually tension between the end users of the resources and the IT staff. Often this is exacerbated by the different language IT professionals use, lack of career paths for users and IT staff across the organization, perceived unresponsiveness to urgent requests (but that sometimes are not really urgent), and perceived technical obsolescence (some recent college graduate is always discovering a new software package that will apparently solve all problems like magic). In this context, the notion of a remote, efficient, experienced outsourcer is particularly compelling.

- **Other Factors.** We found a variety of other drivers for outsourcing in specific situations. Some companies with a low-technology culture appeared to have trouble attracting and retaining high-technology IT staff. Outsourcing offered a way to gain these skills without getting involved in the complex management issues they were not skilled in and did not want to manage.

A midsize high-tech firm needed to develop and run a series of critically important applications. Outsourcing gave it access to skills it could not attract to its organization. Managers felt that outsourcing had substantially reduced their corporate risk while giving them needed access to specialized knowledge.

One large organization felt it was getting a level of commitment and energy that would have been difficult to gain from an in-house unit. In its outsourcing arrangement, it was an extenal reference for the outsourcer, which was growing rapidly. Good performance on the contract was critical for the outsourcer to get the kind of market growth it wanted.

Still another firm was frustrated by its inability to get its products to market faster. Its in-house resources, limited in size and training, were simply not moving fast enough. Outsourcing gave it a boost of adrenalin to build the IT infrastructure for a two-thirds improvement in time to market.

WHEN TO OUTSOURCE IT

When do the benefits of outsourcing outweigh the risks? Our research suggests that there are five factors that tip the scale one way or the other. Each factor is fundamentally linked to the basic research models in the IT field.[10]

POSITION ON THE STRATEGIC GRID

The strategic grid is a framework that shows IT's strategic relevance to a company at a particular time.[11] It assesses two dimensions: (1) the Company's current dependence on computers or networks, and (2) the future importance of computer applications under development. In Table 2, we have generalized the two dimensions. First is the degree of the company's current dependence on information — that is, the extent to which business operations are dependent on reliable, real-time information processing. Second is the future importance of innovative information resource management — that is, the extent that future competitive position is dependent on known initiatives requiring innovative computer applications.

Outsourcing operational activities is generally attractive, particularly as the budget grows and the contract becomes more important to the outsourcer. The more the firm is operationally dependent on IT, the more sense outsourcing makes. The bigger the firm's IT budget, however, the higher in the customer organization the decisions will be made, and thus the more careful the analysis must become. At the super-large scale, the burden falls on the outsourcer to show it can bring more intellectual firepower to the task.

When the application's development portfolio is filled with maintenance work or projects, which are valuable but not vitally important to the firm, transferring these tasks to a partner holds few strategic risks. However, as the new systems and

Table 2 Strategic grid for information resource management

	High	
Current Dependence on Information	Factory - uninterrupted service-oriented information resource management. *Outsourcing Presumption*: Yes, unless company is huge and well managed. Reasons to consider outsourcing: ● Possibilities of economies of scale for small and midsize firms. ● Higher quality service and backup. ● Management focus facilitated. ● Fibre-optic and extended channel technologies facilitate international IT solutions.	Strategic information resource management. *Outsourcing Presumption*: No. Reasons to consider outsourcing: ● Rescue an out-of-control internal IT unit. ● Tap source of cash. ● Facilitate cost flexibility. ● Facilitate management of divestiture.
	Support-oriented information resource management. *Outsourcing Presumption*: Yes. Reasons to consider outsourcing: ● Access to high IT professionalism. ● Possibility of laying off is of low priority and problematic. ● Access to current IT technologies. ● Risk of inappropriate IT architectures reduced.	Turnaround information resource management. *Outsourcing Presumption*: No. Reasons to consider outsourcing: ● Internal IT not capable in required technologies. ● Internal IT not capable in required project management skills.

Low   Importance of Sustained, Innovative   High
Information Resource Development

processes increasingly come to deliver potentially significant differentiation and/or massive cost reduction, the outsourcing decision comes under more and more scrutiny, particularly when the firm possesses a large, technically innovative, well-run IT organization. The potential loss of control, loss of flexibility, and inherent delays in dealing with a project management structure that cuts across two organizations become much more binding and of greater concern. There are examples, like General Dynamics, where outsourcing was successful, but it was more the exception than the rule.

As shown in Table 2, for companies in the support quadrant, the outsourcing presumption is *yes*, particularly for the large firms. For companies in the factory quadrant, the presumption is *yes*, unless they are huge and perceived as exceptionally well managed. For firms in the turnaround quadrant, the presumption is *no;* it represents an unnecessary, unacceptable delegation of competitiveness. For companies in the strategic and turnaround quadrants, the presumption is *no;* not facing a crisis of IT competence, companies in the strategic quadrant will find it hard to justify outsourcing under most circumstances. Subcritical mass in potentially core differentiating skills for the firm, however, are one important driver that might move such a company to consider outsourcing.

For larger multidivision firms, this analysis suggests that various divisions and clusters of application systems can legitimately be treated differently (ie, strategic differentiated outsourcing). For example, an international oil company outsourced its operationally troublesome Brazilian subsidiary's IT activities while keeping the other items in-house. Similarly, because of the dynamic nature of the grid, firms under profit pressures after a period of sustained strategic innovation (in either the transforming or strategic quadrants) are good candidates for outsourcing as a means to clean up their shop and procedures. This was true for one large high-technology organization that saved over $100 million by outsourcing.

DEVELOPMENT PORTFOLIO

The higher the percentage of the systems development portfolio in maintenance or high-structured projects, the more the portfolio is a candidate for outsourcing.[12] (High-structured projects are those in which the end outputs are clearly defined, there is little opportunity to redefine them, and little or no organizational change is involved in implementing them.) Outsourcers that have access to high-quality, cheap labor pools (in, for example, Russia, India, or Ireland) and good project management skills can consistently outperform, on both cost and quality, a local unit that is caught in a high-cost geographic area and lacks the contacts, skills, and confidence to manage extended relationships. The growth of global fiber-optic networks has made all conventional thinking on where work should be done obsolete. For example, Citibank does much of its processing work in South Dakota, and more than 50,000 programmers are working in India on software development for US and European firms.

High-technology, highly structured work (ie building a vehicle tracking system) is also a strong candidate for outsourcing, because the customer needs staff people with specialized, leading-edge technical skills. These technical skills are widely available in countries such as Ireland, India, and the Philippines.

Conversely, large, low-structured projects pose very difficult coordination problems for outsourcing. (Low-structured projects are those in which the end outputs and processes are susceptible to significant evolution as the project unfolds.) Design is iterative, as users discover what they really want by trial and error. As noted earlier, this work requires that the design team be physically much closer to the consumers, thus eliminating significant additional savings. The work can, of course, be outsourced, but it requires more coordination to be effective than the projects we just described. One firm outsourced a large section of this work to a very standards-oriented outsourcer as a way of bringing discipline to an undisciplined organization.[13]

ORGANIZATIONAL LEARNING

The sophistication of a firm's organizational learning substantially facilitates its ability to manage an outsourcing arrangement in the systems development area effectively. A significant component of many firms' applications development portfolios are projects related to business process reengineering or organization transformation. [14] Process reengineering seeks to install very different procedures for handling transactions and doing the firm's work. Organizational transformation tries to redesign where decisions in the firm are made and the type of controls used. The success of both types of projects depends on getting internal staff people to radically change the way they work and often involves significant downsizing as well. While much of this restructuring relies on new IT capabilities, at the heart it is an exercise in applied human psychology where 70 percent of the work falls disappointingly short of target.

Responsibility for this type of development work (low structure by its very nature) is the hardest to outsource, although there is an extraordinary consulting industry that is assisting its facilitation. A firm with substantial experience in restructuring will have less difficulty in defining the dividing line between the outsourcer and the company in terms of responsibility for success. Firms that have not yet worked on these projects will find that outsourcing significantly complicates an already difficult task. The more experience the firm has had in implementing these projects, the easier the outsourcing will be.

A FIRM'S POSITION IN THE MARKET

The farther a company is from the network era in its internal use of IT, the more useful outsourcing is as a way to close the gap. The DP era and early micro era firms often do not have the IT leadership, staff skills, or architecture to quickly move ahead. The outsourcer cannot just keep its old systems running but must drive forward with contemporary practice and technology. The advanced micro era firms are more likely to have internal staff skills and perspectives to leap to the next stage by themselves. The world of client/server architecture, the networked organization, and process redesign is so different from the large COBOL systems and stand-alone PCs of 1985 that it is often prohibitively challenging for a firm to easily bridge the ten-year gap by itself. For firms in this situation, it is not worth dwelling on how the firm got where it is but, rather, how to extricate itself.

CURRENT IT ORGANIZATION

The more IT development and operations are already segregated in the organization and in accounting, the easier it is to negotiate an enduring outsourcing contract. A stand-alone differentiated IT unit has already developed the integrating organizational and control mechanisms that are the foundation for an outsourcing contract. Separate functions and their ways of integrating with the rest of the organization already exist. Cost accounting processes have been hammered out. While both sets of protocols may require significant modification, there is a framework in place to deal with them.

When there are no protocols, developing an enduring contract is much more complex, because the firm must establish both the framework for resolving the issue and the specific technical approaches. This structure facilitated the General Dynamics implementation effort tremendously; the lack of this structure in another high-technology firm extended the resulting outsourcing process over a period of years, with a diminution of savings and a complex conversion.

STRUCTURING THE ALLIANCE

Establishing the parameters of the outsourcing arrangement at the beginning is crucial. The right structure is not a guarantee of success, but the wrong structure will make the governance process almost impossible. Several factors are vital to a successful alliance.

CONTRACT FLEXIBILITY

From the customer's viewpoint, a ten-year contract simply cannot be written in an iron-clad, inflexible way.[15] The arrangements we have examined have changed over time, often radically. Evolving technology, changing business economic conditions, and emergence of new competitive services make this inevitable. The necessary evolutionary features of the contract make the alliance's cognitive and strategic fit absolutely crucial. If there is mutual interest in the relationship and if there are shared approaches to problem solving, the alliance is more likely to be successful. If these do not exist, a troublesome relationship may emerge.

No matter how much detail and thought goes into drafting the contract, the resulting clauses will provide imperfect protection if things go wrong. Indeed, the process of contract drafting (which often takes six to eight months) is likely to be more important than the contract. At this phase, one side gains insights into the other's values and the ability to redirect emphasis as the world changes. Kodak has already altered its outsourcing arrangements as both business circumstances and technologies changed (see the boxed example on outsourcing at Kodak). General Dynamics had eight contracts to provide for different divisions evolving in separate ways.

STANDARDS AND CONTROL

One concern for customers is that they are handing control over an important part of the firm's operations to a third party. This is particularly true if IT innovation is vital to the firm's success or if the firm is very dependent on IT for smooth daily operations. A company must carefully address such concerns in the outsourcing agreement.

Control in some ways is just a state of mind. Most organizations accustom themselves to loss of control in various settings, as long as the arrangement is working out well and the supplier is fully accountable. However, it is worth noting that vital parts of a firm's day-to-day operations have always been controlled by others. Electricity, telephone, and water are normally provided by third parties; interruption in their support can severely cripple any organization in a very short time. Providing sustained internal backup is often impractical or impossible. In the case of a hotel, for example, failure of either electricity or water for more than twenty-four hours is enough to guarantee its closing until the situation is rectified. The managers at a major chemical company who were particularly concerned about loss of control were brought up short by one of us who asked to see its power-generating facilities and water wells (of course, they had neither).

Disruption of operations support has immediate and dramatic implications for many firms. It is also a short-term area where firms are likely to feel comfortable about their protection if carefully structured. Conversely, putting innovation and responsibility for new services and products in the hands of a third party is correctly seen as a risky, high-stakes game. As we discuss later, in outsourcing, these issues are much more capable of being resolved for the firms in the factory and support quadrants (see Table 2), where innovation is much less important, than for firms in the turnaround and strategic quadrants (unless they are midsize and looking for access to critical innovation skills that they cannot command on their own). A company must carefully develop detailed performance standards for systems response time, availability of service, responsiveness to systems requests, and so on. Only with these standards in place can the company discuss the quality of support and new trends.

AREAS TO OUTSOURCE

A company can outsource a wide selection of IT functions and activities. Data center operations, telecommunications, PC acquisition/maintenance, and systems development are all examples of pieces that can be outsourced individually. Continental Illinois outsourced everything, while Kodak kept systems development but outsourced, in separate contracts, data center operations, communication, and acquisition management of PCs. At its core, outsourcing is more an approach than a technique. As we noted earlier, significant portions of a firm's IT software development activities have been routinely outsourced for years. What is at stake here is a discontinuous major shift to move additional portions of a firm's IT activities outside the firm. Between the current situation and total outsourcing lie a variety of different scenarios. When assessing partial outsourcing, managers frequently ask the following questions:

Outsourcing at Kodak

In January 1994, Warren McFarlan interviewed Vaughn Hovey, director of information processing services at Eastman Kodak Company, to learn how a highly publicized IT outsourcing decision was working, four years after its implementation.

McFarlan: *How would you describe your relationship with IBM?*

Hovey: Collaborative. Within the broad outlines of the contract, we try very hard to be partners.

How do you manage the relationship?
In many ways. We have a management board of senior IBM and Kodak managers, including our CIO. We meet at least twice a year, one-and-a-half days at a time. We focus on the strategic elements of the relationship, how we are doing on the agreement, and progress on key projects. Recently, we presented our analysis of how it has worked out during the past four years, and we committed to continuing. We also have a monthly advisory council, which includes ten Kodak application development managers who deal with more tactical and operational issues.

Has the contract changed much in the past four years?
Yes, a great deal. We have put in place twelve amendments to deal with the inclusion of additional business unit computer installations and leveraged opportunities in our international operations. The original arrangement was for the United States and Canada only. We have since extended it to Japan, Germany, France, England, Mexico, and Brazil. We have worked very closely with IBM to develop an approach and understanding on how to do this in a multilingual and multicultural environment. We are both breaking new ground.

What pieces are critical for you to control?
IT architecture and strategic direction. These are the critical items Kodak must control to meet our business objectives. We have a five-person team to manage the relationship. They work through all contract enhancements, monitor progress on service levels and quality improvements, and coordinate any major changes.

What is the biggest challenge you face today?
The continuous commitment to the spirit of partnership. During the past four years, we have had two CIOs and total turnover of our coordination team, except for me and one other person. Similarly, there has been almost total turnover in the IBM management team. Two years ago, we went through an intense team-rebuilding and recommitment effort. There has been enough turnover since then that it is almost time to do it again. In a changing world, a partnership requires sustained work on recommitment.

Do you think the contract will last the full ten years?
We are very satisfied with its results. At the same time, it was developed in a very different technological environment by two firms operating in more prosperous economic circumstances. Client/server was not even in the popular terminology then. I anticipate that both of us will want to sit down and restructure the agreement to deal with the new realities. It is a different technology and a new concept of business that we are dealing with.

You have received a great deal of publicity from this.
Yes, it is interesting how outside visitors have reacted to it. Four years ago, we got a great deal of skepticism from other CIOs over this. The questions were of the "You are out of your mind. Why did you do it?" variety. Today, they are "You have been at it for four years. You seem to be making it work. What is the key to your success?"

Are there any other things to learn from your experience?
Outsourcing is a collaborative relationship that has to be worked on. The lawyers are very helpful in structuring a contract. Our job is to make sure we don't need them throughout the year. When the inevitable financial tensions arise, we have been able to have a "closed door" meeting of several financial people from both sides and share our mutual objectives and useful spreadsheet data. Both sides feel a lot better when it is over. Clear expectations are important, but flexibility and personal communications are vital.

- Can the proposed outsourced piece be separated easily from the rest of the firm, or will the complexities of disentanglement absorb most of the savings?
- Does the piece require particular specialized competencies, which we either do not possess or lack the time and energy to build?
- How central are the proposed outsourced pieces to our firm? Are they either more or less significant to the firm's value chain than the other activities and, thus, deserve different treatment?

Total outsourcing is not necessary for attracting a supplier's attention, but the portion to be outsourced must be meaningful enough so that the vendor will pay attention to it. Several organizations we studied had spun off bits and pieces of their activities to various organizations in a way that engendered enormous coordination costs among multiple organizations. These contracts were also very small in relation to the outsourcers' other work, and we had significant concerns about their long-term viability (in one case, the firm has already insourced again).

COST SAVINGS

Some CIOs believe that the firm's IT activities are so well managed or so unique that there is no way to achieve savings through outsourcing, or for the vendor to profit. This may be true. But two caveats are important. First, only if several outsiders study outsourcing with senior management sponsorship are you ensured an honest, realistic viewpoint. Having a study done objectively under the sponsorship of the local IT organization can be very difficult. The IT operation may see an outsourcing recommendation as so deeply disruptive that the study may be negatively biased from the start. Additionally, since consultants retained by the IT organization are often dependent on it for future billings, either consciously or unconsciously, they may skew the results. One firm's internally initiated IT study, done by a consultant, purported to show that it was 40 percent more efficient than the average firm in its industry. Needless to say, IT's control of the evaluation process led to general management's skepticism; the study is being redone under different sponsorship.

Disinterested professionals can make a real contribution in evaluating cost savings. A major aerospace firm recently retained a consulting firm to help it design and manage the outsourcing review process. Doing an audit in this area is also difficult. Because situations change rapidly and new priorities emerge, it is usually impossible to determine what the results would have been if the alternative had been selected. Thus the IT organization may be tempted to anticipate internal efficiencies so that IT outsourcing does not appear to be viable.

SUPPLIER STABILITY AND QUALITY

How a supplier will perform over a decade is an unanswerable question, and one of the most critical a customer must ask. In ten years, technologies will change beyond recognition, and the supplier that does not have a culture that encourages relentless modernization and staff retraining will rapidly become a liability as a strategic partner. In addition, the stability of the outsourcer's financial structure is critical. Cash crunches, subchapter 11, or worse are genuine nightmares for customers. This issue is complicated by the reality that once a firm outsources, it is very hard to insource again, once the firm's technical and managerial competence have evaporated. While it is difficult to move quickly from one outsourcer to another (the only practical alternative), if a firm considers the possibility in advance, it can mitigate the risks. Some of the best bids come from newcomers trying to crack the market.

Problems are intensified if the way a firm uses technology becomes incompatible with the outsourcer's skill base. For example, a firm in the factory quadrant that selects an operationally strong outsourcer may be in trouble if it suddenly moves toward the strategic quadrant and its partner lacks the necessary project management and innovation skills to operate there.

Finally, there is a potential, built-in conflict of interest between the firm and outsourcer that must be carefully managed so it does not become disabling. The outsourcer makes its money by lengthening leases, driving down operational costs, and charging premium prices for new value-added services. Conversely, the customer has no empathy for the joys of harvesting old technology benefits (one of the reasons it got out of the business in the first place) and also wants rapid access to cheap, high-quality project development skills on demand. Managing this tension is complex, imperfect, and very delicate and must be covered in the contract. Both firms must make a profit. The more the customer moves to the strategic quadrant, the harder it is to ensure a good fit with an outsourcer.

MANAGEMENT FIT

Putting together a ten-year, flexible, evolving relationship requires more than just technical skill and making the numbers work. A shared approach to problem solving, similar values, and good personal chemistry among key staff people are critical determinants of long-term success. Various outsourcers have very different management cultures and styles. It is worth giving up something on the initial price to ensure that you find a partner with whom you can work productively over a long term. The information gained in the tortuous six-to-eight-month process of putting an alliance together is crucial for identifying the likelihood of a successful partnership. Of course, this chemistry is a necessary, but insufficient, condition for ultimate success. Realistically, it is corporate culture fit that is most important, since, after several years, the key people in the initial relationship will have moved to other assignments.

CONVERSION PROBLEMS

The period of time for an outsourcing study and conversion is one of great stress for a company's staff. Uncertainties about career trajectories and job security offer the possibility of things going awry. All the expertise a firm gains when acquiring another is vital during conversion. The sooner plans and processes for dealing with staff career issues, outplacement processes, and separation pay are dealt with, the more effective the results will be. Almost invariably, paralyzing fears of the unknown are worse than any reality.

MANAGING THE ALLIANCE

The ongoing management of an alliance is the single most important aspect of outsourcing's success. We have identified four critical areas that require attention.

THE CIO FUNCTION

The customer must retain a strong, active CIO function. The heart of the CIO's job is planning — ensuring IT resources are at the right level and appropriately distributed. This role has always been distinctly separate from the active line management of networks, data centers, and systems development, although it has not always been recognized as such. These line activities, as noted earlier, have been successfully outsourced in a variety of companies. In a fully outsourced firm, however, sustained internal CIO responsibility for certain critical areas must be maintained. (For an example, see the boxed example on the evolution at Kodak.)

- **Partnership/Contract Management.** As we described earlier, outsourcing does not take place in a static environment. The nature of the technologies, external competitive situations, and so on are all in a state of evolution. An informed CIO who actively plans and deals with the broad issues is critical to ensuring that this input is part of the alliance so it can continuously adapt to change. The evolving Kodak contract gives ample evidence of this.

- **Architecture Planning.** A CIO's staff must visualize and coordinate the long-term approach to interconnectivity. Networks, standard hardware/software conventions, and database accessibility all need customer planning. The firm can delegate execution of these areas, but not its viewpoint of what it needs to support the firm in the long term. The wide range of management practice in firms that do not outsource complicates this. One insurance company we studied supported a network of 15,000 PCs, 18 e-mail systems, and literally hundreds of support staff to maintain its networks. Its CIO stated succinctly, "Even if technology costs 'zero', we cannot continue in this way."

- **Emerging Technologies.** A company must develop a clear understanding of emerging technologies and their potential applications. To understand new technology, managers must attend vendor briefings and peer group seminars and visit firms currently using the new technology. Assessing the hardware/software network alternatives and their capabilities requires an understanding of what is in the market and where it is going. This cannot be delegated to a third party or assessed by sitting in one's office.

Similarly, identifying discontinuous applications and the opportunities and problems posed by them is critical. At one large pharmaceutical organization, the CIO's staff was vindicated when it became clear that they had first spotted business process redesign as an emerging area, funded appropriate pilot projects (which were skillfully transferred to line management), and finally repositioned the firm's entire IT effort. (Users and an outside systems house executed the project, with the CIO playing the crucial initiator role.) Clearly, an outsourcer has an incentive to suggest new ideas that lead to additional work, but delegating responsibility for IT-enabled innovation in strategic and turnaround firms is risky because it is such an important part of the value chain.

- **Continuous Learning.** A firm should create an internal IT learning environment to bring users up to speed so they are comfortable in a climate of continuous IT change. An aerospace firm felt this was so important that, when outsourcing, it kept this piece in-house.

PERFORMANCE MEASUREMENTS

Realistic measurement of success is generally very hard, so a company must make an effort to develop performance standards, measure results, and then interpret them continuously. Individual firms bring entirely different motivations and expectations to the table. In addition, many of the most important measures of success are intangible and play out over a long period of time. Hard, immediate cost savings, for example, may be measurable (at least in the short run), but simplification of the general management agenda is impossible to assess.

The most celebrated cases of outsourcing have evolved in interesting ways. Of Kodak's three selected vendors, while the major one remains intact, another of the vendors has gone through several organizational transformations, triggered by financial distress. General Dynamics, in the first eighteen months, has spun off three of its divisions, along with their contracts. It is too early to determine the outcomes. EDS and GM took years to work out an acceptable agreement; ultimately several very senior EDS managers resigned.

A major power company recently postponed an outsourcing study for a year. Its general managers believed that the internal IT staff and processes were so bloated that, while outsourcing IT would clearly produce major savings, they would still be leaving money on the table. Consequently, in 1993, they reduced their IT staff from 450 to 250 and reduced the total IT expenditure level by 30 percent. With the "easy" things now done, they are now entertaining several outsourcing proposals to examine more closely what additional savings and changes in their method of operation would be appropriate.

MIX AND COORDINATION OF TASKS

As we noted earlier, the larger the percentage of a firm's systems development portfolio devoted to maintaining legacy systems, the lower the risk of outsourcing the portfolio. The question becomes, can we get these tasks done significantly faster and less expensively? The larger the percentage of large, low-structured projects in the systems development portfolio, the more difficult it becomes to execute a prudent outsourcing arrangement and the more intense the coordination work to be done. Large systems development projects that use advanced technology play directly to the outsourcers' strengths. Conversely, issues that relate to structure (and thus close, sustained give and take by users) require so much extra coordination that many outsourcing benefits tend to evaporate.

On the one hand, the costing systems, implicit in the outsourcing contracts that use hard dollars, force users to be more precise in their systems specifications early on (albeit a bit resentfully) and thus cut costs. On the other hand, evolving a sensible final design requires trial and error and discussion. Both the contract and the various geographic locations of the outsourcer's development staff can inhibit

---

An Outsourcer's Viewpoint

In February 1994, Warren McFarlan interviewed Van Honeycutt, president of CSC.

McFarlan: *What are an outsourcer's keys to success?*
Honeycutt: There are three. First and foremost is maintaining your reputation. Outsourcing is a very small town. CEOs are the most important references, and a failed relationship has an overwhelming negative impact. Second is getting our managers to work with the client's key executives. In the best sense, this is a strategic alliance. Third is managing capital and financial planning. Outsourcing, unlike systems integration, is a very capital-intensive business.

What has surprised you most in the past five years?
You need world-class IT skills to get through the door. Realistically, however, they are a necessary, but insufficient condition. Effectiveness demands under-standing the customers' long-term strategy, how IT fits into the execution of this strategy, and designing an approach to deal with it. The key to establishing our relationship with General Dynamics was understanding that it was at a crossroads in the defense industry and that an outsourcing alliance had to have great organizational flexibility. This led us to propose a very different relationship structure than we had originally planned. We don't sell MIPS but, rather, IT as a strategic enabler.

What is the most important aspect in structuring an alliance?

---

discussion and lead to additional costs if not carefully managed. Managing the dialogue across two organizations with very different financial structures and motivations is both challenging and, at the core, critical to the alliance's success. Concerns in this area led Kodak to *not* outsource development. Other firms, such as British Aerospace, did, after careful analysis.

CUSTOMER-OUTSOURCER INTERFACE

The importance of the sensitive interface between the company and the outsourcer cannot be overestimated. First, outsourcing can imply delegation of final respon-sibility to the outsourcer. The reality is that oversight simply is not delegatable, and, as we noted earlier, a CIO and supporting staff need to manage the agreement and relationships. Additionally, the interfaces between customer and outsourcer are very complex and should occur at multiple levels, as noted in both boxed examples. At the most senior levels, there must be links to deal with major issues

Working out a flexible partnership. Culture and fit are crucial. If we can't make that happen, it won't work out well, and we will have tied up a lot of capital in an unproductive relationship. The arrangements we have ultimately not pushed to consummation have failed on this point. At the end, the lawyers can help us formalize the agreement, but they are never part of our early discussion.

How do you adapt your arrangement to changing technology?
Every one of our contracts has evolved in scope, economics, and approach to technology. Realistically, technology such as client/server architecture is coming but, in many cases, more slowly than some believe. Good faith and restructuring with a view to being economically beneficial to both parties are key. For example, at Lockheed, Hughes, and Martin Marietta, our contracts have evolved sharply to meet changing needs and emerging technologies.

What do you worry about most?
Ensuring that, in a fast-moving world, we maintain both our technical edge and delivery skills. World-class execution is the foundation for the rest of the relationship.

How close does CSC remain to senior client management?
No matter how large or small the client, each quarter, our senior team staff meets with the client's CEO and CFO to review progress. At least once a year, Bill Hoover [CSC chairman] or I meet with most of the CEOs. This form of partnership demands that personal links be maintained from the top to the bottom of both organizations.

of policy and relationship restructuring, while, at lower levels, there must be mechanisms for identifying and handling more operational and tactical issues. For firms in the strategic quadrant, these policy discussions take place at the CEO level and occasionally involve the board of directors.

Both the customer and outsourcer need regular, full-time relationship managers and coordinating groups lower in the organization to deal with narrow operational issues and potential difficulties. These integrators are crucial for managing different economic motivations and friction. The smaller the firm in relationship to the outsourcer's total business, the more important it is that these arrangements be specified in advance before they get lost in other priorities.

During the past five years, an entirely different way of gaining IT support for outsourcing has emerged. While outsourcing is not for everyone, some very large and sophisticated organizations have successfully made the transition. What determines success or failure is managing the relationship less as a contract and more as a strategic alliance.

REVIEW AND DISCUSSION QUESTIONS

1. Explain the range of potential difficulties that may make IT outsourcing agreements problematic.

2. What are the key factors that may drive a firm to outsource some or all of its IT function?

3. Explain the concept, and the advantages, of managing an IT outsourcing partnership as a strategic alliance.

REFERENCES

1. R.L. Huber, "How Continental Bank Outsourced Its 'Crown Jewels,'" *Harvard Business Review,* January-February 1993, pp. 121-129.

For a critical discussion of the outsourcing phenomenon, see:

R.A. Bettis, S.P. Bradley, and G. Hamel, "Outsourcing and Industrial Decline," *Academy of Management Executive,* February 1992, pp. 7-22.

A library search on "outsourcing information technology" articles for the past year and a half identified over 700 articles, almost all describing IT outsourcing as reported in the various industry trade journals.

2. For a discussion of the impact of outsourcing, see:

L. Loh and N. Venkatraman, "Diffusion of Information Technology Outsourcing: Influence Sources and the Kodak Effect," *Information Systems Research* 4 (1992):334-358.

3. See "Kodak's Outsourcing Deal Brings Risks — And Not Just for Kodak," *The Business Week Newsletter for Information Executives,* August 1989; and

D. Norton, H. Pfendt, G. Biddle, and R. Connor, "A Panel Discussion on Outsourcing," *Stage by Stage,* 25 January 1990, pp. 13-16.

4. "General Dynamics and Computer Sciences Corporation: Outsourcing the IS Function" (A), (B), (C), (D) (Boston: Harvard Business School, Publishing Division, 1993).

5. The theory of what transactions are best conducted within the firm and outside the firm has been comprehensively covered. See:

O.E. Williamson, *Markets and Hierarchies* (New York: Free Press, 1975).

For further contributions on the inefficiencies of hierarchies, see:

H. Leibenstein, *Inside the Firm: Inefficiencies of Hierarchy* (Cambridge, Massachusetts: Harvard University Press, 1987).

For the notion of a new form of relationship evolving among firms, see:

R. Johnson and P.R. Lawrence, "Beyond Vertical Integration: The Rise of the Value-Adding Partnership," *Harvard Business Review,* July-August, 1988, pp. 94-104.

For further discussion of the nature of the evolving firm, see:

J.L. Badaracco, Jr., *The Knowledge Link: How Firms Compete Through Strategic Alliances* (Boston: Harvard Business School Press, 1991).

For a discussion of the process of managing strategic alliances, see:

M.Y. Yoshino, *Managing Strategic Alliance* (Boston: Harvard Business School Press, 1994).

Finally, for a discussion of competitive strategy and the role of strategic alliances, see:

M.E. Porter, *Competitive Advantage* (New York, Free Press 1985).

6. Porter (1985).

7. See R.L. Nolan, "Managing the DP Crisis," *Harvard Business Review,* March-April 1979, pp. 115-126; and

R.L. Nolan, D.C. Croson, and K. Seger, "Note on Stages Theory Today" (Boston: Harvard Business School, Publishing Division, 1993).

8. See S.P. Bradley, J.A. Hausman, and R.L. Nolan, ed., *Globalization, Technology & Competition* (Boston: Harvard Business School Press, 1993).

9. See L. Loh, "Determinants of Information Technology Outsourcing: A Cross-Selectional Analysis," *Journal of Management Information Systems* 9 (1992): 7-24.

10. See K.P. Arnett and M.C. Jones, "Firms That Choose Outsourcing: A Profile," *Information Management* 26 (1994): 179-188.

11. For a discussion of the strategic grid, see:

F.W. McFarlan, J.I. Cash, and J.L. McKenney, *Corporate Information Systems Management* (Homewood, Illinois: Richard D. Irwin, 1992).

McFarlan developed the framework in 1982 see:

F.W. McFarlan, J.L. McKenney, and P. Pyburn, "The Information Archipelago — Plotting a Course," *Harvard Business Review,* January-February 1983, pp. 145-160.

We have generalized the two dimensions of strategic importance. The operations dimension has been generalized from dependence of the company on the computer for processing transactions to overall dependence of the company on sustained real-time processing of overall business processes. We term this dimension "information intensity." See:

M.E. Porter and V.E. Millar, "How Information Gives you Competitive Advantage, *Harvard Business Review,* July-August 1985, pp. 149-160.

The second dimension of the strategic grid that we generalized was the importance of new applications development. Here we generalize applications development to the importance of innovative information resource management. Indeed, in-house applications development is one aspect of this dimension, but modern development initiatives commonly involve a number of outside partners as well.

12. See McFarlan et al. (1992).

13. For additional issues in outsourcing development, see:

"The Managing of Partnering Development in IS Outsourcing," *Proceedings of the Twenty-Sixth Annual Hawaii International Conference on Systems Sciences* 4 (1992): 518-527.

14. See M. Hammer and J. Champy, *Reeingeering the Corporation* (New York: Harper Collins, 1993); and

T. Davenport *Process Innovation* (Boston: Harvard Business School Press, 1993).

15. For a discussion of issues involved in an outsourcing contract, see:

W.B. Richmond and A. Seidmann, "Software Development Outsourcing Contract: Structure and Business Value," *Journal of Management Information Systems* 10 (1993): 57-72.

10 MANAGING UNDERSTANDINGS:
POLITICS, SYMBOLISM, NICHE MARKETING AND THE QUEST FOR LEGITIMACY IN IT IMPLEMENTATION

ANDREW D. BROWN *

Traditionally, the implementation of a new computerized information system has been viewed as a largely rational and technical process. Increasingly, however, it is being recognized that there are also more subtle cultural and political forces to be managed when large IT-based systems are being introduced. Within this paper, Andrew D. Brown focuses upon the political processes through which 'legitimacy' was sought for a new multi-million pound information system within a large UK hospital. In particular, he discusses how politics played a key role in the 'niche marketing' of different sets of system benefits to different categories of hospital employee.

INTRODUCTION

This paper draws on the literatures concerned with interpretive approaches to understanding organizations and IT to provide an analysis of how a large acute hospital dealt with the implementation of a Hospital Information Support System (HISS). The paper focuses on the micropolitical processes by which the sponsors and supporters of the system managed other hospital stakeholders' perceptions of it. This hypocritical exercise in power, while only partially successful, played a crucial role in legitimating the HISS, thus helping to overcome resistance and ensure the system's ultimate acceptance. Our understanding of each of these separate issues has reached a fair degree of sophistication with studies of politics in organizations (Baldridge, 1971; Pettigrew, 1973; Pfeffer & Leong, 1977; Pfeffer & Salancik, 1974), organizational symbolism (Pfeffer, 1981; Turner, 1986) and organizational legitimacy (Brunsson, 1989; Kamens, 1977; Meyer & Rowan,

* THE JUDGE INSTITUTE OF MANAGEMENT STUDIES, UNIVERSITY OF CAMBRIDGE.
REPRINTED WITH PERMISSION FROM, ORGANIZATION STUDIES, VOL. 16 PART 6, 1995.

1977) now well established. This paper suggests that longitudinal interpretive research which is analytically concerned with political processes and symbolic acts in pursuit of legitimacy may yield valuable insights into how individuals come to understand and attribute meaning to their work organization (see Brown, 1994).

There has been very little systematic analysis concerning how organizational members draw on characteristics of their culture — its history, myths and metaphors — to legitimate their exercise of power over other members (Conrad, 1983). What information we do possess has largely been produced by researchers who have engaged in 'processual' or 'contextualist' organizational analysis (Knights & Murray, 1992; Mintzberg, 1978; Pettigrew, 1985), in which tradition this research was conceived and conducted. This paper examines patterns of interaction and the content of the communicative relations between the sponsors and supporters of the HISS and other key (in the sense of being either recognized opinion-formers or holders of senior positions) individuals in an attempt to discover how organizational knowledge is negotiated (Pfeffer & Salancik, 1974; Thompkins & Cheney, 1983; Yukl & Wexley, 1971). The paper illustrates how, in their attempts to gain user acceptance for the HISS, a select group of individuals managed to engineer others' understandings of the system through calculated argument, control over the flow of information, and symbolic acts (Clegg, 1975, 1981), so that they viewed it more favourably than might otherwise have been the case.

The theoretical approach adopted by this research regards organizations as socially constructed phenomena (Berger & Luckmann, 1966) which may be analysed as systems of shared meaning sustained through social, political and symbolic processes (Pfeffer, 1981 Smircich, 1983). Fundamental to human organizing is the creation of meanings which shape actions, events and work environments, and foster personal identities through a complex alchemy of socialization processes and interpersonal relationships (Eisenberg & Riley, 1988). These shared meanings are manifested in the myths, metaphors and stories organizational members tell and the rules of behaviour to which they conform, and analysis of such symbolic phenomena can provide insights into the taken-for-granted and pre-conscious 'deep structure' of power within an organization (Clegg, 1981; Foucault, 1972; Giddens, 1979). Indeed, political manipulation through strategic communication (Williams & Goss, 1975), symbolic domination through language (O'Barr, 1984; Banks, 1985), and the behaviour-constraining effects of rites and stories (McGee, 1980; Kirkwood, 1983; Smith, McLaughlin & Smith-Altendorf, 1985; Eisenberg, 1984; Wilkins, 1983) are all well documented.

While some have sought to understand the management of IT as a purely technical and rational process it is clear that managers attach themselves to certain practices and social constructions of technology, markets and organization, that IT strategies are often accidental in their formation and the result of political struggles and unforeseen circumstances (Swan & Clark, 1992), and that the implementation of such strategies is often motivated by the material and career prospects of individuals and groups seeking to secure, protect and advance their own selfish interests (Keen, 1981; Knights & Murray, 1992). Technological artifacts are thus social constructions or 'equivoques' (Weick, 1990) that possess a high degree of 'interpretative flexibility' (Pinch and Bijker, 1987: 29) and concerning which social groups with their different interests and resources tend to have different views. Kling (1987) and Kling and Iacono (1984), for example, have noted that some organizational participants find developments in IT attractive because they interpret them as leading to their increased control, speed, and discretion over work or an improvement in their bargaining capabilities. With specific reference to IT in health care settings the necessity for sensitivity to the political context, especially the distribution of power and the use of language, has been stressed by Markus and Pfeffer (1983), Barley (1986), and Willcocks and Mark (1989). In all this it is clear that social constructions are the tools of political action.

This paper examines how proponents of the HISS managed to structure and inform individuals' understandings of the system in order to facilitate their acceptance of it. The primary means by which this was accomplished was face-to-face discussion with key individuals supplemented by team briefing meetings, articles in the in-house magazine, a new HISS-specific broadsheet, extensive training programmes, and a variety of formal and informal seminars and presentations. Much of the implementation team's communication was framed at the strategic level, and included particular normative views of the way the organization was and should be (Walsham, 1993; Smircich & Stubbart, 1985). Rather than 'force' one all-embracing vision of what the HISS would mean for the hospital, however, the implementation team were careful to tailor the messages they transmitted to the audience in hand. In practice, what this meant was that they engaged in a concerted niche marketing campaign which crucially involved the withholding, slanting and emphasizing of selected information in a sophisticated micropolitical process (March & Simon, 1958; Tversky & Kahneman, 1974). That the sponsors and supporters of the HISS themselves referred to these activities as 'marketing' or 'sales' processes was important, because it masked (both for them and for others) the extent to which they were embroiled in a political process in an organization where 'politics' was considered a derogatory term. On the face of it this finding would seem to contradict the dominant view that IS strategies tend to embody one very general vision which can be incorporated into a variety of personal enactments (Walsham, 1993), though evidence for the 'broad vision' approach was found in some organization-wide written communications.

The political activities of the HISS implementation team, centred on the manipulation of meanings and understandings and symbolically referred to by them as 'sales' or 'marketing' activities was designed to legitimate the system. It has been persuasively argued that organizations continually seek to gain and maintain legitimacy because then they find it easier to secure resources and unrestricted access to markets, their environment exhibits greater stability, and their survival prospects are considerably enhanced (Meyer & Rowan, 1977). Similarly, organization leaders must legitimate themselves and their strategies in order to ensure that employee acquiescence, enthusiasm and commitment are maintained (Pfeffer, 1981). Legitimacy is also a problem for IT systems, which are often seen as expensive to purchase, difficult to implement, time consuming to operate, and of marginal significance to the well being of the organization and the pursuit of its mission. In this instance the perceived requirement to legitimate the HISS was complicated by the need felt by the implementation team and the Trust board to legitimate themselves in what was a fractious organization. This paper attempts to shed some light on the detailed micropolitical processes by which individuals' perceptions and understandings may be influenced by symbolic action and niche marketing in pursuit of personal, system and organization legitimacy.

CASE STUDY: MANAGING UNDERSTANDINGS

RESEARCH DESIGN

This research was designed and conducted from within the interpretive perspective ('inquiry from the inside'), in which the researcher was immersed in a stream of organizational events (Evered & Louis, 1981) in an inductive attempt to generate 'thick description' (Geertz, 1973), the categories and hypotheses of which were constantly revised and reformulated through an iterative process of interaction and integration of data with observed experiences (Putnam, 1983: 44). The result is an ethnographic account which is firmly grounded in the data from which it has been derived (Glaser, 1978; Glaser & Strauss, 1965a,b; 1967; Martin & Turner, 1986; Strauss, 1987; Turner, 1981, 1983). A total of 11 semi-structured interviews were conducted, mostly with senior and influential individuals, over a period of 18 months. The interviews were of between sixty and ninety minutes duration, and were recorded on audio tapes before being transcribed by the researcher and subjected to analysis. None of the eleven respondents expressed any reservations concerning the capture of data on audio cassettes, and informal (untaped) conversations with these and other individuals reinforced the impression that the taped data were reliable.

Access to the organization was initially gained via the chief information officer who, in conjunction with other senior members of the HISS team, identified likely candidates for interview. At each of the interviews the respondent was invited to name other individuals who they thought should be researched, and these new leads were followed-up wherever possible. Given the vast size of the hospital and the heavy workloads of staff it was impossible to formally interview all relevant employees, and instead every opportunity was taken to converse informally with individuals (such as the director of operational services, the medical records manager, estates department manager, and many of their more junior staff, among others) as the opportunity arose. In addition, a wealth of supplementary documentary material was collected and observations of interactions between participants were made. Documentation concerning HISS had been produced both by the NHS Executive (mostly in the form of information pamphlets and briefing packs) and the HISS team (newsletters, information bulletins, strategy reports and a contract with a software company) much of which was available to the researcher for analysis. The research design was thus longitudinal, though with some retrospective reconstruction of events, (Knights & Murray, 1992), contextual and processual. In these ways it was hoped to overcome some of the methodological deficiencies of the literature on organizational symbolism, which some have observed 'has thusfar distinguished itself more for its theoretical vision than for its empirical rigor' (Eisenberg & Riley, 1988: 144).

PROLEGOMENON

The case study organization ('The City') was a large acute hospital (1500 beds) which sprawled over a 95 acre site. A major UK teaching hospital with a long and distinguished history the organization, and specifically the events described, here need to be understood in the context of more general processes of change that were/are characteristic of the UK National Health Service (NHS). Towards the end of the 1980s the Conservative Goverment led by Margaret Thatcher began to implement a series of reorganizations of the NHS in an attempt to make it more competitive and cost effective (Keen & Buxton, 1991; Levitt & Wall, 1992; Pettigrew, Ferlie & McKee, 1992). Central to this intent was the transformation of what was essentially one giant organization into separate purchasers and suppliers, and the strengthening of management at all levels. In this new structure hospitals like The City were able to opt out of control by local administrative bodies (called District Health Authorities) and become independent self-governing NHS Trusts, accountable directly to Government ministers. In fact The City had gained Trust status in April 1992, and as a result a Trust board headed by a chief executive (who in this instance was a trained nurse) had been set up. As a result of this transformation in the organization's governance, together with the uncertainties associated with a host of related change programmes that were being implemented as this research was conducted, the hospital was in a bewildering state of flux. The demands of the HISS project were additional to these other pressures, and complaints of role overload were frequently made by respondents.

The HISS project was conceived and financed by the NHS Executive (which has important coordinating and strategic roles viz. all sub-parts of the NHS), and was one of a range of IT initiatives it controlled. A HISS is an integrated IT environment able to meet the real-time operational and information needs of both health care professionals and their professional managers. While The City was invited to be a pilot site for HISS as early as February 1989, bureaucratic and political processes associated with realizing such large projects meant that it was not until early 1992 that the hospital was at last able to proceed. The interim was spent in seemingly interminable discussions with senior civil servants in the NHS Executive and Department of Health, district and regional health care officials, and potential IT contractors (Digital, IBM and Oracle). The result was a general sense of pessimism that the project would never be actioned followed (once the contract had been signed) by feelings of relief accompanied by fatigue.

With a £10.1 million contract signed (which would fund the first of five project phases) supervision of the project within the hospital was delegated to a HISS project manager (a professional pharmacist) who began to recruit an implementation team (expected to peak at 75 members). This team worked in conjunction with the software company Oracle which was to write the bespoke software required. A few months after the contract had been signed a chief information officer was recruited whose brief was to ensure delivery of HISS on time and on budget. The reporting relationship between the project manager and chief information officer was extremely unclear and a continual source of conflict which was brokered by the director of finance and information to whom they both reported. Twelve months later the chief information officer had been effectively marginalized, and the position of the project manager was considerably strengthened. The director of finance and information chaired a 'steering committee' consisting of directors and a few senior managers which monitored and directed progress on HISS. In practice, five 'working parties' set up under the auspices of the steering committee were more important in terms of their direct influence on implementation issues. These working parties were in turn responsible for initiating 'action teams' in each hospital department whose brief it was to facilitate actual physical implementation of the system. It is important to note that The City already had a large number of sophisticated IT systems in operation in the departments, and that familiarity with IT was one of the factors that had originally prompted the NHS Executive to offer the HISS opportunity to the organization.

The City hospital was a highly fragmented and political entity in which certain departments and groups of professionals wielded considerable influence. While the move to Trust status did seem to have strengthened the position of the executive directors, the Trust board (and especially the chief executive), were recognized to be in a highly exposed position. Thus although the board had considerable formal powers in practice they were constrained by the need to satisfy the demands of powerful internal constituencies, the Government and public opinion. What this meant was that the board was highly sensitive to internal and external criticism, and this sensitivity seemed to be an active constraint on their willingness to force through change. For example, the board had no access to the departments' medical audit data (which were held on stand alone departmental systems), and were unwilling to insist that they should do, or that this information be fed-in to the HISS. This was despite the fact that this information was recognized to be vital for the effective management of the hospital.

MANAGING UNDERSTANDINGS: THE STRATEGY

Data collection for this project commenced ten months after the contract for the HISS had been signed by The City, the software company and the NHS Executive.

By this time all senior staff had been made aware (through various written communications, briefing meetings, and word-of-mouth) that a large IT system was to be developed and implemented during the course of the next few years. Progress on HISS had, however, been slow, and it was only now that the first part of the first phase of the system (office automation) was being piloted. While individuals possessed variable amounts of knowledge concerning the specifics of the HISS project most sought to understand events by means of analogies with past similar-type implementations (Swan & Clark, 1992; Neustadt & May, 1986):

> Having been through this phase of a system being developed and implemented once before I'd know that there will be a big dip before we get up to people saying 'oh well, that's useful, that's worthwhile' (Director of Quality, TS1 8.2.93, 5).

> [The long time scales do] not surprise me because it took us years to implement our lab system. So something the size of the HISS system, I don't expect it to happen overnight by any stretch of the imagination (Chief Haematologist, TS1 2.3.93, 19).

> It's having installed a couple of computer systems in the lab, in theory it sounds very easy. In practice when you come to do it, the practicalities are more difficult than the theory (Business Manager, Pathology, TS1 3.2.93, 3).

The tendency of individuals to use past events to interpret current and likely future occurrences, and the power of this form of retrospective analogical reasoning to set expectations, increase feelings of control, and reduce anxiety levels, has been widely commented upon (Berger & Luckmann, 1966; Isabella, 1990; Schutz, 1967; Weick, 1979). These understandings and evaluations, often confused and poorly thought-through as they were, provided the implementation team with a matrix of opportunities and constraints in their attempts to reduce resistance. Here we are primarily concerned with the efforts of the HISS implementation team and the system's other sponsors and supporters to obviate negative perceptions of the HISS and substitute more optimistic assessments of the implications of the system tailored to the specific values and concerns of key individuals and stakeholder groups. This was an exercise in power (loosely described as a 'marketing' or 'selling' campaign) which involved the deliberate withholding and distorting of information and appeals to rational self-interest supported by symbolic rites of rationalization and legitimation in the form of training programmes, and the overt support of senior executives. That the sponsors and supporters of HISS defined their political role in marketing/selling terms was clear from their descriptions of their activities:

> We marketed it very carefully (HISS Project Manager, TS1 5.2.93, 26).

> I think the benefits of HISS have been adequately sold to those staff who were around about the time that the procurement process was going on (Director of Finance and Information, TS1 8.2.93, 7).

For internal management of the roll-out process in terms of selling people on using the system is the Steering Committee (Chief Information Officer, TS1 2.2.93, 14).

In their attempts to legitimate the HISS the implementation team employed four principal arguments: (i) that it would lead to improvements in the quality of health care provided; (ii) that it would enable cost savings to be made; (iii) that it would not be the cause of any job losses; and (iv) that it would be a source of strategic advantage. Not all of these arguments were deployed all the time. There was an explicit recognition by the implementation team that organizations are not monolithic entities, but rather coalitions of participants with different (and often conflicting) interests and priorities (Putnam, 1983). What is more, the team were sensitive to the need to understand the interests and priorities of different groups and offer them relevant and acceptable tailored versions of their arguments:

> I think it [HISS] must have legitimacy. But of course it will have to be legitimated to each group of users independently by their sponsors (Director of Radiology, TS1 12.2.93, 28).

> You have to be aware of what your target for today is looking for and then adjust your pitch to that. And if you cross over you are in deep deep trouble. We're careful on that (HISS Project Manager, TS1 5.2.93, 23).

The implementation team thus understood their role as requiring a sophisticated niche marketing campaign that offered each stakeholder group an interpretation of the HISS that it would find acceptable and legitimate. In fact within the hospital only two important broad interest groups were implicitly identified by the team: those whose primary concern was the quality of health care provision (including nurses and clinicians), and those whose work interest was in managerial issues of control, economy and efficiency (among them the Trust board and business managers). A third internal group that may loosely be referred to as support staff and which consisted of porters, secretaries and those working in medical records was identifiable as being principally concerned with issues of job security, but were not thought to be crucial to the successful implementation of the HISS. Additionally, a fourth constituency, involving a variety of external individuals and organizations (such as the NHS Executive, the Department of Health, a central HISS team, other parts of the NHS and the IT industry in general) were also the target of considerable 'marketing/sales' efforts:

> The trick with those particular staff [clinicians] is that you don't go in there saying you could save them three nurses and whatever — it's the clinical benefits which again are easy to point out (HISS Project Manager, TS1 5.2.93, 23).

> . . . emphasis[ing] the financial benefits — that goes to a different body. You talk about that when your talking to the Trust board and the finance directors and people outside the Trust (HISS Project Manager, TS1 5.2.93, 23).

There has been a very strong commitment on the site by the chief executive. She reiterates at every induction course that there will be no redundancies through HISS (Chief Information Officer, TS2 2.2.92, 22).

I think it [HISS] signifies a good strategic direction that we should be taking because good management rests so much on good information. And if we get the information right in terms of content, accuracy, and above all its timeliness and relevance, then that gives us a much better basis for making good decisions . . . (Director of Quality, TS1 8.2.93, 18).

Furthermore, in order to ensure system legitimacy the team considered that their explanations should not just rely on abstract arguments but make reference to particular problems and concrete examples which individuals could more easily associate with and comprehend. In part this seemed to be a reaction to the commonly held view that IT systems were not directly relevant to the business of health care, but it may also have reflected a tacit realization that mass acceptance of the HISS required tailored explanations that were not only plausible and meaningful but 'real'. In an organization in which rumours regarding HISS had been circulating for years and yet no physical evidence for it had been witnessed, the practice of providing realistic problem-solution scenarios may well have been instrumental in persuading people to regard HISS as a helpful inevitability against which it was irrational to resist:

I would find the problems and I would say 'right that's your problem, how can we help solve that problem?' If you go along and say this new wonderful system is going to do all these things for you people are not interested because you don't make it real for them (Director of Quality, TS1 8.2.93, 9).

I always use the phrase 'I don't think it's a HISS system, it's a HOSS system — Hospital Operational Support System'. It's getting into the key of what they are doing and its relevant to what they want to do. It solves problems that they've had and they can see . . . . It's not some airy fairy system that's going in just for the glory of some hi tech department in the corner (HISS Project Manager, TS1 5.2.93, 20).

They have to understand that amongst their key objectives HISS is an objective — but it is also a delivery mechanism which they can use to advantage to fulfil their own objectives (Chief Information Officer, TS3 29.6.94, 2).

It was clear that in deliberately tailoring their arguments, the team's legitimation strategies also involved the conscious omission of certain information from their discussions (Pettigrew, 1972). For example, the HISS had built-in to it a rule base which could help junior doctors with the diagnosis and treatment of patients. This was not being mentioned because of perceived political problems centred on issues of deskilling. As the chief information officer stated, 'The system has the capability perhaps to deskill (that would be one way of describing it) part of the medical role — another way of describing it is it's a means of helping' (Chief Information Officer, TS2 2.2.94, 23). Similarly, the facility that HISS offered for evaluating the cost efficiencies of different clinicians was not being communicated. This further underscores the extent to which the implementation team understood their political role as being as much interpretational as operational (Daft & Weick, 1984). In Isabella's (1990) terminology it indicates an awareness of the need to manage others' understandings of the HISS as they progress through the four interpretational stages (anticipation, confirmation, culmination and aftermath) which she has identified.

While the clinicians espoused an interest in the quality of patient care they had other interests, notably in evading effective control, which remained largely implicit. One specific area that HISS threatened to regulate was theatre lists (the order in which patients were operated upon): this was the source of considerable disquiet in certain parts of the hospital where the potentially dangerous practice of changing these lists was clearly 'endemic'. Clinician resistance additionally focused on the waiting list module, which threatened to wrest control over waiting lists from clinicians. Some of the support staff, for example the porters, also voiced concerns over the quality of patient care while apparently harbouring anxieties about being subject to more stringent control measures as a result of HISS. The issue of patient care, which commanded almost universal support as a legitimate concern, seemed to be employed as a smokescreen for some highly resistant groups which feared that the HISS would diminish their professional autonomy and leave them open to control from the Trust board:

> They think . . . that it will mean that they [clinicians] will actually be controlled by computer . . . . (Director of Radiology, 12.2.93, 7).

> . . . we have a waiting list module now, and it's been scheduled to take a year to run that out across the hospital . . . . It's going to take a year because the way in which doctors work their waiting lists at the moment is different. There's nothing different about the technology, they are all card indexes. But they all want to control them (Chief Information Officer, TS3 29.6.94, 1).

> We hope that it [HISS] will do what we want it to do as a department . . . . We want HISS . . . to work for us rather than being imposed on us . . . . We don't want to lose control of the way that we organize our portering staff (Support Services Manager, TS1 15.2.93, 4).

The reluctance of the clinicians and porters to discuss issues of control (other than with the researcher) and the deliberate omission of control issues from the arguments of the implementation team meant that questions regarding control, autonomy and discretion were not being openly debated. The unwillingness of any group to raise the profile of emotive control issues combined with the implementation team's largely successful efforts to convince people that HISS would improve the quality of patient care meant that open resistance to HISS was negligible. However, it did not mean that resistance was not a major factor influencing the likely outcome of events, merely that the resistance, based as it was on interests that did not command hospital-wide support as legitimate, was passive and covert:

> [The resistance is] passive and quiet — the soggy sponge . . . . The problem as I see it is that the clinicians have actually dropped out of it — I think I'm the only one person who's left on the medical side (Director of Radiology, TS1 12.2.93, 9,29).

As the data collection for this project came to an end in mid 1994 there were considerable grounds for optimism at the City Hospital: the first phase of the HISS programme had been completed, all the bespoke software had been written for the pilot sites, and the task of modifying some of the generic programmes to fit the needs of different departments was well in hand. The position of the IT function had recently been strengthened by the appointment of an IT director (a board level appointment), who assumed all those IT-related responsibilities that had until then been the preserve of the non-specialist finance and information director. In addition, the contract of the chief information officer had not been renewed, and his departure seemed likely to reduce the scope for personal antagonism within the IT function. However, funding for the second phase of the HISS had not yet been granted, and further development of the project was on hold until a National Audit Office assessment of the first phase (which was yet to commence) had been completed.

DISCUSSION

To summarize, the events described here illustrate how the sponsors and supporters of a large IT system attempted to render dominant their multiple interpretations of it in order to establish its legitimacy. These multiple interpretations were devised in order to satisfy the various interests and requirements of different stakeholder groups. The activities of the implementation team can thus be interpreted as moves in a micropolitical game in which the understandings of significant individuals were manipulated so that they had more favourable opinions of the HISS than might otherwise have been the case. This crucially involved not just the specific tailoring of communications to meet the concerns of those influenced but the withholding of key information regarding the implications the HISS had for control over individual and departmental discretion and its potential for 'deskilling' junior doctors. The research presented here has thus exemplified some of the means by which power relations are created, legitimated and sustained. These points require further amplification and analysis.

The project was a vehicle for communicating new sets of power relations that success, if it came, would legitimate in due course (Gagliardi, 1986). For individuals in the HISS implementation team the project represented an opportunity to establish their personal reputations as achievers, as technical specialists, and as key to the hospital's long term IT strategy. Attempts at manipulation were the embodiment of a 'politico-symbolic dialectic' (Cohen, 1974: 35), with the symbolic talk of a 'marketing/sales' campaign acting as a rationalizing facade for the advancement of political interests. This was a highly ambiguous process in which individuals were invited to think of themselves as being 'informed' rather than influenced or persuaded. The fact that the senior members of the implementation team were well known and established figures in the hospital, that they knew and understood the interests, values and lexicons of the people they were dealing with, and their insistent one-to-one pattern of communication with opinion formers and those holding senior positions all served to favour the enactment of their interpretations, and help 'reify a particular social structure with ramifications for the maintenance of a particular power order' (Rosen, 1985: 33).

For the Trust board, and especially the chief executive and finance and information director, the project was a means of impressing vital external constituencies (notably senior figures in the Department of Health and NHS Executive) whose good opinions were crucial to the development of their NHS careers (Buren, 1962). As the chief executive of The City observed, 'I was told if you want a career in the NHS you make this [HISS] work' (Chief Executive, TS1, 12). More than this, the HISS was a means of capturing and disseminating departmental information which senior managers thought when fully operational had the potential to usurp control over information from the departments and their feeder systems. The hospital's specialist IT function could thus hope to benefit from its much increased strategic importance, while the Trust board looked forward to being provided with the information it required to realize control over the organization (see Zuboff, 1988). According to the HISS project manager the system will 'allow us to know what we are doing: I defy anyone to tell you what's happening at the moment' (HISS Project Manager, TS1 5.2.93, 36).

That the implementation team conceived and described their activities as a 'sales' or 'marketing' (rather than 'political') campaign was significant. While The City was recognized to be a highly political entity, strong cultural norms made overt political activity unwise. In order to circumvent such taboos the team chose to describe their activities using the more neutral (in the cultural context of the hospital) terms 'marketing' and 'sales', which shielded them from accusations that they were playing politics. Interestingly, the respondents themselves seemed unaware that in attempting to gain acceptance for HISS they were in fact engaged in an exercise in power, and it is tempting to suggest that by regarding their role as one of marketeers or salesmen they were able to engage in a form of self-deception concerning the extent to which they were embroiled in political manipulation. Indeed, it is arguable that this was an important psychological dynamic which contributed to their success, for if they had recognized their actions to be overtly political it is doubtful whether they could have played out their role with conviction. According to this interpretation of meanings and events the belief that they were engaged in a sales/marketing campaign that was essentially apolitical was a myth, a self-deception that was necessary in order to engage in self-confident action (Schwartz, 1985: 35) and which permitted them to offer explanations for their activities which were ego-supportive and ego-preservative (Staw, 1980).

The activities described in this paper clearly illustrate that 'sharing a language with other persons provides the subtlest and most powerful of all tools for controlling the behavior of . . . other persons to one's advantage' (Morris, 1949: 214). The meaning of a word is the set of ways in which it is used (Parkinson, 1968; Wittgenstein, 1974), and local variations between organizations seems inevitable. For example, it has been suggested that what is meant by phrases such as 'high quality', and 'good service' vary substantially between firms (Schein, 1985). In this case the most senior members of the implementation team were (with a few notable exceptions) people with considerable experience of The City hospital, and who employed the same lexicon as their colleagues in other parts of the organization (Pondy, 1978: 93). Indeed, it was noticeable that the chief information officer, who had only recently been recruited, experienced considerable difficulties because of his lack of awareness of the meanings and understandings attributed to HISS by those steeped in the culture and traditions of the NHS. The importance of the subtle use of language in determining effectiveness by enhancing credibility and managing influence did, however, seem to be appreciated and exploited by the HISS project manager. In sum, there was evidence that members of the implementation team understood (at least at a tacit level) that to be effective they had to invest the HISS (and HISS related activities) with meanings that other employees would consider legitimate and which would encourage acceptance of the system (Pondy, 1978: 94).

The implementation team's deliberate policy of tailoring their arguments to match the interests and aspirations of individuals while simultaneously being careful to omit other information they believed to be relevant to those actors indicates the extent to which hypocritical actions and intentions dominate organizational life (Brunsson, 1989). While not wishing to over-emphasize what was surely very normal behaviour, there were clear instances of hypocrisy worthy of attention. This paper has suggested that in order to encourage acceptance of the system the team needed to convince what were often highly sceptical individuals that its product (the HISS) would offer net benefits while at the same time maintaining a healthy social symbolic accord with these actors. This meant that the inconsistent demands of various groups had to be satisfied in order to promote organized action (the continued piloting and implementation of the HISS), something which required considerable political acumen. The most interesting examples of this centred on the team's decision not to mention the HISS's rule base facility for evaluating the cost effectiveness of clinicians, or indeed the control implications of the system generally, with either medical or support staff. Hypocritical action may therefore be interpreted as a 'rational' response to the conflicting demands of different coalitions, for in this case it was only by acting hypocritically that they could hope to promote and maintain legitimacy for themselves and the HISS.

Conclusions

This paper has focused on the micropolitical behaviour of an IT implementation team who attempted to gain acceptance for their multiple interpretations of the system through a hypocritical process involving symbolic action, myth-making and control over the flow of information. Each interpretation was designed to legitimate the system with respect to particular stakeholder groups by appealing to either their actual or espoused interests as perceived by the implementation team. The key to the success of this venture was the use of the marketing/selling metaphor as a rationalizing (obfuscating) facade. It is interesting to note that the marketing/selling terminology itself seemed to be of relatively recent origin in the hospital, and provides evidence for the sectoral transference of concepts from the private to the public sector. This 'new' terminology had very positive connotations within the hospital where it was used to describe activities that everyone could agree were rational and legitimate, and it is tempting to suggest that this interpretation reflected a naivety regarding what marketing/selling often involves, a naivety that may only be a temporary feature of the cultural life of The City.

This research has illustrated 'technology as equivoque', as something which requires 'ongoing structuring and sensemaking' if it is to be effectively managed (Weick, 1990: 2). The HISS was a 'self-evident artifact' to which people accommodated (Weick, 1990: 21) under the influence of the project team. While the HISS seemed likely to alter the scripts of actors, and traditional institutional patterns of signification, legitimation and domination (see, for example, Barley, 1986), it was by no means clear that such major changes would occur, or that if large scale change did occur, that it would conform to the desires of the HISS project team and senior hospital executives. We should recall that technology is not only a cause but also a consequence of structure: people create structural constraints, which then constrain them (Turner, 1987). In other words, technology alters and is altered by ongoing social and political processes that shape the meaning of artifacts through scripts, culture and tradition. Thus the fact that HISS had tremendous control capabilities did not mean that the system would actually be used for control purposes. Indeed, there was some evidence to indicate that aspects of the system were being subverted, not used, and diverted to other purposes by certain groups. What was going to 'happen next' at The City was, therefore, far from certain.

Acknowledgement

The helpful comments and advice of Mick Rowlinson and three anonymous reviewers are gratefully acknowledged.

REVIEW AND DISCUSSION QUESTIONS

1. Identify the arguments in favour of the implementation of the HISS within The City.

2. Explain why the concept of 'niche marketing' the various benefits of the HISS to different interest groups came to be adopted.

3. Discuss what reservations the following interest groups may have harboured against the implementation of the HISS, the potential legitimacy of such reservations, and how they were or could have been overcome by the implementation team.

   • Hospital managers
   • Doctors and nurses
   • Porters and other support staff

REFERENCES

Baldridge, J.V. 1971 *Power and conflict in the university*. N.Y.: Wiley.

Banks, S. 1985 'Toward viewing organizational cultures as semiotic texts.' Unpublished paper, University of Southern California.

Barley, S.R. 1986 'Technology as an occasion for structuring: Evidence from observations of CT Scanners and the social order of Radiology departments', *Administrative Science Quarterly* 31: 78-98.

Berger, P.L. & T. Luckmann 1966 *The social construction of reality*. Garden City: Doubleday.

Brown, A.D. 1994 'Politics, symbolic action and myth-making in pursuit of legitimacy', *Organization Studies* 15/6, 861-878.

Brunsson, N. 1989 *The organization of hypocrisy: Talk, decisions and actions in organizations*. Chichester, England: John Wiley & Sons.

Buren 1962 Cited in E. Harvey and R. Mills 'Patterns of organizational adaptation:a political perspective' in *Power in organizations* M.N. Zald (ed.),181-213, Vanderbilt University Press 1970.

Clegg, S. 1975 *The theory of power and organization*. London: Routledge & Kegan Paul.

Clegg, S. 1981 'Organizations and control', *Administrative Science Quarterly* 26: 545-562.

Cohen, A. 1974 *Two dimensional man: an anthropology of power and symbolism in complex society*. London: Routledge & Kegan Paul.

Conrad, C. 1983 'Organizational power, faces and symbolic forms' in *Communication in organizations, an interpretive approach* L.L. Putnam and M.E. Pacanowsky, (eds.), 173-194. Beverley Hills: Sage.

Daft, R.L. & Weick, K.E. 1984 'Toward a model of organizations as interperative systems', *Academy of Management Review, 9(2), 284-295.*

Eisenberg, E.M. 1984 'Ambiguity as strategy in organizational communication', *Communication Monographs* 51: 227-242.

Eisenberg, E.M. & Riley P., 1988 'Organizational symbols and sense-making', in the *Handbook of organizational communication* G.M. Goldhaber & G.A. Barnett (eds),131-150. Norwood, N.J.: Ablex Publishing Corporation.

Evered, R. & M. Louis 1981 'Alternative perspectives in the organizational sciences: "inquiry from the inside and "inquiry from the outside", *Academy of Management Review* 6:385-396.

Foucault 1972 *Power/knowledge: Selected interviews and other writings*. New York: Pantheon Books.

Gagliardi, P. 1986 'The creation and change of organizational cultures: A conceptual framework', *Organization Studies* 7/2: 117-134.

Geertz, C. 1973 *The interpretation of cultures*. NY: Basic Books.

Giddens, A. 1979 *Central problems in social theory*, Berkeley: University of California Press.

Glaser, B.G.1978 *Theoretical sensitivity: advances in the methodology of grounded theory*. Mill Valley, California: Sociology Press.

Glaser, B.G. & A. Strauss 1965a *Awareness of dying*. Chicago: Aldine Publishing.

Glaser, B.G. & A. Strauss 1965b 'Temporal aspects of dying as a non-scheduled status passage', *American Journal of Sociology* 71: 48-59.

Glaser, B.G. & A. Strauss 1967 *The discovery of grounded theory: Strategies for qualitative research*. N.Y.: Aldine Publishing.

Isabella, L.A. 1990 'Evolving interpretations as a change unfolds: how managers construe key organizational events', *Academy of Management Journal* 33/1: 7-41.

Kamens, D.H. 1977 'Legitimating myths and educational organization: The relationship between organizational ideology and formal structure', *American Sociological Review* 42: 208-219.

Keen, P.G.W. 1981 'Information systems and organizational change', *Communications of the ACM* 24/1: 24-32.

Keen, T.P.J. & Buxton, M. 1991 *Hospitals in transition, the resource management experiment, Milton Keynes: Oxford University Press.*

Kirkwood, W. 1983 'Storytelling and self-confrontation: Parables as communication strategies', *Quarterly Journal of Speech*, 69: 58-74.

Kling, R. 1987 'Defining the boundaries of computing across complex organizations', in: *Critical issues in information systems research*, 307-362. R. Boland & R.Hirschheim (eds.), N.Y.: Wiley

Kling, R. & Iacono, S. 1984 'The control of information systems developments after implementation', *Communications of the ACM* 27/12: 1218-1226

Knights, D. & Murray, F. 1992 'Politics and pain in managing information technology' *Organization Studies* 13/2: 211-228.

Law, J. 1987 'Technology and heterogeneous engineering: The case of Portuguese expansion', in: *The social construction of technological systems*. Bijker, W.B., Hughes, T.P. and Pinch, T. (eds.), 111-134. Cambridge, MA: The MIT Press.

Levitt, R. & Wall, A. 1992, *The reorganized National Health Service*, London: Chapman & Hall.

McGee, M.C. 1980 'The "ideograph": A link between rhetoric and ideology', *Quarterly Journal of Speech* 55: 1-16.

March, J.G. & H.A. Simon 1958 *Organizations*. New York: John Wiley & Sons.

Markus, M.L. & Pfeffer, J. 1983 'Power and the design and implementation of accounting and control systems', *Accounting, Organizations and Society* Vol.8 No.2/3: 205-218.

Martin, P. & B.A. Turner 1986 'Grounded theory and organizational research' *Journal of Applied Behavioral Science* 22/2: 141-157.

Meyer, J.W. & B. Rowan 1977 'Institutionalized organizations: formal structure as myth and ceremony', *American Journal of Sociology* 83: 340-363.

Mintzberg, H. 1978 'Patterns in strategy formation', *Management Science* 24/9: 934-948.

Morris, C.W. 1949. *Signs, language and behavior.* NY: Prentice-Hall.

Neustadt, R.E. & May, E.R. 1986 *Thinking in time: the uses of history for decision makers,* New York: Free Press.

O'Barr, W. M. 1984 'Asking the right questions about language and power' in *Language and power* C. Kramarae, M. Schultz, & W.M. O'Barr (eds.), 260-280. Beverly Hills: Sage.

Parkinson, G.H.R. 1968 *The theory of meaning.* London: OUP.

Peters, T.J. 1978 'Symbols, patterns, and settings: An optimistic case for getting things done', *Organizational Dynamics* 7: 2-23.

Pettigrew, A.M. 1972 'Information control as a power resource', *Sociology* 6: 187-204.

Pettigrew, A.M. 1973 *The politics of organizational decision-making.* London: Tavistock.

Pettigrew, A.M. 1985 *The awakening giant: continuity and change at ICI.* Oxford: Basil Blackwell.

Pettigrew, A.M., Ferlie, P. & McKee, C. 1992 *Shaping strategic change, making change in large organizations; the case of the National Health Service.* London: Phase Publications Inc.

Pfeffer, J. 1981 'Management as symbolic action: the creation and maintenance of organizational paradigms', *Research in Organizational Behavior* 3: 1-52.

Pfeffer, J. & A. Leong 1977 'Resource allocation in united funds: examination of power and dependence', *Administrative Science Quarterly* 18: 449-461.

Pfeffer, J. & G.R. Salancik 1974 'Organizational decision making as a political process: the case of a university budget', *Administrative Science Quarterly* 19: 135-151.

Pinch, T.J. & W.E. Bijker 1987 'The social construction of facts and artifacts: or how the sociology of science and the sociology of technology might benefit each other', in *The social construction of technological systems.* Bijker, W.B., Hughes, T.P. and Pinch, T. (eds.), 17-50. Cambridge, MA: The MIT Press.

Pondy, L.R. 1978 'Leadership is a language game', in *Leadership: where else can we go?* M.W. McCall & M.M. Lombardo (eds.) 87-101. Durham, N.C.: Duke University Press.

Putnam, L.L. 1983 'The interpretive perspective, an alternative to functionalism' in *Communication in organizations, an interpretive approach* L.L. Putnam and M.E. Pacanowsky, (eds.), 31-54. Beverley Hills: Sage.

Rosen, M. 1985 'Breakfast at spiro's: dramaturgy and dominance', *Journal of Management* 11/2: 31-48.

Schein, E.H. 1985 *Organizational culture and leadership.* San Francisco, California: Jossey Bass.

Schutz, A. 1967 *The phenomenology of the social world.* Evanston, Ill: Northwestern University Press.

Schwartz, H.S. 1985 'The usefulness of myth and the myth of usefulness; A dilemma for the applied organizational scientist', *Journal of Management* 11/1: 31-42.

Smircich, L. 1983 'Organizations as shared meanings' in *Organizational symbolism.* L.R. Pondy, P.J. Frost, G. Morgan, and T.C. Dandridge (eds.), 55-65. Greenwich, Conn.: JAI Press.

Smircich, L. & C. Stubbart 1985 'Strategic management in an enacted world', *Academy of Management Review* 10/4: 724-736.

Smith, S., McLaughlin, M. & Smith-Altendorf, D. 1985 'A cultural themes perspective: Approaches to the use of stories in the study of the organizational socialization process.' Paper presented at the Annual Meeting of the International Communication Association, Honolulu, Hawaii.

Staw, B.M. 1980 'Rationality and justification in organizational life' in *Research in organizational behavior* B.M. Staw & L.L. Cummings (eds.), 45-80 Vol.2, Greenwich, Conn.: JAI Press.

Strauss, A. 1987 *Qualitative analysis for social scientists.* Cambridge: Cambridge University Press.

Swan, J.A. & Clark, P. 1992 'Organizational decision-making in the appropriation of technological innovation: cognitive and political dimensions', *European Work and Organizational Psychologist* 2/2: 103-127.

Thompkins, P.K. & G. Cheney 1983. 'Account analysis of organizations, decision making and identification' in *Communication in organizations, an interpretive approach* L.L. Putnam and M.E. Pacanowsky, (eds.), 123-146. Beverley Hills: Sage.

Turner, B. 1981 'Some practical aspects of qualitative data analysis: one way of organising the cognitive processes associated with the generation of grounded theory', *Quality and Quantity* 15: 225-247.

Turner, B. 1983 'The use of grounded theory for the qualitative analysis of organizational behaviour', *Journal of Management Studies* 20/3: 333-348.

Turner, B. 1986. 'Sociological aspects of organisational symbolism', *Organization Studies*, 7/2: 101-115.

Turner, J.H.1987 'Analytical theorizing' in *Social theory today* A. Giddens and J.H. Turner (eds.), Stanford, Calif: Stanford University Press. Cited in Weick, K.E. 1990 'Technology as equivoque: Sense making in new technologies', in *Technology and Organisations* P.S. Goodman and L.S. Sroull (eds.), 1-44. San Francisco: Jossey Bass.

Tversky, A. & Kahneman, D. 1974 'Judgement under uncertainty: Heuristics and biases', *Science* 185:1124-1131.

Walsham, G. 1993 *Interpreting information systems in organizations*, Chichester: John Wiley & Sons.

Weick, K.E. 1979 *The social psychology of organizing* (2nd ed.). Reading: Addison-Wesley.

Weick, K.E. 1990 'Technology as equivoque: Sense making in new technologies', in *Technology and organisations* P.S. Goodman and L.S. Sproull (eds.), 1-44. San Francisco: Jossey Bass.

Wilkins, A.W. 1983. 'Organizational stories as symbols which control the organization' in *Organizational symbolism.* L.R. Pondy, P.J. Frost, G. Morgan, & T.C. Dandridge, (eds.), 81-92. Greenwich, Conn: JAI Press.

Willcocks, L.P. & Mark, A.L. 1989 'IT systems implementation: research findings from the public sector', *Journal of Information Technology* 4/2: 92-103.

Williams, M.L. & Goss, B. 1975 'Equivocation: Character insurance', *Human Communication Research*,1: 265-270.

Wittgenstein, L. 1974 *Philosophical investigations* (G.E.M. Anscombe, Trans). Oxford: Basil Blackwell.

Yukl, G.A. & K.N. Wexley 1971 *Readings in organizational and industrial psychology.* NY: Oxford University Press.

Zuboff, S. 1988 *In the age of the smart machine.* NY: Basic Books.

11 THE NEW INDUSTRIAL ENGINEERING:
INFORMATION TECHNOLOGY AND BUSINESS PROCESS REDESIGN

THOMAS H. DAVENPORT *
JAMES E. SHORT **

Business process redesign and information technology have long been 'natural partners', yet their marriage has rarely been fully exploited. Within this paper, the authors use a variety of case examples to explore the IT/business process redesign relationship. In particular they contend that, whilst IT has been underexploited in the past, where IT has been used to cross previous boundaries, enormously beneficial customer-driven processes have arisen as a result.

At the turn of the century, Frederick Taylor revolutionized the workplace with his ideas on work organization, task decomposition, and job measurement. Taylor's basic aim was to increase organizational productivity by applying to human labor the same engineering principles that had proven so successful in solving the technical problems in the work environment. The same approaches that had transformed mechanical activity could also be used to structure jobs performed by people. Taylor came to symbolize the practical realizations in industry that we now call industrial engineering (IE), or the scientific school of management.[1] In fact, though work design remains a contemporary IE concern, no subsequent concept or tool has rivalled the power of Taylor's mechanizing vision.

As we enter the 1990s, however, two newer tools are transforming organizations to the degree that Taylorism once did. These are *information technology* — the capabilities offered by computers, software applications, and telecommunications — and *business process redesign* — the analysis and design of work flows and processes within and between organizations. Working together, these tools have the potential to create a new type of industrial engineering, changing the

* ERNST AND YOUNG
** MIT SLOAN SCHOOL OF MANAGEMENT

REPRINTED FROM SLOAN MANAGEMENT REVIEW, 31(4) SUMMER 1990, BY PERMISSION OF PUBLISHER.

way the discipline is practised and the skills necessary to practice it.

This article explores the relationship between information technology (IT) and business process redesign (BPR). We report on research conducted at MIT, Harvard, and several consulting organizations on nineteen companies, including detailed studies of five firms engaged in substantial process redesign. After defining business processes, we extract from the experience of the companies studied a generic five-step approach to redesigning processes with IT. We then define the major types of processes, along with the primary role of IT in each type of process. Finally, we consider management issues that arise when IT is used to redesign business processes.

IT IN BUSINESS PROCESS REDESIGN

The importance of both information technology and business process redesign is well known to industrial engineers, albeit as largely separate tools for use in specific, limited environments.[2] IT is used in industrial engineering as an analysis and modelling tool, and IEs have often taken the lead in applying information technology to manufacturing environments. Well-known uses of IT in manufacturing include process modelling, production scheduling and control, materials management information systems, and logistics. In most cases where IT has been used to redesign work, the redesign has most likely been in the manufacturing function, and industrial engineers are the most likely individuals to have carried it out.

IEs have begun to analyze work activities in non-manufacturing environments, but their penetration into offices has been far less than in factories. IT has certainly penetrated the office and services environments — in 1987 *Business Week* reported that almost 40 percent of all U.S. capital spending went to information systems, some $97 billion a year — but IT has been used in most cases to hasten office work rather than to transform it.[3] With few exceptions, IT's role in the redesign of nonmanufacturing work has been disappointing; few firms have achieved major productivity gains.[4] Aggregate productivity figures for the United States have shown no increase since 1973.[5]

Given the growing dominance of service industries and office work in the Western economies, this type of work is as much in need of analysis and redesign as the manufacturing environments to which IT has already been applied. Many firms have found that this analysis requires taking a broader view of both IT and business activity, and of the relationships between them. Information technology should be viewed as more than an automating or mechanizing force; it can fundamentally reshape the way business is done. Business activities should be viewed as more than a collection of individual or even functional tasks; they should be broken down into processes that can be designed for maximum effectiveness, in both manufacturing and service environments.

How can IT support business processes?

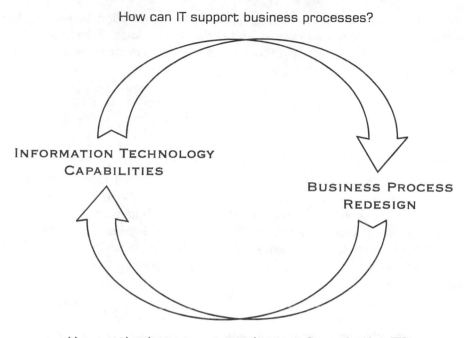

INFORMATION TECHNOLOGY
CAPABILITIES

BUSINESS PROCESS
REDESIGN

How can business processes be transformed using IT?

Figure 1 The recursive relationship between IT capabilities and business process redesign.

Our research suggests that IT can be more than a useful tool in business process redesign. In leading edge practice, information technology and BPR have a recursive relationship, as Figure 1 illustrates. Each is the key to thinking about the other. Thinking about information technology should be in terms of how it supports new or redesigned business processes, rather than business functions or other organizational entities. And business processes and process improvements should be considered in terms of the capabilities information technology can provide. *We refer to this broadened, recursive view of IT and BRP as the new industrial engineering.*

Taylor could focus on workplace rationalization and individual task efficiency because he confronted a largely stable business environment; today's corporations do not have the luxury of such stability.[6] Individual tasks and jobs change faster than they can be redesigned. Today, responsibility for an outcome is more often spread over a group, rather than assigned to an individual as in the past. Companies increasingly find it necessary to develop more flexible, team-oriented, coordinative, and communication-based work capability. In short, rather than maximizing the performance of particular individuals or business functions, companies must maximize interdependent activities within and across the entire organization.

Such business processes are a new approach to coordination across the firm; information technology's promise — and perhaps its ultimate impact — is to be the most powerful tool in the twentieth century for reducing the costs of this coordination. [7]

WHAT ARE BUSINESS PROCESSES?

We define business processes as a set of logically related tasks performed to achieve a defined business outcome. This definition is similar to Pall's "The logical organization of people, materials, energy, equipment, and procedures into work activities design to produce a specified end result (work product)."[8]

A set of processes forms a business system — the way in which a business unit, or a collection of units, carries out its business. Processes have two important characteristics:

- They have customers; that is, processes have defined business outcomes, and there are recipients of the outcomes. Customers may be either internal or external to the firm.
- They cross organizational boundaries; that is, they normally occur across or between organizational subunits. Processes are generally independent of formal organizational structure.

Common examples of processes meeting these criteria include.

- developing a new product;
- ordering goods from a supplier;
- creating a marketing plan;
- processing and paying an insurance claim; and
- writing a proposal for a government contract.

Ordering goods from a supplier, for example, typically involves multiple organizations, and functions. The end user, purchasing, receiving, accounts payable, etc., and the supplier organization are all participants. The user could be viewed as the process's customer. The process outcome could be either the creation of the order, or, perhaps more usefully, the actual receipt of the goods by the user.

Our examples so far are of large-scale processes that affect whole organizations or groups. There are more detailed processes that meet the definitional criteria above. These might include installing a windshield in an automobile factory, or completing a monthly departmental expense report. IT-driven process redesign can be applied to these processes, but the implications of redesigning them may be important only in the aggregate. In many of the firms studied, analyzing processes in great detail was highly appropriate for some purposes, for example, the detailed design of an information system or data model to support a specific work process. However, the firms that were truly beginning to redesign their business functions took a broader view of processes.

A BRIEF HISTORY OF PROCESS THINKING

Process thinking has become widespread in recent years, due largely to the quality movement. Industrial engineers and others who wish to improve the quality of operations are urged to look at an entire process, rather than a particular task or business function. At IBM, for example, "process management will be the principal IBM quality focus in the coming years".[9] But process discussions in the quality movement's literature rarely mention information technology. Rather, the focus is usually on improving process control systems in a manufacturing context; when IT is discussed, it is in the context of factory floor automation. Recent IE literature also borders on process thinking when advocating cross-functional analysis,[10] although, as we will discuss, cross-functional processes are only one possible type of process.

Other than quality-oriented manufacturing process redesign, most processes in major corporations have not been subject to rigorous analysis and redesign. Indeed, many of our current processes result from a series of ad hoc decisions made by functional units, with little attention to effectiveness across the entire process. Many processes have never even been measured. In one manufacturing company studied, for example, no one had ever analyzed the elapsed time from a customer's order to delivery. Each department (sales, credit checking, shipping, and so on) felt that it had optimized its own performance, but in fact the overall process was quite lengthy and unwieldy.

Even fewer business processes have been analyzed with the capabilities of IT in mind. Most business processes were developed before modern computers and communications even existed. When technology has been applied, it is usually to automate or speed up isolated components of an existing process. This creates communication problems within processes and impediments to process redesign and enhancement. For example, in a second manufacturing firm studied, the procurement process involved a vendor database, a materials management planning system, and accounts payable and receivable systems, all running on different hardware platforms with different data structures. Again, each organizational subunit within the process had optimized its own IT application, but no single subunit had looked at (or was responsible for) the entire process. We believe the problems this firm experienced are very common.

REDESIGNING BUSINESS PROCESSES WITH IT: FIVE STEPS

Assuming that a company has decided its processes are inefficient or ineffective, and therefore in need of redesign, how should it proceed? This is a straightforward activity, but five major steps are involved: develop the business vision and process objectives, identify the processes to be redesigned, understand and measure the existing process, identify IT levers, and design and build a prototype of the new process (see Figure 2). We observed most or all of these steps being performed in companies that were succeeding with BPR. Each step is described in greater detail below.

DEVELOP BUSINESS VISION AND PROCESS OBJECTIVES

In the past, process redesign was typically intended simply to "rationalize" the process, in other words, to eliminate obvious bottlenecks and inefficiencies. It did not involve any particular business vision or context. This was the approach of the "work simplification" aspect of industrial engineering, an important legacy of Taylorism. An example of the rationalization approach appears in a 1961 "Reference Note on Work Simplification" from the Harvard Business School:

> A good manager asks himself *why* things are done as they are, extending his enquiry to every aspect of the job and the surroundings in which it is performed, from the flow of paper work to the daily functioning of his subordinates . . . He is expected to supply the stimulus and show that job improvement or simplification of work is not only important but also is based on commonsense questioning aimed at uncovering the easiest, most economical way of performing a job.[11]

Our research suggests strongly that rationalization is not an end in itself, and is thus insufficient as a process redesign objective. Furthermore, rationalization of highly decomposed tasks may lead to a less efficient overall process. Instead of task rationalization, redesign of entire processes should be undertaken with a specific business vision and related objectives in mind.

In most successful redesign examples we studied, the company's senior management had developed a broad strategic vision into which the process redesign activity fit.[12] At Xerox, for example, this vision involved taking the perspective of the customer and developing systems rather than stand-alone products; both required cross-functional integration. At Westinghouse, the vision consisted largely of improving product quality. Ford's involved adopting the best practices of Japanese automobile manufacturers, including those of Mazda, of which it is a partial owner.

Each of these visions implied specific objectives for process redesign. The most likely objectives are the following:

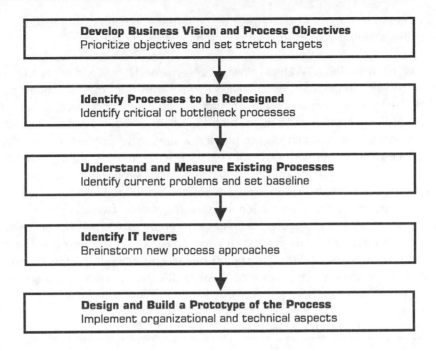

Figure 2 Five steps in business process redesign.

- **Cost reduction.** This objective was implicit in the "rationalization" approach. Cost is an important redesign objective in combination with others, but insufficient in itself. Excessive attention to cost reduction results in tradeoffs that are usually unacceptable to process stakeholders. While optimizing on other objectives seems to bring costs into line, optimizing on cost rarely brings about other objectives.

- **Time reduction.** Time reduction has been only a secondary objective of traditional industrial engineering. Increasing numbers of companies, however, are beginning to compete on the basis of time.[13] Processes, as we have defined them, are the ideal unit for a focused time reduction analysis. One common approach to cutting time from product design is to make the steps begin simultaneously, rather than sequentially, using IT to coordinate design directions among the various functional participants. This approach has been taken in the design of computers, telephone equipment, automobiles, and copiers (by Digital Equipment, AT&T Bell Labs, Ford and Xerox, respectively).

- **Output quality.** All processes have outputs, be they physical — such as in manufacturing a tangible product — or informational — such as in adding data to a customer file. Output quality is frequently the focus of process improvement in manufacturing environments; it is just as important in service industries. The specific measure of output quality may be uniformity, variability, or freedom from defects; this should be defined by the customer of the process.

- **Quality of worklife (QWL)/learning/empowerment.** IT can lead either to greater empowerment of individuals, or to greater control over their output. Zuboff points out that IT-intensive processes are often simply automated, and that the "informating" or learning potential of IT in processes is often ignored.[14] Moreover, Schein notes that organizations often do not provide a supportive context for individuals to introduce or innovate with IT.[15] Of course, it is rarely possible to optimize all objectives simultaneously, and in most firms, the strongest pressures are to produce tangible benefits. Yet managers who ignore this dimension risk failure of redesigned processes for organizational and motivational factors.

Some firms have been able to achieve multiple objectives in redesigning processes with IT. American Express, for example, set out to improve the cost, time and quality of its credit authorization process by embedding the knowledge of its best authorizers in an "Authorizer's Assistant" expert system. This successful redesign led to a $7 million annual reduction in costs due to credit losses, a 25 percent reduction in the average time for each authorization, and a 30 percent reduction in improper credit denials.

Finally, all firms found it was important to set specific objectives, even to the point of quantification. Though it is difficult to know how much improvement is possible in advance of a redesign, "reach should exceed grasp." Setting goals that will stretch the organization will also provide inspiration and stimulate creative thinking. For example, a company might decide to reduce the time to bring new products to market by 80 percent. In the accounts payable process at Ford, the "stretch" goal was to eliminate invoices — to pay suppliers upon receipt of their products or services. This goal has been achieved with the help from an information system to confirm expected deliveries at the loading dock. As a result, Ford has eliminated three-quarters of the jobs in accounts payable.

IDENTIFY PROCESSES TO BE REDESIGNED

Most organizations could benefit from IT-enabled redesign of critical (if not *all*) business processes. However, the amount of effort involved creates practical limitations. Even when total redesign was the ultimate objective, the companies we studied selected a few key processes for initial efforts. Moreover, when there was insufficient commitment to total redesign, a few successful examples of IT-enhanced processes became a powerful selling tool.

The means by which processes to be redesigned are identified and prioritized is a key issue. This is often difficult because most managers do not think about their business operations in terms of processes. There are two major approaches. The *exhaustive* approach attempts to identify all processes within an organization and then prioritize them in order of redesign urgency. The *high-impact* approach attempts to identify only the most important processes or those most in conflict with the business vision and process objectives.

The exhaustive approach is often associated with "information engineering" (developed by James Martin in the early 1980s), in which an organization's use of data dictates the processes to be redesigned.[16] For example, one information engineering method, employed at several divisions of Xerox, involves identifying business activities and the data they require using a data-activity matrix. The clusters of data activity interactions in the cells of the matrix are the organization's major business process. Once processes are identified, Xerox managers prioritize them in the order in which new IT applications support should be provided. Although process identification in some Xerox divisions has taken as little as three months, many companies find this approach very time consuming.

The alternative is to focus quickly on high-impact processes. Most organizations have some sense of which business areas or processes are most crucial to their success, and those most "broken" or inconsistent with the business vision. If not, these can normally be identified using senior management workshops, or through extensive interviewing.[17] At IBM, the salesforce was surveyed to determine the relative importance of various customer support processes; the generation of special bids emerged as the highest priority and was the first process to be redesigned.

Companies that employed the high-impact approach generally considered it sufficient. Companies taking the exhaustive approach, on the other hand, have not had the resources to address all the identified processes; why identify them if they cannot be addressed? As a rough rule of thumb, most companies we studied were unable to redesign and support more than ten to fifteen major processes per year (i.e., one to three per major business unit); there was simply not enough management attention to do more. And some organizations have abandoned the exhaustive approach.[18]

Whichever approach is used, companies have found it useful to classify each redesigned process in terms of beginning and end points, interfaces, and organization units (functions or departments) involved, particularly including the customer unit. Thinking in these terms usually broadens the perceived scope of the process. For example, a sales manager may be aware that there are inefficiencies in customer order entry. A skilled process consultant might decide that the whole process — negotiating, receiving, and fulfilling orders — needs to be redesigned. Whether the problem is broken down into three processes or viewed as one is not important; expanding the *scope* of the process analysis is the key issue.

High-impact processes should also have owners.[19] In virtually all the process redesigns we studied, an important step was getting owners to buy in to both the idea and the scope of process redesign at an early state. In several companies, managers felt that the process owner's job should be either above the level of the functions and units involved, or, if on the same level, that the owner should be willing — and able — to change the status quo. The difficulty, however, is that some processes only come together at the CEO level. In this situation, the CEO should designate a senior manager as owner and invest him or her with full authority. Processes that are fully contained within a single function or department can normally be owned by the manager of that area.

UNDERSTAND AND MEASURE EXISTING PROCESSES

There are two primary reasons for understanding and measuring processes before redesigning them. First, problems must be understood so that they are not repeated. Second, accurate measurement can serve as a baseline for future improvements. If the objective is to cut time and cost, the time and cost consumed by the untouched process must be measured accurately. Westinghouse Productivity and Quality Center consultants found that simply graphing the incremental cost and time consumed by process tasks can often suggest initial areas for redesign. These graphs look like "step functions" showing the incremental contribution of each major task.

This step can easily be overemphasized, however. In several firms, the "stretch" goal was less to eliminate problems or bottlenecks than to create radical improvements. Designers should be informed by past process problems and errors, but they should work with a clean slate. Similarly, the process should not be measured for measurement's sake. Only the specific objectives of the redesign should be measured. As with the high-impact process identification approach, an 80-20 philosophy is usually appropriate.

IDENTIFY IT LEVERS

Until recently, even the most sophisticated industrial engineering approaches did not consider IT capabilities until after a process had been designed. The conventional wisdom in IT usage has always been to first determine the business requirements of a function, process, or other business entity, and then to develop a system. The problem is that an awareness of IT capabilities can — and should — influence process design. Knowing that product development teams can exchange computer-aided designs over large distances, for example, might affect the structure of a product development process. The role of IT in a process should be considered in the early stages of its redesign.[20]

Several firms accomplished this using brainstorming sessions, with the process redesign objectives and existing process measures in hand. It was also useful to have a list of IT's generic capabilities in improving business processes. In the broadest sense, *all* of IT's capabilities involve improving coordination and information access across organizational units, thereby allowing for more effective management of task interdependence. More specifically, however, it is useful to think about IT capabilities and their organizational impacts in nine different ways (see Table 1).

Table 1 IT capabilities and their organizational impacts

Capability	Organizational Impact/Benefit
Transactional	IT can transform unstructured processes into routinized transactions
Geographical	IT can transfer information with rapidity and ease across large distances, making processes independent of geography
Automational	IT can replace or reduce human labor in a process
Analytical	IT can bring complex analytical methods to bear on a process
Informational	IT can bring vast amounts of detailed information into a process
Sequential	IT can enable changes in the sequence of tasks in a process, often allowing multiple tasks to be worked on simultaneously
Knowledge Management	IT allows the capture and dissemination of knowledge and expertise to improve the process
Tracking	IT allows the detailed tracking of task status, inputs, and outputs
Disintermediation	IT can be used to connect two parties within a process that would otherwise communicate through an Intermediary (internal or external)

There are undoubtedly other important IT capabilities that can reshape processes. Organizations may want to develop their own lists of capabilities that are specific to the types of processes they employ. The point is twofold: IT is so powerful a tool that it deserves its own step in process redesign, and IT can actually create new process design options, rather than simply support them.

DESIGN AND BUILD A PROTOTYPE OF THE PROCESS

For most firms, the final step is to design the process. This is usually done by the same team that performed the previous steps, getting input from constituencies and using brainstorming workshops. A key point is that the actual design is not the end of the process. Rather, it should be viewed as a prototype, with successive iterations expected and managed. Key factors and tactics to consider in process design and prototype creation include using IT as a design tool, understanding generic design criteria and creating organizational prototypes.

- **IT as a Design Tool.** Designing a business process is largely a matter of diligence and creativity. Emerging IT technologies, however, are beginning to facilitate the "process" of process design. Some computer-aided systems engineering (CASE) products are designed primarily to draw process models. The ability to draw models rapidly and make changes suggested by process owners speeds redesign and facilitates owner buy-in. Some CASE products can actually generate computer code for the information systems application that will support a modeled business process.

Several Xerox divisions, for example, are moving directly from process modeling to automated generation of computer code for high-priority processes. They report improved productivity and high user satisfaction with the resulting systems. A further benefit is that when the business process changes, the IS organization can rapidly modify the affected system. Use of code generation products generally presumes that process designers will use the exhaustive approach to process identification.

- **Generic design criteria.** Companies used various criteria for evaluating alternative designs. Most important, of course, is the likelihood that a design will satisfy the chosen design objectives. Others mentioned in interviews included the simplicity of the design, the lack of buffers or intermediaries, the degree of control by a single individual or department (or an effective, decentralized coordinative mechanism), the balance of process resources, and the generalization of process tasks (so that they can be performed by more than one person).

- **Organizational prototypes.** Mutual Benefit Life's (MBL) redesign of its individual life insurance underwriting process illustrates a final, important point about process design. At MBL, underwriting a life insurance policy involved 40 steps with over 100 people in 12 functional areas and 80 separate jobs. To streamline this lengthy and complex process, MBL undertook a pilot project with the goal of improving productivity by 40 percent. To integrate the process, MBL created a new role, the case manager. This role was designed to perform and coordinate all underwriting tasks centrally, utilizing a workstation-based computer system capable of pulling data from all over the company. After a brief start-up period, the firm learned that two additional roles were necessary on some underwriting cases: specialists such as lawyers or medical directors in knowledge-intensive fields, and clerical assistance. With the new role and redesigned process, senior managers at MBL are confident of reaching the 40 percent goal in a few months. This example illustrates the value of creating organizational prototypes in IT-driven process redesign.

Creating prototypes of IT applications has already gained widespread acceptance. Advocates argue that building a prototype of an IT change usually achieves results faster than conventional "life cycle" development, and, more important, that the result is much more likely to satisfy the customer. Building prototypes of business process changes and organizational redesign initiatives can yield similar benefits. [21] The implications of this extension are that process designs, after agreement by owners and stakeholders, would be implemented on a pilot basis (perhaps in parallel with existing processes), examined regularly for problems and objective achievement, and modified as necessary. As the process approached final acceptance, it would be phased into full implementation.

DEFINING PROCESS TYPES

The five steps described above are sufficiently general to apply to most organizations and processes. Yet the specifics of redesign vary considerably according to the type of process under examination. Different types require different levels of management attention and ownership, need different forms of IT support, and have different business consequences. In this section, we present three different dimensions within which processes vary.

Understanding and classifying the different types of processes is important because an organization can appear to be a seamless web of interconnected processes. With various process *types* in mind, a manager can begin to isolate particular processes for analysis and redesign, including activities that, without process thinking, might otherwise be overlooked.

Three major dimensions can be used to define processes (see Figure 3). These are the organizational entities or subunits involved in the process, the type of objects manipulated, and the type of activities taking place. We describe each dimension and resulting process type below.

DEFINING PROCESS ENTITIES

Processes take place between types of organizational entities. Each type has different implications of IT benefits.

Interorganizational processes are those taking place between two or more business organizations. Increasingly, companies are concerned with coordinating activities that extend into the next (or previous) company along the value-added chain. [22] Several U.S. retail, apparel, and textile companies, for example, have linked their business processes to speed up reordering of apparel. When Dillard's (department store) inventory of a particular pants style falls below a specified level, Haggar (apparel manufacturer) is notified electronically. If Haggar does not have the cloth to manufacture the pants, Burlington Industries (textile manufacturer) is notified electronically. As this example of electronic data interchange (EDI) illustrates, information technology is the major vehicle by which this interorganizational linkage is executed.

For most companies, simple market relationships are the most common source of interorganizational processes. All the tasks involved in a selling-buying trans-

Process Dimension and Type	Typical Example	Typical IT Role
Entities		
Interorganizational	Order form from a supplier	Lower transaction costs; eliminate intermediaries
Interfunctional	Develop a new product	Work across geography; greater simultaneity
Interpersonal	Approve a bank loan	Role and task integration
Objects		
Physical	Manufacture a product	Increased outcome flexibility; process control
Informational	Create a proposal	Routinizing complex decisions
Activities		
Operational	Fill a customer order	Reduce time and costs; increase output quality
Managerial	Develop a budget	Improve analysis; increase participation

Figure 3 Types of processes.

action form a critical process for sellers, and an increasingly important one for buyers seeking higher quality, cost efficiency, and responsiveness. Yet much of the focus has been on a simple transaction level, rather than on an interorganizational business process level. Again, how EDI is used illustrates this point.

Buyers and sellers have used EDI largely to speed up routine purchasing transactions, such as invoices or bills of materials. Few companies have attempted to redesign the broader procurement process — from the awareness that a product is needed, to the development of approved vendor lists, or even to the delivery and use of the purchased product. In the future, sellers will need to look at all buyer processes in which their products are involved.

Moreover, many firms will need to help the buyer improve those processes. Du Pont's concept of "effectiveness in use" as the major criterion of customer satisfaction is one leading approach to measuring the effectiveness of interorganizational processes. Du Pont is motivated not simply to sell a product, but to link its internal processes for creating value in a product, to its customer's processes for using the product. This concept led Du Pont to furnish EDI-provided Material

Safety Data Sheets along with the chemicals it sells to its customers to ensure their safe use.

Westinghouse used an interorganizational process approach in dealing with Portland General Electric (PGE), a major customer of power generation equipment. PGE managers called upon Westinghouse's Productivity and Quality Center, a national leader in process improvement, to help them implement EDI, but the Westinghouse team asked if it could analyze the entire process by which PGS procured equipment from Westinghouse and other suppliers. They found that, while implementing EDI could yield efficiencies on the order of 10 percent, changing the overall procurement process, including using EDI and bypassing the purchasing department altogether for most routine purchase orders, could lead to much greater savings. In one case, the time to execute a standard purchase order, for example, could be reduced from fifteen days to half a day; the cost could be reduced from almost $90 to $10.

A second major type of business process is *interfunctional*. These processes exist within the organization, but cross several functional or divisional boundaries. Interfunctional processes achieve major operational objectives, such as new product realization, asset management, or production scheduling. Most management processes — for example, planning, budgeting, and human resource management — are interfunctional.

Many manufacturing companies that focused on quality improvement found that producing quality products and services required addressing difficult interfunctional issues. Yet most firms have never even listed their key interfunctional processes, let alone analyzed or redesigned them, with or without the aid of IT.

Two companies that recently analyzed their key interfunctional business processes are Baxter Healthcare Corporation and US Sprint Communications Company. Baxter's 1985 merger with American Hospital Supply provided the context for a major analysis of key business strategies, and the alignment of the IT infrastructure with those strategies.[23] As part of a seven-month IT planning effort, the company defined twenty-nine major interfunctional processes and analyzed the current and future role of IT in supporting them. For example, in the distribution area, the company identified order entry, inventory, warehouse management, purchasing, transportation, and equipment tracking as key processes. The success of this IT planning effort led Baxter to incorporate the process definition approach into its annual corporate planning process.

At US Sprint, well-publicized problems with the customer billing system prompted the company's IT function to develop a model of information flows for the entire business as part of a comprehensive systems improvement program. This model defined the critical information and key interfunctional processes necessary to run the business. Sprint is now assigning ownership to key processes and continuing to identify improvements — and ways to measure them — in each process. The systems improvement program raised the IT organization's composite internal quality index by more than 50 percent in one year.[24]

A major problem in redesigning interfunctional processes is that most information systems of the past were built to automate specific functional areas or parts of functions. Few third-party application software packages have been developed to support a full business process. Very few organizations have modeled existing interfunctional processes or redesigned them, and companies will run into substantial problems in building interfunctional systems without such models.

Interpersonal processes involve tasks within and across small work groups, typically within a function or department. Examples include a commercial loan group approving a loan, or an airline flight crew preparing for takeoff. This type of process is becoming more important as companies shift to self-managing teams as the lowest unit of organization. Information technology is increasingly capable of supporting interpersonal processes; hardware and communications companies have developed new networking-oriented products, and software companies have begun to flesh out the concept of "groupware" (e.g., local area network-based mail, conferencing, and brainstorming tools).[25]

Several companies, including GM's Electronic Data Systems (EDS), are exploring tools to facilitate the effectiveness of meetings and small group interactions. At EDS, the primary focus is on enhancing the interpersonal processes involved in automobile product development. The company's Center for Machine Intelligence has developed a computer-supported meeting room, and is studying its implications for group decision making and cooperative work.[26]

We should point out that IT can make it possible for employees scattered around the world to work as a team. As an example, Ford now creates new car designs using teams that have members in Europe, Central America, and the United States. Because Ford has standardized computer-aided design systems and created common data structures for the design process, engineers can share complex three-dimensional designs across the Atlantic. Similarly, a small team at Digital Equipment used the company's electronic mail and conferencing capabilities to build the core of a new systems integration business. The team was scattered around the United States and Europe and only rarely met in person.

DEFINING PROCESS OBJECTS

Processes can also be categorized by the types of objects manipulated. The two primary object types are physical and informational. In physical object processes, real tangible things are either created or manipulated; manufacturing is the obvious example. Informational object processes create or manipulate information. Processes for making a decision, preparing a marketing plan, or designing a new product are examples.

Many processes involve the combination of physical and informational objects. Indeed, adding information to a physical object as it moves through a process is a common way of adding value. Most logistical activities, for example, combine the movement of physical objects with the manipulation of information concerning their whereabouts. Success in the logistics industry is often dependent on the close integration of physical and informational outcomes; both UPS and Federal Express, for example, track package movement closely.

The potential for using IT to improve physical processes is well known. It allows greater flexibility and variety of outcomes, more precise control of the process itself, reductions in throughput time, and elimination of human labour. These benefits have been pursued for the past three decades. Still, manufacturing process flows are often the result of historical circumstance and should usually be redesigned before further automation is applied. This is particularly true in low volume, job shop manufacturing environments.[27] Redesigners of physical processes should also consider the role of IT in providing information to improve processes; Shoshana Zuboff has described this "informating" effect in detail for the paper industry.[28]

Strangely, the proportion of informational processes already transformed by IT is probably lower than that of physical processes. True, legions of clerks have become unemployed because of computers. But the majority of information processes to which IT has been applied are those involving high volume and low complexity. Now that these processes are well known even if not fully conquered, the emphasis needs to shift to processes that incorporate semistructured and unstructured tasks and are performed by high-skill knowledge workers. Relevant IT capabilities include the storage and retrieval of unstructured and multimedia information, the capturing and routinizing of decision logic, and the application of far-flung and complex data resources. A computer vendor's advertising videotape, for example, illustrates how artificial intelligence and "hypertext," or mixed-media databases, combine to lead a manager through the process of developing a departmental budget. The IT capabilities in the video are available today, but they are rarely applied to such information-intensive yet unstructured processes.

Defining Process Activities

Our examples of business processes have involved two types of activities: operational and managerial. Operational processes involve the day-to-day carrying out of the organization's basic business purpose. Managerial processes help to control, plan, or provide resources for operational processes. Past uses of IT to improve processes, limited as they are, have been largely operational. We will therefore focus almost entirely on managerial processes in this section.[29]

Applying IT to management *tasks* is not a new idea. The potential of decision support systems, executive support systems, and other managerial tools has been discussed for over twenty years. We believe, however, that the benefits have not been realized because of the absence of systematic process thinking. Few companies have rigorously analyzed managerial activities as processes subject to redesign. Even the notion of managerial activities involving defined outcomes (a central aspect of our definition of business processes) is somewhat foreign. How

IT-Driven process redesign at Rank Xerox UK

Rank Xerox UK (RXUK), a national operating company of Xerox Corporation, has undertaken the most comprehensive IT-driven process redesign we have studied. The process was led by David O'Brien, the division's managing director, who arrived at the company in 1985. O'Brien quickly came to two realizations; first, the company needed to focus on marketing "office systems" in addition to its traditional reprographic products; and second, the company's strong functional culture and inefficient business processes would greatly inhibit its growth. He began to see his own organization as a place to test integrated office systems that support integrated business processes; if successful, he could use RXUK as a model for customers.

The company began to redesign its business in 1987. In a series of offsite meetings, the senior management team reappraised its external environment and mission, then identified the key business processes needed if the company was to achieve its mission. The group began to restructure the organization around cross-functional processes, identifying high-level objectives and creating task forces to define information and other resource requirements for each process. It created career systems revolving around facilitation skills and cross-functional management rather than hierarchical authority. O'Brien decided to keep a somewhat functional formal structure, because functional skills would still be needed in a process organization and because the level or organizational change might have been too great with a wholly new structure.

The level of change was still very high. Several senior managers departed because they could not or would not manage in the new environment. Two new cross-functional senior positions, called "facilitating directors," were created, one for organizational and business development, the other for process management, information systems, and quality. O'Brien took great advantage of the honeymoon period accorded to new CEOs, but managing the change still required intense personal attention:

> Of course, this new thinking was in sharp contrast to some of the skills and attitudes of the company. We were introducing a change in management philosophy in a company that, in many ways, was very skillful and effective, but in a different product-market environment. We faced all the issues of attitudinal change and retraining that any such change implies. We were moving to a much more integrated view of the world and had to encourage a major shift in many patterns of the existing culture. This meant a very hard, tough program of selling the new ideas within the organization as well as an extensive and personal effort to get the new messages and thinking to our potential customers.*

---

* DAVID O'BRIEN, QUOTED IN B. DENNING AND B. TAYLOR, "RANK XEROX UK OFFICE SYSTEMS STRATEGY (C): DEVELOPING THE SYSTEMS STRATEGY," (HENLEY ON THAMES, ENGLAND: HENLEY — THE MANAGEMENT COLLEGE CASE STUDY, SEPTEMBER 1988). OTHER RANK XEROX UK INFORMATION COMES FROM PERSONAL INTERVIEWS.

As the key processes were identified and their objectives determined, the company began to think about how information technology (its own and from other providers) could enable and support the processes. The facilitating director of processes and systems, Paul Chapman, decided that the firm needed a new approach to developing information systems around processes. His organization used the information engineering approach discussed earlier and worked with an external consultant to refine and confirm process identification. They uncovered 18 "macro" business processes (e.g., logistics) and 145 "micro" processes (e.g., fleet management). The senior management team reconvened to prioritize the identified processes and decided that seven macro processes had particular importance: customer order life cycle, customer satisfaction, installed equipment management, integrated planning, logistics, financial management, and personnel management. It selected personnel management as the first process to be redesigned because this was viewed as relatively easy to attack and because personnel systems were crucial in tracking the development of new skills. The personnel system has now been successfully redesigned, using automated code generation capabilities, in substantially less time than if normal methods had been used.

RXUK's financial situation began to improve as it redesigned its business processes. The company emerged from a long period of stagnation into a period of 20 percent revenue growth. Jobs not directly involved with customer contact were reduced from 1,100 to 800. Order delivery time was, on average, reduced from thirty-three days to six days. Though many other market factors were changing during this time, O'Brien credits the process redesign for much of the improvement.

Other Xerox divisions heard of RXUK's success with process redesign and began efforts of their own. Xerox's U.S. product development and marketing divisions now have major cross-functional teams performing process redesign. Paul Chapman has been loaned to Xerox corporate headquarters, where he is heading a cross-functional team looking at corporate business processes. Commitment to IT-driven process redesign by Xerox senior corporate management is also growing.

would such managerial processes as deciding on an acquisition or developing the agenda for the quarterly board meeting be improved if they were treated as processes — in other words, measured, brainstormed, and redesigned with IT capabilities?

The generic capabilities of IT for reshaping management processes include improving analytic accuracy, enabling broader management participation across wider geographical boundaries, generating feedback on actions taken (the managerial version of "informating" a process), and streamlining the time and resources a specific process consumes. Texas Instruments and Xerox's corporate headquarters provide excellent examples.

Texas Instruments has developed an expert system to facilitate the capital budgeting process. Managers in a fast-growing and capital-intensive IT division were concerned that the time and experience necessary to prepare capital budget request packages would become an obstacle to the division's growth. The packages were very complex and time consuming, and few employees had the requisite knowledge to complete them accurately. The expert system was developed by two industrial engineers with expertise in both the technology and the budget process.

TI's system has radically improved the capital budget request process. Requests prepared with the system require far less time than the manual approach and conform better to the company's guidelines. One experienced employee reported a reduction in package preparation time from nine hours to forty minutes; of the first fifty packages prepared with the system, only three did not conform to guidelines, compared to an average of ten using a manual approach.[30]

At Xerox Corporation headquarters, IT has been used to improve the review of division strategic plans. Prior to the development of the company's Executive Information System (EIS), the planning process was somewhat haphazard; each division prepared its planning documents in a different format and furnished different types of information to corporate headquarters. Plans often came in too late for the corporate management committee to review them before the quarterly or annual review meeting. The EIS was developed to include standard information formats and a user friendly graphical interface enabling fast comprehension. Divisional plans are now developed on the EIS and delivered instantaneously over Xerox's network to all corporate management committee members. These members can now read and discuss the plans beforehand and can move directly to decisions at the review meetings. The workstations are even used in the meetings themselves, allowing revisions to be made and agreed upon before adjournment. As one manager put it, " . . . [the system] lets us communicate at higher speed and in greater depth."[31]

MANAGEMENT ISSUES IN IT-ENABLED REDESIGN

Companies have found that once a process has been redesigned, several key issues remain. These include the management role in redesigned activity, implications for organization structure, new skill requirements, creating a function to perform IT-enabled BPR, the proper direction for the IT infrastructure, and the need for continuous process improvement. We discuss each below.

MANAGEMENT ROLES

Perhaps the greatest difficulty in IT-driven redesign is getting and keeping management commitment. Because processes cut across various parts of the organization, a process redesign effort driven by a single business function or unit will probably encounter resistance from other parts of the organization. Both high-level and broad support for change are necessary.

To perform the five redesign steps described above, several companies created a cross-functional task force headed by a senior executive. These task forces included representatives from key staff and line groups likely to be affected by the changes, including IT and human resources. It was particularly important that the customer of the process be represented on the team, even when the customer was external. The team composition was ideal if some members had some record of process or operations innovation involving IT.

As the redesign teams selected processes and developed objectives, they needed to work closely with the managers and staff of the affected units. Managing process change is similar to managing other types of change, except that its cross-functional nature increases the number of stakeholders, thereby increasing the complexity of the effort.

It was also important to have strong, visible commitment from senior management. Employees throughout the organization needed to understand that redesign was critical, that differences of opinion would be resolved in favour of the customer of a process, and that IT would play an important role. In many cases, the CEO communicated any structural implications of the redesign effort.

An example of the importance of the CEO's role is found at GUS Home Shopping, the largest home shopping company in Europe. GUS undertook a $90 million project to redesign its logistical processes with IT. Redesign objectives involved both cost and time: to be able to sell a product within five minutes of its arrival on the loading dock, and to be able to deliver a product to the customer's door at an average cost of sixty cents. The company's managing director commented on his role in meeting these objectives:

> To change our business to the degree we have [done] demands integration. How involved should the managing director get in designing computer systems? My view is totally, because he's the one who can integrate across the entire organization.[32]

PROCESS REDESIGN AND ORGANIZATIONAL STRUCTURE

A second key issue is the relationship between process orientation and organizational structure. Certainly someone must be in charge of implementing a process change, and of managing the redesigned process thereafter. But process responsibilities are likely to cut across existing organizational structures. How can process organization and traditional functional organization be reconciled?

One possible solution is to create a new organization structure along process lines, in effect abandoning altogether other structural dimensions, such as function, product, or geography. This approach presents risks, however; as business needs change, new processes will be created that cut across the previous process-based organization. This does not mean that a process-based structure cannot be useful, but only that it will have to be changed frequently.

While no firm we studied has converted wholly to a process-based structure, a few organizations have moved in this direction. For example, Apple Computer recently moved away from a functional structure to what executives describe as an IT-oriented, process-based, customer satisfaction-driven structure called "New Enterprise". The company relishes its lack of formal hierarchy; Apple managers describe their roles as highly diffuse, and team and project based.

A more conservative approach would be to create a matrix of functional and process responsibilities. However, because of the cross-functional nature of most processes, the functional manager who should have responsibility for a given process is not always easy to identify. The company may also wish to avoid traditional functional thinking in assigning process responsibilities. For example, it may be wiser to give responsibility for redesigning supplies acquisition to a manager who uses those supplies (i.e., the customer of the process), rather than to the head of purchasing.

NEW SKILL REQUIREMENTS

For process management to succeed, managers must develop facilitation and influence skills. Traditional sources of authority may be of little use when process changes cut across organizational units. Managers will find themselves trying to change the behaviour of employees who do not work for them. In these cases, they must learn to persuade rather than to instruct, to convince rather than to dictate. Of course, these recommendations are consistent with may other organizational maxims of the past several years; they just happen to be useful in process management as well.[33]

Several organizations that are moving towards IT-driven process management are conducting programs intended to develop facilitation skills. These programs encourage less reliance on hierarchy, more cross-functional communication and cooperation, and more decision making by middle- and lower-level managers. Such a program at American Airlines is being used to build an organizational infrastructure at the same time a new IT infrastructure is being built.

AN ONGOING ORGANIZATION

Organizations that redesign key processes must oversee continuing redesign and organizational "tuning," as well as ensure that information systems support process flows. In most companies, the appropriate analytical skills are most likely to be found in the IT function. However, these individuals will also require a high degree of interpersonal skills to be successful as the "new industrial engineers." The ideal group would represent multiple functional areas, for example, information systems, industrial engineering, quality, process control, finance, and human resources.

There are already some examples of such process change groups. Silicon Graphics has created a specific process consulting group for ongoing process management; it is headed by a director-level manager. At United Parcel Service, process redesign is traditionally concentrated in the industrial engineering function. The UPS group is incorporating IT skills in the IE function at a rapid rate, and creating task forces with IT and IE representation for process redesign projects. Federal Express has gone even further, renaming its IE organization the "Strategic Integrated Systems Group," placing it within the Information Systems function, and giving it responsibility for designing and implementing major IT-driven business changes.

PROCESS REDESIGN AND IT ORGANIZATION

Just as information technology is a powerful force in redesigning business processes, process thinking has important implications for the IT organization and for the technology infrastructure it builds. Though few IT groups have the power and influence to spearhead process redesign, they can play several important roles. First of all, the IT group may need to play a behind-the-scenes advocacy role, convincing senior management of the power offered by information technology and process redesign. Second, as demand builds for process redesign expertise, the IT group can begin to incorporate the IE-oriented skills of process measurement, analysis, and redesign, perhaps merging with the IE function if there is one. It can also develop an approach or methodology for IT-enabled redesign, perhaps using the five steps described above as a starting point.

What must the information systems function do technologically to prepare for process redesign? IT professionals must recognize that they will have to build most systems needed to support (or enable) processes, rather than buy them from software package vendors, because most application packages are designed with particular functions in mind. IT professionals will need to build robust technology platforms on which process-specific applications can be quickly constructed. This implies a standardized architecture with extensive communications capability between computing nodes, and the development of shared databases. However, like the organization strategies for process management described above, these are appropriate technology strategies for most companies, whether or not they are redesigning processes with IT.

CONTINUOUS PROCESS IMPROVEMENT

The concept of process improvement, which developed in the quality movement, requires first that the existing process be stabilized. It then becomes predictable, and its capabilities become accessible to analysis and improvement.[34] Continuous process improvement occurs when the cycle of stabilizing, assessing, and improving a given process becomes institutionalized.

IT-enabled business process redesign must generally be dynamic. Those responsible for a process should constantly investigate whether new information technologies make it possible to carry out a process in new ways. IT is continuing to evolve, and forthcoming technologies will have a substantial impact on the processes of the next decade. The IT infrastructure must be robust enough to support the new applications appropriate to a particular process.

SUMMARY

We believe that the industrial engineers of the future, regardless of their formal title or the organizational unit that employs them, will focus increasingly on IT-enabled redesign of business processes. We have only begun to explore the implications and implementation of this concept, and only a few companies have ventured into the area. Many companies that have used IT to redesign particular business processes have done so without any conscious approach or philosophy. In short, the actual experience base with IT-enabled process redesign is limited.

Yet managing by customer-driven processes that cross organizational boundaries is an intuitively appealing idea that has worked well in the companies that have experimented with it. And few would question that information technology is a powerful tool for reshaping business processes. The individuals and companies that can master redesigning processes around IT will be well equipped to succeed in the new decade — and the new century.

REVIEW AND DISCUSSION QUESTIONS

1. Explain what is meant by business process redesign.

2. Why are business process design and IT 'natural partners'?

3. Discuss the potential to redesign a currently manual business process via IT application within an organization of which you have some experience.

REFERENCES

The authors wish to acknowledge the support of the Center for Information Systems Research at the MIT Sloan School, Harvard Business School's Division of Research, and McKinsey & Company. They are also grateful for the comments of Lynda Applegate, James Cash, Warren McFarlan, John Rockart, Edgar Schein, and Michael S. Scott Morton.

1. L. Gulick, "Notes on the Theory of Organizations," in L. Gulick and L. Urwick, eds., *Papers on the Science of Administration* (New York: Institute of Public Administration, 1937), p. 9.

2. S. Sakamoto, "Process Design Concept: A New Approach to IE," *Industrial Engineering,* March 1989, p. 31.

3. "Office Automation: Making it Pay Off," *Business Week,* 12 October 1987, pp. 134-146. For an alternative perspective, see

R. E. Kraut, ed., *Technology and the Transformation of White-Collar Work* (Hillsdale, New Jersey: Lawrence Erlbaum Associates, 1987).

4. G. W. Loveman, "An Assessment of the Productivity Impact of Information Technologies" (Cambridge, Massachusetts: MIT Sloan School of Management, Management in the 1990s, Working Paper 90s: 88-054, July 1988). Loveman studied microeconomic data from manufacturing firms to estimate econometrically the productivity impact of IT in the late 1970s and early 1980s. In finding no significant positive productivity impact from IT, he argues that his findings in manufacturing raise serious questions about impacts in nonmanufacturing firms as well.

Baily and Chakrabarti (1988) studied white-collar productivity and IT as one part of a broader inquiry into poor productivity growth. They found no evidence of significant productivity gain. See M. N. Baily and A. Chakrabarti, *Innovation and the Productivity Crisis* (Washington, D.C.: Brookings Institution, 1988).

5. Loveman (1988);

Baily and Chakrabarti (1988).

See also L. C. Thurow "Toward a High-Wage, High Productivity Service Sector" (Washington, D.C.: Economic Policy Institute, 1989).

6. Robert Horton, who became chairman and chief executive of British Petroleum in March 1990, argues that his major concern in setting BP's course in the next decade is "managing surprise." Horton's belief is that the external business environment is so unpredicatable that surprise, rather than managed change, is inevitable. See R. Horton, "Future Challenges to Management," *MIT Management,* Winter 1989, pp. 3-6.

7. T. Malone, "What is Coordination Theory?" (Cambridge, Massachusetts: MIT Sloan School of Management, Centre for Coordination Science, Working Paper No. 2051-88 February 1988);

K. Crowston and T. Malone, "Information Technology and Work Organization" (Cambridge, Massachusetts: MIT Sloan School of Management, Center for Information Systems Research, Working Paper No. 165, December 1987).

8. G. A. Pall, *Quality Process Management* (Englewood Cliffs, New Jersey: Prentice-Hall, 1987). Our definition also complements that of Schein, who focuses on human processes in organizations — e.g., building and maintaining groups, group problem solving and decision making, leading and influencing, etc.

See E. H. Schein, *Process Consultation: Its Role in Organization Development,* Vol. 1, 2nd ed.. (Reading, Massachusetts: Addison-Wesley, 1988).

9. E. J. Kane, "IBM's Total Quality Improvement System" (Purchase, New York: IBM Corporation, unpublished manuscript), p.5.

10. See, for example, M. F. Morris and G. W. Vining, "The EI's Future Role in Improving Knowledge Worker Productivity," *Industrial Engineering,* July 1987, p. 28.

11. "Reference Note on Work Simplification" (Boston: Harvard Business School, HBS Case Services #9-609-0601961, 1961).

12. The relationship between business vision and IT has been explored by several researchers under the auspices of the MIT Sloan School's five-year "Management in the 1990s" research program. An overview volume is scheduled for publication by Oxford University Press in August 1990.

13. See, for example, G. Stalk, Jr., "Time — The Next Source of Strategic Advantage," *Harvard Business Review,* July-August 1988, pp. 41-51.

14. S. Zuboff, *In the Age of the Smart Machine* (New York: Basic Books, 1988).

15. E. H. Schein, "Innovative Cultures and Organizations" (Cambridge, Massachusetts: MIT Sloan School of Management, Management in the 1990s, Working Paper 90s:88-064, November 1988).

16. Information engineering and other redesign approaches based on data modeling are necessarily limited in scope. More than data is exchanged in many process relationships. Note too that many companies have used information engineering methods *without* a specific process orientation.

17. Examples of IT planning approaches where high-impact objectives and/or goals are defined include critical success factors (CSFs) and business systems planning (BSP). See J. F. Rockart, "Chief Executives Define Their Own Data Needs," *Harvard Business Review,* March-April 1979, pp. 81-93; and IBM, *Information Systems Planning Guide,* 3rd ed. (Business Systems Planning Report No. GE20–05527–2, July 1981).

18. D. Goodhue, J. Quillard, and J. Rockart, "Managing the Data Resource: A Contingency Perspective" (Cambridge, Massachusetts: MIT Sloan School of Management, Center for Information Systems Research, Working Paper No. 150, January 1987).

19. J. F. Rockart, "The Line Takes the Leadership — IS Management in a Wired Society," *Sloan Management Review,* Summer 1988, pp. 57-64.

20. J. C. Henderson and N. Venkatraman, "Strategic Alignment: A Process Model for Integrating Information Technology and Business Strategies" (Cambridge, Massachusetts: MIT Sloan School of Management, Center for Information Systems Research, Working Paper No. 196, October 1989).

21. Dorothy Leonard-Barton introduced the concept of organizational prototyping with regard to the implementation of new information technologies. See D. Leonard-Barton, "The Case for Integrative Innovation: An Expert System at Digital," *Sloan Management Review,* Fall 1987, pp. 7-19.

22. R. Johnston and P. R. Lawrence, "Beyond Vertical Integration — The Rise of the Value-Adding Partnership," *Harvard Business Review,* July-August 1988, pp. 94-101. See also N. Venkatraman, "IT-Induced Business Reconfiguration: The New Strategic Management Challenge" (Cambridge, Massachusetts: Paper presented at the annual conference of the MIT Center for Information Systems Research, June 1989).

23. T. J. Main and J. E. Short, "Managing the Merger: Building Partnership through IT Planning at the New Baxter," *Management Information Systems Quarterly,* December 1989, pp. 469-486.

24. C. R. Hall, M. E. Friesen, and J. E. Short, "The Turnaround at US Sprint: The Role of Improved Partnership between Business and Information Management," in progress.

25. R. R. Johansen, *Groupware: Computer Support for Business Teams* (New York: The Free Press, 1988). Also see C. V. Bullen and R. R. Johansen, "Groupware: A Key to Managing Business

Teams?" (Cambridge, Massachusetts: MIT Sloan School of Management, Center for Information Systems Research, Working Paper No. 169, May 1988).

26. See L. M. Applegate, "The Center for Machine Intelligence: Computer Support for Cooperative Work" (Boston: Harvard Business School Case Study No. 189-135, 1988, rev. 1989).

27. J. E. Ashton and F. X. Cook, "Time to Reform Job Shop Manufacturing," *Harvard Business Review,* March-April 1989, pp. 106-111.

28. See cases on "Tiger Creek," "Piney Wood," and "Cedar Bluff" in S. Zuboff (1988); other industries discussed by Zuboff primarily involve information processes.

29. One might consider managerial processes synonymous with informational processes. Certainly the vast majority of managerial processes, such as budgeting, planning, and human resource development, involve informational objects. Yet it is important to remember that informational processes can be either operational or managerial, so we believe that this separate dimension of process types is warranted.

30. A case study describes the process and the creation of the expert system. See "Texas Instruments Capital Investment Expert System" (Boston: Harvard Business School Case Study No. 188-050, 1988).

31. Some aspects of this process improvement are described in L. M. Applegate and C. S. Osborne, "Xerox Corporation: Executive Support Systems" (Boston: Harvard Business School Case Study No. 189-134, 1988, rev. 1989).

32. R. I I. C. Pugh, address to McKinsey & Co. information technology practice leaders, Munich, Germany, June 1989.

33. See, for example, A. R. Cohen and D. L. Bradford, "Influence without Authority: The Use of Alliances, Reciprocity, and Exchange to Accomplish Work," *Organizational Dynamics,* Winter 1989, pp. 4-17.

34. See G. A. Pall (1987).

12 MANAGING BY WIRE

STEPHAN H. HAECKEL *
RICHARD L. NOLAN **

Just as airline pilots now 'fly by wire' — using complex IT systems to control their aircraft — so systems enabling 'management by wire' are starting to be developed. Within this paper, Stephen Haeckel and Richard Nolan discuss how organizations in a variety of circumstances have developed IT systems to enable them to better cope with modern market demands, and hence boost their 'corporate IQ'.

Flexibility and responsiveness now rule the marketplace. Rather than follow the make-and-sell strategy of industrial-age giants, today's successful companies focus on sensing and responding to rapidly changing customer needs. Information technology has driven much of this dramatic shift by vastly reducing the constraints imposed by time and space in acquiring, interpreting, and acting on information.

Responding to the competitive dynamic created by information technology, many large companies have drastically downsized, divested, and outsourced to reduce the costs and complexity of their operations. Yet simply reducing the size of a corporation is not the solution. As CEO Jack Welch has said, GE's Goal is not to become smaller but to "get that small-company soul and small-company speed inside our big-company body." We believe that corporate size is worth saving. Market power, not bureaucratic clumsiness, can again become the dominant quality of a large corporation. But in order to survive in a sense-and-respond world, big companies must consider a strategy that we call managing by wire.

In aviation, *flying by wire* is a response to the changes introduced by jet-engine technology in the 1950s. It means using computer systems to augment a pilot's ability to assimilate and react to rapidly changing environmental information. Today heads-up displays (computer-generated pictures projected onto the pilot's

* DIRECTOR OF STRATEGIC STUDIES, IBM ADVANCED RESEARCH INSTITUTE.
** HARVARD BUSINESS SCHOOL, AND EX-CHAIRMAN OF NOLAN, NORTON AND COMPANY.
REPRINTED BY PERMISSION OF HARVARD BUSINESS REVIEW, SEPTEMBER–OCTOBER 1993, PP.122–132.

helmet visor) present selected abstractions of a few crucial environmental factors, like oncoming aircraft and targets. Instrumentation and communication technologies aid in evaluating alternative responses. And when the pilot makes a decision, say to take evasive action by banking sharply to the left, it's the computer system that intercepts the pilot's command and translates it into the thousands of detailed orders that orchestrate the plane's behavior in real time.

When pilots fly by wire, they're flying informational representations of airplanes. In a similar way, managing by wire is the capacity to run a business by managing its informational representation. Manage-by-wire capability augments, instead of automating, a manager's function. Fly-by-wire technology — and by extension managing by wire — integrate pilot and plane into a single coherent system. The role and accountabilities of the pilot become an essential part of the design. Autopilot, or complete automation, is used only in calm, stable flying conditions. The system design allows for considerable flexibility in pilot behavior, including the ability to override the technology if, for instance, a sudden storm arises.

Like a plane at mach speeds, a company must be able to respond to threats in real time. In today's turbulent business environment, strategies have to be implemented in tactical timeframes. In response to his challenge, top-level managers need to view information technology in a new light. Rather than investing in isolated IT systems — such as e-mail, reservation systems, or inventory control systems — a company must invest in the IT capabilities that it will need to manage by wire.

The ideal manage-by-wire implementation uses an enterprise model to represent the operations of an entire business. Based on this model, expert systems, databases, software objects, and other technical components are integrated to do the equivalent of flying by wire. The executive crew then pilots the organization, using controls in the information cockpit of the business. Managers respond to the readouts appearing on the console, modifying the business plan based on changes in external conditions, monitoring the performance of delegated responsibilities, and sending directions to subsidiary units such as manufacturing and sales.

Of course, if the enterprise model represents the wrong reality — or is incomplete, out of date, or operating on bad data — the outcome could be catastrophic, like putting engines in reverse at 30,000 feet. Creating a robust model of a large business organization is an extremely challenging undertaking. But companies like Mrs. Fields Cookies, Brooklyn Union Gas, and a financial services organization that we will call Global Insurance have already demonstrated the feasibility of representing large portions of businesses in software. These companies manage by wire to varying degrees, from "hardwiring" automated processes at Mrs. Fields Cookies to a complete enterprise model that codifies business strategy at Global Insurance.

Many companies have spent decades automating pieces of their businesses, scattering networks and incompatible computer platforms throughout their organizations. But the empowered, decentralized teams of the information economy need a unified view of what's happening within an organization. Coherent behaviour requires more than blockbuster applications and network connections; it must be governed by an enterprise model that codifies the corporation's intent and "how we do things around here." More important, a coherent mode should include "how we change how we do things around here." Adding the institutional ability to adapt in a dynamic environment has become a survival imperative for most companies. And this ability will ultimately differentiate a manage-by-wire strategy from the static make-and-sell strategies of the past.

HARDWIRING A BUSINESS

Over the last three decades, companies have used information technologies in increasingly sophisticated ways to run parts of a business. From the mainframe complexes of the 1960s to the client/server platforms of today, computers already help executives manage by automating business processes, from payroll to cash-dispensing. In fact, a company like Mrs. Fields can build an extensive representation of its business by automating procedures, that is, by codifying them in software.

In small companies, the model of "how we do things around here" often resides in the minds of a few people. Under these conditions, if senior executives are willing to sacrifice some flexibility and delegate the technical design to IT professionals, it's possible to represent enough of the business in software to manage by wire. For example, Mrs. Fields Cookies has captured a significant amount of its well-defined business in software. Its hardwired processes resemble the autopilot capability of a fly-by-wire system.

In 1978, when Debbi Fields opened her second cookie store in San Francisco (45 miles away from her first store in Palo Alto), she confronted the logistical problems of maintaining hands-on-management at remote locations. She and her husband Randy, a skilled computer professional, had ambitious plans that would prevent Debbi from personally overseeing each store. They needed a strategy that would let them know what was going on in hundreds of dispersed locations and at the same time ensure that local managers responded to daily challenges in the same way Debbi Fields would. In this case, Randy Fields had the technical expertise to implement in software the way Debbi Fields worked. He created the software at a reasonable cost and much more quickly than most traditional large-company IT groups could have.

Now with more than 800 stores, including franchises around the world, the central management of Mrs. Fields uses software to issue instructions and advice to store managers. Each morning, local managers project sales for the day and enter information into a personal computer: for example, day of the week, season and local weather conditions. The software analyzes this data and responds with hourly instructions on what to do to meet the day's objectives: how many batches of different cookies to mix and bake; how to adjust the mixtures as the actual pattern of customer buying unfolds; when to offer free samples; how to schedule workers; and when to reorder chocolate chips.

There are a few fundamental principles that define Mrs. Field's business concept: a thorough articulation of "how we do things around here;" a conviction that quality must be centrally controlled; and a dedication to knowledge sharing between central management and local store managers. As a matter of policy, the company integrates all of its information in one database and has one set of guidelines about how things are done the Mrs. Fields way. Because this vision is so clearly articulated, and because the company's business niche is relatively well-defined and stable, top management has, in effect, created an informational representation of Debbi Fields in each store.

Yet a manage-by-wire system that hardwires much of a business can turn out to be too rigid. For example, because its software was designed to describe the behaviour of US store managers, Mrs. Fields faced a number of challenges when it expanded into Europe and Asia, where different labor laws, languages, and supplier contracts had to be taken into account. In addition to the adjustments required to accommodate a wider range of local environments, falling profit margins forced the company to become more flexible in the way it applied information technology to running its daily business at remote locations.

Responding to these new conditions, Mrs. Fields Software (a separate business unit) developed a second generation of software, called the Retail Operations Intelligence system. ROI contained modules for inventory control, scheduling daily activities, interviewing and hiring, repair and maintenance, financial reporting, lease management, and e-mail. Senior management believes that ROI can be adapted to a variety of retail and service organizations. In fact, Mrs. Fields sold ROI to Burger King in 1992.

But at Mrs. Fields, top management relies on its IT division to translate business strategy into software. If senior executives want to change how the business runs, IT professionals must change the procedural software code. Because the cookie business doesn't change significantly from day to day — and employee turnover in a retail outlet like Mrs. Fields is high — it makes sense to run basic store operations as close to autopilot as possible. But most larger companies compete in more dynamic environments than Mrs. Fields, and, therefore, a corporate business model must do more than connect hardwired processes. It must also specify the roles and accountabilities of the people involved, incorporate the unplanned activity that can take up to 80% of a working day, and build in sufficient latitude for individual decision-making.

INSTITUTIONALIZING FLEXIBILITY

Large organizations have become too complex for any individual, even the most brilliant executive, to keep complete models of the business in mind. Whether individually or collectively, managers of companies with hundreds of millions in revenue and tens of thousands of employees can't track everything that happens, much less coordinate millions of elements into a timely, coherent response. In fact, they never could, which is why functional hierarchies were originally created.

The old chain of command was designed for a relatively stable — and now increasingly rare — make-and-sell business. But many fast-growing sense-and-respond companies never adopted functional hierarchies in the first place. Instead, in the process of expanding, they have used IT-enabled networks as the tendons that hold the skeleton and muscles of the company together. Large companies, attempting to compete with agile niche players, are heading in the opposite direction of hardwiring operations. Rather than explicitly specifying "do it this way," many executives are empowering employees to "do it the way you know how." However, without coordination, accountability, and shared objectives, this approach can often lead to paralysis rather than coherent company-wide behavior.

The need for flexibility drove the $1 billion utility, Brooklyn Union Gas of New York to a radically different strategy. By the early 1980s, Brooklyn Union's 1971 Customer-Related Information System (CRIS) had become obsolete. Among other things, the Public Service Commission had begun requiring utilities to treat certain customers — for example, the elderly and disabled — in different ways. Top-level executives were also convinced that micromarketing increasingly customized service offerings was essential to Brooklyn Union's competitive survival. But the practices and policies of 1971 had become petrified in software procedures that were finally rendered obsolete by the dynamic environment that the company faced in the 1980s.

A $2 million initial attempt to upgrade CRIS failed. Finally, after spending more than three years on feasibility studies, design, and prototype systems, senior management agreed to let the IT department completely redo CRIS. The project began in the spring of 1987 and was completed by January 1990 at a cost of $48 million. In this case, the manage-by-wire implementation resulted not from a new business design by management but from the systems being redesigned by a talented group of IT professionals.

The IT department chose to implement the new system using object-oriented programming. Objects are reusable software building blocks: sets of instructions that programmers can reassemble for a variety of different operations. CRIS now contains 650 such objects that create, in various combinations, 10,000 appropriate actions in 800 distinct business situations. These actions cover everything from meter reading and cash processing to collection, billing, credit, and field service orders. Brooklyn Union has now codified a substantial part of its customer-related business behavior in these software combinations. And because of the IT department's flexible, building-block approach to software, the system is much easier to modify than a hardwired one.

But at Brooklyn Union, as at Mrs. Fields, the IT department functions as the intermediary between customer-related management policy and its execution. The IT shop translates into software an understanding of management's business changes. It does this by defining the conditions that dictate legitimate combinations of software objects. These conditions may relate to business policy, legal requirements, or common-sense logic: for example, "You can't cut off service to an elderly customer before x months," or "You can't bill a customer if you haven't installed a meter."

Brooklyn Union exemplifies how computers can be used to create and manage building blocks of business activity that can then be combined and recombined into a variety of responses. However, senior executives are still disconnected from direct influence over the software that determines how their company handles customers. In fact, it is middle managers, rather than senior executives, who are managing by wire. And in the sense that the IT department acts as intermediary, Brooklyn Union has not moved beyond the practices of many large companies.

Not that top management at Brooklyn Union feels shortchanged. Its IT experts had the vision and ability to build in exceptional flexibility by using object-oriented software. As a result, new capabilities can now be created by extensively reusing existing software objects and adding only those required for specific additional functions. A proposal for a new engineering system, for instance, estimated that up to 30% of the software objects that were required to implement the system already existed in CRIS. More important, CRIS has delivered on top management's mandate against obsolescence, allowing Brooklyn Union to respond to market change and new opportunities in a timely way and at a reasonable cost.

CREATING AN ENTERPRISE MODEL OF A BUSINESS

Mrs. Fields's and Brooklyn Union's IT strategies demonstrate that manage-by-wire implementations vary from business to business, depending on size and complexity. A company's complexity is a function of how many information sources it needs, how many business elements it must coordinate, and the number and type of relationships that exist among those elements. We think of a company's corporate IQ as its institutional ability to deal with complexity, that is, its ability to capture, share, and extract meaning from marketplace signals. Corporate IQ directly translates into three IT infrastructure imperatives for connecting, sharing, and structuring information (see Chart 1 "How 'Smart' Is a Company in a Complex World?").

In most large companies, a low IQ results from change occurring so rapidly that keeping computer applications up to date is neither feasible nor affordable. Low IQs are particularly prevalent when processes have been automated over decades without any framework to integrate disparate applications and databases. At Mrs. Fields, where there are few information sources and clear and unchanging employee roles, ROI creates high corporate IQ in an environment of comparatively low complexity.

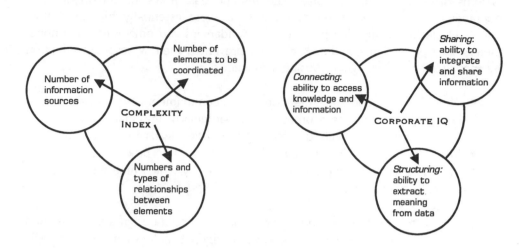

Chart 1 How smart is a company in a complex world?

Brooklyn Union's CRIS is less complete because it captures a smaller percentage of the total business. But this larger company operates in a much more complex industry. Brooklyn Union has a high capacity for sharing information and a comprehensive knowledge base in one important area: customers. Compared with many other large companies — with their disconnected information systems, competing computer platforms, and ill-defined business processes — Brooklyn Union Gas looks like a corporate genius.

But neither Mrs. Fields nor Brooklyn Union has a coherent model that fully maps key processes, how information is interpreted, and who is accountable for what. It is just such a model that can replace the IT department as the intermediary between management policy and execution. In fact, large companies need a coherent enterprise model to raise their corporate IQ.

An enterprise model is a high-level map of a business that guides the writing of computer code and the execution of nonautomated activities. Once procedures, data flows, and employee accountabilities are represented in computers by specific bit patterns and machine states, the map becomes the terrain; in other words, it becomes "real" in cyberspace, that computer-generated realm in which the informational representation of a cookie store or a utility's customer-related activities can be manipulated and modified. Companies can use an enterprise model to leverage a computer's memory and speed; to track and interrelate millions of events and relationships simultaneously; to allow selective sharing of information; and finally, to initiate physical processes.

Of course, enterprise modeling tools have been available from software consultants and vendors for more than 25 years. Used primarily by information systems professionals to lay out procedures and data flows for certain business operations, the first generation of these tools were essentially high-level flow charts. Useful in highlighting procedural redundancies and omissions, they none-theless have several major drawbacks that prevented their widespread adoption by management for designing business functions:

- They fail to incorporate the notions of commitment and human ac-countability in business processes, a particularly important omission because procedure without accountability often leads to bureaucracy.
- They don't deal with unstructured work and ad hoc processes.
- They take years to map into computer code, by which time the model is badly out of date.

Clearly, corporate managers, not IT professionals should design a business. And business design extends beyond procedural design; it includes making strategic decisions about what market signals should be sensed, what data or analytical models should be used to interpret those signals, and how an appropriate response should be executed. To faithfully represent management's design, a robust enter-prise model must consistently characterize any process at any scale, exhaustively account for the possible outcomes of every process, and unambiguously specify the roles and accountabilities of the employees involved in carrying them out.

A new generation of enterprise modeling tools that overcomes the drawbacks of traditional modeling tools is now emerging. Admittedly, creating a comprehen-sive information map is no simple task, but the benefits can be substantial, even for small business units. In a test at a large manufacturing company, one of these new enterprise modeling tools was used to map an engineering change process for electronic circuitry. Senior executives considered this process among the best in the organization. However, the new modeling tool not only revealed opportu-nities for procedural improvements, such as removing manufacturing bottlenecks, it also uncovered this startling fact: during the entire operation, not one person in the entire organization made a single commitment on volumes, cost, or delivery dates — only forecasts, estimates, and targets. If accountability isn't specified, business processes lack discipline and predictability, making them difficult to manage. A model that defines both procedures and accountability for outcomes can help managers of large companies do the job of managing.

The new enterprise modeling tools, for example, could make a substantial difference at Brooklyn Union Gas. CRIS uses data models to interpret signals from meter readings, field reports, and cash receipts. But the utility company has yet to develop an enterprise model that allows top managers to define and modify the policies that determine permissible combinations of its reusable software objects. An enterprise model would raise Brooklyn Union's corporate IQ by enhancing the structure of its customer information system. In effect, top-level managers would move into the information cockpit and gain the ability to modify directly how CRIS drives customer-related activities.

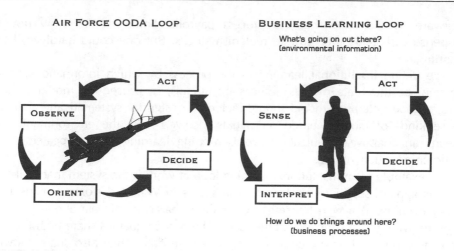

Chart 2 Learning loops

DESIGNING THE INTELLIGENT CORPORATION

To be useful in today's dynamic business environment, an enterprise model must do more than represent a static version of "how we do things around here;" it must also include the capacity to adapt systematically and rapidly. Like the process of piloting a jet fighter, a true manage-by-wire system relies both on an accurate information model and on the organization's ability to learn.

The United States Air Force assesses a pilot's ability to learn with the OODA Loop, a model for the mental processes of a fighter pilot. OODA stands for:

- *Observation* : sensing environmental signals;
- *Orientation* : interpreting those signals;
- *Decision* : selecting from a repertoire of available responses;
- *Action* : executing the response selected.

Fighter pilots with faster OODA Loops tend to win dogfights, while those with slower ones get more parachute practice. Note that the loop is iterative: a continuous cycle in which an action leads to the observation of the results of that action that in turn requires a new orientation, decision, and action. This iterative sequence constitutes a *learning loop* . It contains the four functions essential to any adaptive organism: sensing, interpreting, deciding, and acting. By analogy, an enterprise model for a business that incorporates learning is one that systematically creates and links learning loops (see Chart 2 "Learning Loops").

Recent work on organizational learning focuses on the way that people in a company learn. But what about institutional learning? How much do companies know when the people go home at night? Many companies, with the aid of software, would know how to process payrolls. Some would know how to dispense cash and other how to replenish stocks. But one could hardly call that learning.

We define institutional learning as the process by which information models change, be they data models, forecasting models, or procedural models. Therefore, a good enterprise model should include a design for systematically changing these kinds of models, based on signals received from the environment. That means an adaptive organization avoids running learning loops repeatedly over static information models.

An example of an institutional learning loop at work is the system that Wal-Mart and its apparel suppliers use to replenish stocks in Wal-Mart stores. For instance, every evening, Wal-Mart transmits five million characters of data about the day's sales to Wrangler, a supplier of blue jeans. The two companies share both the data and the model that interprets the meaning of the data. They also share software applications that act on that interpretation to send specific quantities of specific sizes and colours of jeans to specific stores from specific warehouses. The result is a learning loop that lowers logistics and inventory costs and leads to fewer stock outs. And every time the data model is changed to reflect a new fashion season or pricing pattern, both Wal-Mart and Wrangler learn and adapt.

Using technology to integrate how an organization interprets "what's going on out there" with a codification of "how we do things around here" creates an intelligent corporation. The company we call Global Insurance (the real company is disguised) is one of the best examples of managing by wire at this level of sophistication.

A large financial services organization, Global was driven to a fundamental reconceptulization of how it does business because of competition from niche players in the 1980s. The $78 billion company was facing extinction. New polices took two years from conception to consumer, and operational costs were 15% higher than those of smaller competitors, who were luring customers away with innovative offerings. Furthermore, the insurance industry was changing so rapidly that senior executives had little confidence that any specific strategy would keep the company afloat for more than a year or two.

In the late 1980s, rather then investing in a specific business strategy, top-level managers decided to spend $110 million on an IT infrastructure that would allow them to implement any strategy quickly. Senior executives started the project with the development of an enterprise model for the company's two largest business lines: casualty and life insurance. The model linked product development, underwriting, sales, and other functions in a coherent informational representation of "how we do things around here." Information specialists created the model based on senior managers' specifications of the information they wanted to track (observations); the data models needed to interpret the information (orientation); the analytic and decision support provided for underwriters, actuaries, and managers in the field (decision); and, finally how these decisions should be executed via their on-line transaction systems (action).

Using combinations of more than 1,000 software objects, the company created the transactions, activities, and data that would, when properly linked, define any present or future offering in its life or casualty-insurance business lines. "Enrol client," "send premium notice," and "establish risk limit" are examples of these software building blocks.

In addition, data models were developed to interpret the market research, transaction history, demographic, and economic information that Global collected from the field, external databases, and internal operations. Data models are explicit renderings of the way an application program, or a collection of these programs, views the world. When these models are used to create databases, they institutionalize specific ways of interpreting raw data. Elaborate data models are worth fortunes to banks, airlines, food manufacturers, and large retailers like Wal-Mart, because they help these companies reorient themselves continually.

At Global, a decision-support system used the patterns its data models revealed to trigger exception reports or approval requests that then appeared on managers' terminals. For instance, a manager whose product was losing ground to a new competitive offering would have the option of modifying the existing policy or creating an entirely new one. This process was codified by expert systems that contain legal, logical, and business constraints: for example, "we will not underwrite an aggregate risk for a single client that is more than x times the client's net worth."

Through this manage-by-wire capability, decision-to-action times have been reduced by 400% to 700%, enabling Global to meet the competition of small niche players. And certain types of decisions can now be carried out in real time. One example: agents, who have their own laptop computers with easy access to Global's electronic network, can customize a policy in a client's living room. They can tailor policies based on a client's specific situation, such as annual income, ages of dependents, or lifestyle preferences.

There was, of course, substantial technological risk associated with Global's project. Still riskier was counting on the ability of managers to specify adequately the hundreds of procedures and dozens of management policies necessary to ensure that Global's responses were consistent with its business goals. The CEO also worried that his information systems team, lacking sufficient business experience, might misinterpret these specifications when they translated business rules into the language of data models and expert systems. It was only through extensive prototyping that senior executives acquired the confidence to transfer processes gradually to the manage-by-wire system.

Along the way, Global has experienced setbacks. Vendor technology was late and slow. Some managers, who implicitly relied on bureaucratic procedures to buffer them from direct accountability for policy changes, resisted the extensive retraining that was designed to put them in the pilot's seat. In fact, many managers didn't make the shift successfully. Some key executives retired or left the company, taking with them crucial knowledge that the rest of the institution hadn't learned because it had never been codified.

But after more than a year's delay and a budgetary overrun, Global has implemented almost all it set out to do technologically. Because its enterprise model wasn't developed with the new generation of modeling tools, changes to the model must still be made by the IT shop. Still, the senior executives who run the life and casualty businesses are managing by wire a large portion of their operations. With a few additional changes, managers will be able to modify underwriting policy themselves through the IT system and have these changes reflected immediately in the policies written by agents.

SETTING GUIDELINES FOR MANAGING BY WIRE

Given the right enterprise model and a technology-enabled capacity to learn, a large company's size can again become a decisive competitive advantage. But to many managers, Global Insurance's successful manage-by-wire strategy will seem unattainable. For one thing, the technical expertise needed to implement such an integrated system may not exist within the company. The ability to change reality by modifying an informational representation of it is possible only with an underlying technological infrastructure that has a high corporate IQ. Indeed, managing by wire requires the long-term commitment of both senior executives and a world-class IT group.

Flying a modern jet airplane is a sophisticated operation. The current generation of fly-by-wire systems requires more than 20 million lines of computer code. Yet if an aviation information model can successfully capture this level of complexity, an enterprise model can do the same for the managers of rapidly changing business units. In fact, adopting a manage-by-wire strategy is nothing less than a change in the nature of strategy itself, from a *plan* to produce specific offerings for specific markets to a *structure* for sensing and responding to change faster than the competition.

Faced with an unpredictable business environment, top managers at Global Insurance were forced to fuse their business and IT strategies. It is imperative that today's senior executives make IT policy an integral part of corporate strategy and intent. Technological knowledge must join the financial and operational know-how of a policy-making manager; otherwise, crucial business decisions will implicitly be delegated to the IT department.

Managers can follow a few guidelines to help them implement a manage-by-wire-system:

Top managers must assess a company's corporate IQ in terms of connecting, sharing, and structuring information. There are three critical attributes of a company's IT infrastructure that determine its corporate IQ. Connecting means the degree to which the IT platform links information sources, media, locations, and users. Since the 1970s, computer networks have sprung up in multiple places for multiple purposes. As a result, many companies today are crisscrossed by dozens of independent networks that are incompatible technically and thus actually inhibit, rather than promote, information sharing. Mere connectivity doesn't necessarily increase productivity or institutional learning. Management must not only determine what the signals should be but also ensure that these signals are understood and shared by the right people and teams.

Sharing makes possible coordinated effort and, therefore, the benefits associated with teamwork, integration, and extended scope. Getting everyone on the same page in a large business requires an institutional capability to share data, interpretations of that data, and specifications of core processes. The added value that this integration can yield underlines a subtle but important distinction: the actual implementation of a breakthrough application, such as an automated airline reservation system like American Airlines' SABRE, may ultimately be less important than how that application is implemented. A stand-alone application is less likely to deliver sustainable competitive advantage than one implemented on an integrated technology platform designed for extensive information sharing. Anyone who receives multiple premium notices on the same day from the same insurance company for different policies is on the receiving end of an unintegrated IT platform.

Structuring holds the most potential for the strategic exploitation of information in the 1990s and beyond. Structure is created by information about information, for instance, how data is classified, organized, related, and used. Tables of contents, indices, and "see also" references are familiar hard-copy examples. The data models of Global Insurance and Wal-Mart structure information by filtering the data that bombards these companies every day.

When information from previously unrelated sources is structured in a meaningful way, human beings become capable of thinking thoughts that were previously unthinkable. Computers that use their speed and memory to reveal patterns in raw data augment the extraordinary capacity of humans to recognize and assign meaning to patterns. For example, through spectral analysis and mathematical equations that model what scientists call the red shift, a computer can process light signals from a remote galaxy to calculate the distance and size of its parts. The results can be displayed in a three-dimensional picture and then rotated. Presentation in this manner allows scientists to "see" a distant galaxy from the back or side and even to discover, as they did recently, a huge void passing through it.

An enterprise model should be expressed in business language, not IT terminology. Management should select and use one business design language and insist on its use throughout the organization. In many companies, a variety of first and second-generation enterprise modeling tools have already been used to capture key processes in different functions or operating units. But in order to create a unified understanding of "how we do things around here" (and, if it makes strategic sense, to facilitate future integration of presently autonomous organizational units), a common business language is required.

Senior executives must determine the highest level at which coherent institutional behaviour adds value. Managers must decide which business units, if well coordinated, could together create more value than the sum of their individual parts. In many respects, this is the strategic task facing managers in a sense-and-respond world. There's no one answer to this crucial issue. Many different approaches have been tried, even in an information-intensive industry like publishing. McGraw-Hill's strategy, for example, it to treat their information systems and certain editorial content as assets to be shared among multiple units. Dun and Bradstreet, on the other hand, views its information and technology as assets to be separated into individual units. In other words, McGraw-Hill shares assets at the enterprise level and Dun and Bradstreet at the business-line level.

Once a company embarks on a manage-by-wire strategy, senior executives must carefully plan the pace of its implementation. Just as information technology has fueled a new competitive dynamic for businesses, the advent of jet-engine technology in the 1950s profoundly affected aviation. By increasing the speed of fighter planes, the jet engine made it impossible for pilots to fly planes manually. But flying by wire didn't happen overnight. In the mid-1950s, no pilot would have felt safe with a sudden and comprehensive introduction of software between the cockpit controls and the physical airplane, even if the technology had existed at the time. In fact, only the latest generation of commercial aircraft truly fly by wire.

Similarly, few executives will feel confident enough to commit their company to managing by wire in one massive effort. How fast and how far they're willing to go will depend on how effectively the software currently mediates management decisions; how much confidence managers have in their IT staff; and how much money and time will it ultimately take to implement the process.

When a target level for coherent institutional behaviour has been defined, common information and technology assets can be leveraged to create economies of scope. But realistically, most companies will model smaller business domains first, such as Brooklyn Union's customer information system. They will then link these domains to cover larger parts of the business, as Global did.

No corporation has implemented a fully integrated manage-by-wire system yet. But growing numbers of companies like Brooklyn Union Gas and Global Insurance are showing that large and complicated business operations can be captured in an information technology structure and used to govern behavior. These companies have already significantly improved their response times and substantially reduced the costs of developing new products and services.

The imminent arrival of a new generation of enterprise modeling tools makes a manage-by-wire strategy plausible. But it will be management's skill in codifying a competitive information model that will determine its success.

AUTHORS' NOTE

The description of CRIS and its management implications has benefited from discussions with Joe Pinnola and Tom Morgan of Brooklyn Union Gas and Ben Konsynski of Emory University, who has written a Harvard Business School case study of Brooklyn Union, "Brooklyn Union Gas: OOPS on Big Iron." In addition, we have based our discussion of new enterprise modeling tools on Alan Scherr's work at IBM, which is described in his article "A New Approach to Business Processes" (*IBM Systems Journal*, February 1993).

REVIEW AND DISCUSSION QUESTIONS

1. Explain what is meant by the term 'management by wire'.

2. What benefits did Mrs. Fields Cookies derive from its ROI system?

3. Explain the concept of an IT-empowered learning loop for boosting 'corporate IQ'.

4. How have the newly developed IT systems at Brooklyn Union Gas and 'Global Insurance' enabled each company to respond more effectively to changing market conditions?

13 OFFICE SPACE, CYBERSPACE AND VIRTUAL ORGANIZATION

CHRISTOPHER BARNATT *

In order to work together, white-collar employees have traditionally had to congregate in expensive and largely under-utilized office buildings. With new developments in computing and telecommunications, this need for a common location may now be relaxed. This final reading discusses what is meant by the term 'virtual organization', together with how the working patterns to be exhibited within such a structure may compare with those isolated within a range of more traditional organizational forms.

Reports, papers and books concerned with 'virtual companies'[1], 'virtual factories'[2], 'virtual offices'[3] and 'virtual corporations'[4] have been appearing with increasing regularity in both the business press and the academic business literature for several years. Little coherence in the definition of such terms has yet to emerge. However, in all cases, the involved writers are concerned with how developments in new technology will allow remote individuals to work together.

As well as journalists and writers, governments are also taking a distinct interest in the virtual organization concept. In the UK, the DTI are currently backing several initiatives charged with both realizing, and raising awareness of, developments in computer supported cooperative work. Their launch event, held in May 1994, even carried the title 'The Virtual Corporation'. Various European initiatives, for example the ESPRIT COMIC project, are sponsoring similar research. The *concept* of the 'virtual organization' is therefore not one that is likely to disappear in the immediate future. No manager or business academic can therefore afford to remain ignorant of the plethora of developments now

* LECTURER IN ORGANIZATIONAL BEHAVIOUR, COMPUTERS AND MANAGEMENT, UNIVERSITY OF NOTTINGHAM, UK. REPRINTED WITH PERMISSION FROM JOURNAL OF GENERAL MANAGEMENT, VOL. 20 NO. 4, SUMMER 1995, PP. 78–91, THE BRAYBROOKE PRESS LTD., HENLEY—ON—THAMES.

bandied together under its contentious metaphorical umbrella. As a resource to both theory and current practice, this paper draws together common themes concerning virtual organizations by exploring the impact of developments in computer and communications technologies upon working practices and organizational structures.

TECHNOLOGY IN CONTEXT

It is all too easy to view developments in technology, and particularly the business *application* of new technological developments, in a rather narrow, incremental fashion. To some degree this is inevitable, as technological concepts can often only be assimilated in manageable 'babysteps'. The transition from a typewriter to a PC boasting desktop publishing, database and electronic mail facilities, for example, is likely to occur in stages. Simply remove the typewriter one day, and offer the full computer suite the next, and you are asking for problems. However, if the PC is initially installed solely for use as a word processor, and only in time comes to be used for database, desktop publishing and electronic mail applications, then success is far more likely to be achieved. Indeed, this is what has occurred in most businesses today, with computer technology having been introduced in increments that have permitted employees the time to cross the conceptual barriers involved. Granted, personal computers (PCs) are now far more powerful and user-friendly than they were ten years ago, yet most of the common genres of computer application we run today have existed in one form or another for over a decade. The message is therefore clear. Where new technology is concerned, both people and organizations need time to adjust to new ways of working. They simply cannot accept everything in one go. They have a need to tread lightly in babysteps.

Once the concept of our largely incremental approach to technological innovation in business is accepted, it becomes clear that we may inadvertently view *all* computing and telecommunications developments in a purely incremental fashion. If this occurs there is an inherent danger of missing out on the wider picture, and not appreciating the true impact that computer technology in particular is making on business today.

Nobody woke up one morning in the 18th century and cried: 'Let's have an industrial revolution!' Instead, technology changed around people over several decades, and we only note the *revolutionary* nature of this period in history with hindsight [5]. It is one of the contentions herein that a similar transition is occurring today with the rise of new working practices that are revolutionary rather than incremental. We run the risk of not being aware of these changes, however, due to the fact that we are caught *within* the transition — the information revolution; the birth of a 'new age' — and hence cannot see the wood for the trees. It is therefore important not to simply launch into an examination of new technological

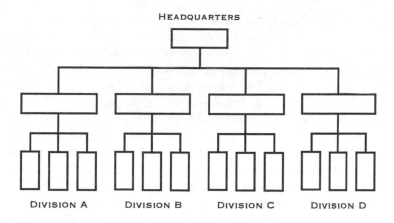

HEADQUARTERS

DIVISION A   DIVISION B   DIVISION C   DIVISION D

Figure 1 A classical hierarchy.

developments, and case examples, without first stepping back to consider the background theory of the evolution of business organizations themselves. When this historical evolutionary backdrop has been presented, the currently *revolution - ary* developments in organizational patterns and functioning may be viewed in their broadest context.

THE EVOLUTION OF ORGANIZATION

From the widespread birth of large industrial organizations in the second quartile of this century until the mid-to-late 1970s, most markets were stable and a 'logic of scale' dominated the philosophy of organizational construction. Indeed, most mass consumer markets, such as those for automobiles and domestic appliances, only arose post WWII, with mass-production assembly lines employed to meet the demand of the largely buoyant consumer economies which had 'never had it so good'. Product differentiation, labour market flexibilities, and the ability to rapidly cope with change, were not items high on the agenda of most organizations. After all, for many years consumers were keen to purchase a product rather than a specific custom item. Large firms, like Ford and General Motors in the automobile industry, therefore chose to adopt vertically-integrated hierarchical structures geared to standardized mass production, and attempted to control as many stages of the production process as possible in order to keep unit costs down. In Ford's case, the company not only operated massive production lines, but also owned railroads to transport its vehicles, a rubber plantation to provide latex for tyre manufacture, and a steel foundry to provide the raw material for car bodies. The multi-divisional structure of large hierarchical firms therefore came to appear as in Figure 1.

Figure 1's depiction of a hierarchy has of necessity been simplified for the sake of clarity in illustration. This said, the figure does highlight the *concept* of a hierarchy, with a clear chain of command running down through every level/division of the organization, each of which is under common ownership and control. In theory, a hierarchy therefore provides an excellent model of production structure, offering both clarity and process integration. In practice, however, large hierarchical organizations have tended to become bureaucratic and cumbersome, with communications from on-high distorted within the red-tape of middle management. Ideas from first line level also often fail to permeate the upper echelons. As environments became more turbulent in the 1970s and 1980s, vertically-integrated hierarchies also proved highly inflexible, as massive sunk-costs had often been incurred in their bid to specialize as greatly as possible in the mass-production of standardized product. In 1972, for example, the Ford Motor Company had constructed a huge, highly specialized engine plant to produce 500,000 V8 engines a year. When the oil crisis hit, the company subsequently found themselves lumbered with a facility geared to the production of gasoline-guzzling engines that consumers were no longer demanding. They consequently had to shut down the facility and move back to a range of smaller and older plants [6]. Other firms have faced similar problems as technologies have advanced apace, more fickle consumer tastes have led to shorter product lifecycles requiring short-term, customized methods of flexible manufacturing, and economic recessions have forced all organizations to consider more innovative and flexible patterns of labour and plant utilization.

Whilst from the 1960s into the 1980s the most popular new 'organic' mode of organizational structure was the matrix organization — a form reliant on shifting project teams with multiple responsibility linkages — in the 1980s an even more flexible organizational pattern emerged. Noted by Miles and Snow in 1986 via observation of the increased incidence of joint ventures, industrial partnerships, and sub-contractual arrangements [7], the so-termed 'dynamic network' operates in an 'outsourcing mode' to 'operationalize' the ideas of the 'brokers' at its core [8]. In essence the resulting structure is a controlled interlinkage of only those parties required for the production of a particular product or service at any particular point in time. The network therefore really is *dynamic*, and such a pattern of flexible organization has now become common across a range of industries. A typical dynamic network may be illustrated as in Figure 2.

The operations of a dynamic network are best explained via example. In the fashion industry, for instance, a network of agents — designers, manufacturers, distributors and those involved in marketing — will come together around a broker core responsible for a particular garment label [9]. Similarly in television or film production, a production team will call upon the services of performing artists, technical facilities houses, contractual services (such as set building) and freelance personnel (like writers and directors), as required for each film, programme or series [10]. Thus, although in the public eye the structure so created may have a clear and unique identity, in practice the involved network dynamically utilizes

Figure 2 A dynamic network.

only the exact facilities it requires as and when it requires them. There is thus little slack in the system, and few (if any) sunk costs to be incurred, with any logic of scale having been abandoned in favour of a new logic of 'flexible specialization'.

Flexible specialization is a concept that at first appears paradoxical. After all, how can an organization be both 'flexible' and 'specialized'? By looking at the dynamic network model, however, the logic is revealed. Viewed in its entirety, a dynamic network is indeed a highly flexible organizational arrangement, capable of adapting rapidly to changing markets, technologies, and demand levels, via coupling agents into or out of its web. When we view the individual agents that service the network core, however, we discover that they are highly specialized in the service they render. Hence, we have the concept of 'flexible specialization', with patterns of specialist agents coordinated by the core of a network that thereby becomes flexible in operation.

The transition from hierarchical firms, geared towards mass production, towards more organic production structures, exhibiting the flexible specialization concept, has been termed the *Second Industrial Divide* [11]. This second industrial revolution — the infotech revolution leading us into a 'Third Age' — will be as extraordinary as the first. It is quite possible, however, that organizational structures such as the dynamic network represent only a transitory structural model as we cross the second industrial divide. As a result of the industrial revolution people moved off the land to concentrate in towns and cities where the new factories were located. In other words, the industrial revolution lead to population *concentration*. As information technologies develop across the second industrial divide, it is quite possible that many people will no longer have to concentrate around their workplace. Instead, a geographically dispersed workforce may once again be exhibited, with electronic links bringing people together in virtual networks when they need or wish to work together. Such virtual organizations therefore carry the concept of flexible specialization a stage further than the dynamic network, which whilst flexible in nature is still limited by the physical location of its broker and agents, and by the complexity of the contractual and monitoring arrangements required between the two.

CHARACTERISTICS OF VIRTUAL ORGANIZATION

Virtual organizations are likely to exhibit a set of common reliances and initial characteristics. In particular it can be noted that virtual organizations:

- Will be reliant on the medium of *cyberspace*
- Will be enabled via new computing and communications developments
- Will initially only exist *across* conventional organizational structures.

The concept of 'cyberspace' is crucial to an understanding of virtual organizational forms. Put simply, cyberspace refers to the *medium* in which electronic communications flow and computer software operates. A little cyberspace therefore exists within every computer or telecommunications system. However, in general, the term is now used to refer to the concept of global systems interconnection whereby every computer and tele-communications network will come to have access to the same 'information space'. When this mass interconnection finally occurs sometime early next century, cyberspace will be a single nexus of electronic data and communications upon which all business operations will be dependent.

First termed by futuristic novelist William Gibson [12], the cyberspace concept is now widely accepted across a range of disciplines. After all, if computers are tools (as most argue) then they have to be tools *to a medium*. Thus, just as a sculptor works *with* a chisel but *in* wood or stone, so present-day office employees work *with* computers but *in* cyberspace [13]. Virtual organizations will therefore be created within the cyberspace medium. To exist, however, they will also require certain enabling software and hardware developments.

Many hard- and softwares already permit forms of remote worker interconnection. By far the most common of these today is electronic mail (e-mail), a system whereby messages and computer files can be 'posted' electronically from computer to computer over a network. Most large organizations now use electronic mail. This not only cuts down on waste paper, and increases the speed and immediacy of messaging systems, but in certain cases is also altering the way in which teams of employees work together. In the giant Microsoft Corporation, for example, e-mail is said to 'carry the culture'. The company is so big, and expanding so rapidly, that it is reliant on e-mail as the glue to hold people together. When new employees are recruited, there is often no attempt made to locate them in the same physical space as other members of their team. Instead, Microsoft's software 'Gods' and 'Goddesses' work through the medium of electronic mail [14]. In a very 'real' sense, the sub-organizations and cultures the company's 12,000+ employees work within are 'virtual' in nature.

Electronic mail aside, various software developments under the heading of 'groupware' permit far more complex and interactive methods of remote employee working. An application called *Lotus Notes*, for example, now reputed to be used by around 750,000 people, allows multiple users interactive access to data files posted centrally on corporate *bulletin boards*. The software also permits interactive dialogues on-screen between many people simultaneously. Thus, with *Notes* or similar groupware, four people in four different locations may conduct a four-way dialogue via their computers whilst simultaneously having access to the same corporate information. Already over 2,500 companies use *Lotus Notes* to allow teamwork to be re-engineered across physical boundaries. Indeed, across industry as a whole, groupware applications are now being adopted with an almost 'unbounded enthusiasm' [15].

Also included under the groupware heading are developments in video-conferencing. Video-conference links allow people in remote locations to see as well as to hear other multiple parties over telecommunications links, and to hence conduct meetings. In many companies, dedicated video-conferencing facilities are now standard and widely utilized. Facilities for PC-based video links are also emerging. One such system is *ProShare* from Intel, which will run on any high-specification personal computer with an appropriate ISDN (integrated services digital network) telephone line, and which sells for only a few thousand pounds. According to Personal Technology Research in Massachusetts, by 1997 the market for video-conferencing equipment is expected to be worth over $10 billion per annum [16].

New generations of video-conferencing technology are also in development. British Telecom's Systems Research Division, for example, is working on a system which incorporates a large screen bisecting a large, 'round' table. Participants sitting before the screen on one side of the table will be able to view remote parties on the screen *as if they were sitting across the same table*. The aim is for participants to 'lose themselves' in the technology, and hence to forget that a video-conference is actually taking place [17].

Around the year 2000, video-conferencing is likely to develop one stage further than British Telecom's large screen system and become totally three dimensional. Rather than just looking at each other upon flat screens, participants will instead don virtual reality helmets that will allow them to be transported into computer-generated graphics worlds in order to hold 'virtual meetings' in cyberspace.

It is clear from the above, that whilst groupware facilities will allow people to be drawn together electronically across cyberspace, the virtual organizational patterns of workers so created are initially likely to exist *across* other organizations. An arbitrary virtual organization may therefore be represented as in Figure 3.

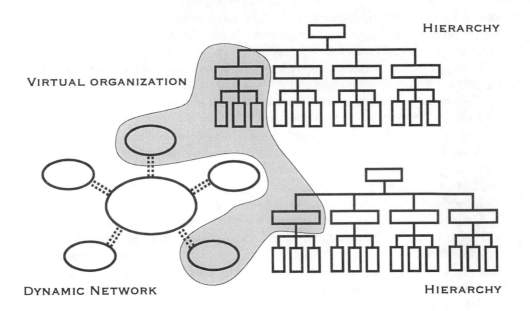

Figure 3 Hierarchy, network and virtual organization.

In Figure 3 we see two conventional hierarchical structures and a dynamic network. Across these organizations, electronic links enable employees to work interactively with those in other companies. Research scientists, for example, may swap data and discuss problems via electronic mail systems (a practice that is known to occur and which is *very* difficult for the employing corporate parent to control). In this sense, electronic webs of virtual organization may 'oil the wheels' of more conventional organizational forms. On the other hand, virtual organizations will also have the potential to become a resource drain, with people employed by one organization but simultaneously being part of virtual webs of interconnection across the electronic arena of cyberspace. In some cases, issues of employee control and information ownership may hence become a nightmare.

VARIANTS OF VIRTUAL ORGANIZATIONAL FORM

The preceding sections suggest that virtual organizations, having no distinct physical form and permitted and limited solely via electronic interconnection across cyberspace, will exist in a wide range of guises. In particular, four key variants of virtual organization may currently be isolated:

- The adoption of homeworking ('telecommuting')
- The development of 'hot desk' environments

- The adoption of 'hotelling'
- The operation of 'virtual teams' enabled via groupware.

The concept of homeworking (or 'telecommuting'), whereby employees use a remote terminal to access their office system, has been discussed for well over a decade. Experiments were conducted in the early 1980s at Rank Xerox in the UK [18], and although homeworking proved technically feasible, employees felt socially isolated when working from home on computers. In the USA, however, greater physical distances have made homeworking more attractive, with around six-million Americans now having formal homeworking arrangements [19].

New groupware technologies will also make homeworking more acceptable. Early homeworking systems simply offered employees green-screen monitors with text-only displays. Whilst providing acceptable business functionality, the technology did nothing to try to bridge the social chasm created by geographic isolation. In modern homeworking systems, however, employees may have the facility to actually see their colleagues on a video screen or in a window on their console display. They may therefore feel less remote and hence more readily accept the homeworking option. Homeworking is also becoming more attractive as new initiatives negate the importance of personal *physical* space at work, with employees instead finding themselves and their work focused within computer systems. For many the difference between working in the office and working at home is therefore becoming more and more superficial. Initiatives working toward the negation of personal physical space currently come under the banners of *hot-desk systems, hotelling* and the operation of *virtual teams*.

Hot-desk systems exist in re-engineered office environments which have removed permanent, individual desks for all employees. In the British Gas Research Centre in Loughborough, for example, employees are reported to arrive in the morning to be allocated a desk for the day. From the workstation on this desk they can access their own electronic mail and computer network files, whilst their personal telephone number will be routed to the telephone on the desk so that they can be contacted by colleagues and access any voice-mail messages. Employees are therefore likely to be working at a different (but identical) desk every day, and alongside different colleagues. All that is unique to them is their telephone number and computer network access. Perhaps not surprisingly, there is a degree of social hostility toward this system [20].

Similar hot-desk arrangements have also been constructed by the Digital Equipment Corporation and IBM. In Digital's 'office of the future' in Stockholm, individual desks have been abandoned, employees carry cordless telephones, and computer consoles are freely available that pull down on flexibars from the ceiling when individuals need access to the central system. Any personal space is limited to the inside of a drawer in a bank of cabinets in which employees may store individual possessions. If meetings need to be held, general rooms for this purpose are available [21].

IBM's system encapsulating hot-desk arrangements is entitled *SMART*, standing for Space, Morale And Remote Technology. At Bedford Lakes on the outskirts of London, the company has divided individual workspaces into four classifications: managers' offices, permanent workstations for administrative staff, hot-desk facilities for mobile consultants, and finally 'touch-down' desks to be used by staff visiting the office for short periods of time [22].

The concept of the touch-down desk leads us to consider a development related to hot-desk termed 'hotelling'. This system, recently reported to be in use by consultants Ernst & Young, relies on the fact that if workers spend the majority of their working lives out with clients, then they have no need for a permanent desk in their parent company. Employees such as consultants therefore rely on their clients to provide a desk — effectively using client facilities like a hotel — and stay in contact with colleagues via computer links and voice mail. When an employee does need to work back at base, they simply call in to a 'concierge', letting them know when they will be arriving and for how long. A cubicle is then allocated for duration of the worker's 'visit', on which their name will be emblazoned by the time they arrive. Like its sister hot-desk arrangement, the hotelling concept relies on a company-wide computer network, high-specification (and often portable) computer hardware, and a nationwide voice-mail system [23].

A final and associated example of this genre of remote working concerns the operation of 'virtual teams'. Mercury Telecommunications, in an attempt to cope with its massive expansion, has opted for virtual teamworking, with people collaborating closely but in a variety of locations. Whether at home, in the car, at a customer's office, a third-party site, in a branch office or in headquarters, employees are unified via highly sophisticated information technology, and by skilled team coordinators who foster a strong sense of common identity and mission. Again a 'base office' providing 'touch-down' facilities as and when required constitutes a key element of the system [24].

A REVOLUTION IN OFFICE PRODUCTIVITY

All of the above examples have two characteristics in common. Firstly, they all rely on computing and communications technologies to bring people together. New technological developments may therefore be defined as the 'pull factor' moving more and more people toward working patterns with no strong reliance on common physical space. Secondly, the above examples also all allow a reduction of white-collar overheads, with work displaced as greatly as possible from office space (common physical buildings) into cyberspace (computing and electronic communications links). The 'push factor' toward new technology-enabled remote working practices is therefore seen as part of a traditional desire to reduce fixed costs.

As Bruce Lloyd highlighted in 1990, whilst around half the Western world's employees work in office buildings, these buildings (constituting a large percentage of asset base for most companies) are highly unproductive. Most workers only spend around 40 hours a week in their office, which, when combined with holidays, means that the office capital asset is only used effectively for around 21% of its lifetime. In contrast, many production facilities (assembly lines, mines, transport systems and so forth) run around the clock for the majority of the year [25]. Any developments that will allow office space to be shared (with initiatives such as hot-desk and hotelling arrangements), or perhaps negated altogether (via homeworking and virtual team arrangements), will therefore clearly be welcomed by corporate accountants. Most companies today have little fat left to slice from their production and distribution operations. For efficiency to improve in a cut-throat business environment, pressures may therefore be great to adopt *any* new technological development that will save even a small percentage of the massive resource expenditure directed into office buildings by almost all large organizations. What's more, the savings can be considerable. Ernst & Young, for example, having adopted hotelling arrangements for staff in their New York and Chicago branches, now only have to provide one office per three consultants, and as a result have reduced office space by 25%. Once hotelling is adopted across the United States, the company expects cost savings in the region of $40million a year [26].

ENTERING VIRTUAL REALITY

With such potential cost savings in mind, many new groupware technologies to permit far more complex and interactive computer supported cooperative work (CSCW) are receiving serious attention. Perhaps most notably, the concept of *virtucommuting* is being increasingly discussed. Put simply, virtucommuting involves people donning virtual reality clothing (such as a head-mounted display and a dataglove) which will allow them to disappear into a virtual reality — a virtual working environment — created in computer graphics. Many people will be able to remotely access each virtual working environment, thus allowing cooperative and useful work to be undertaken. Software engineers Steve Pruitt and Tom Barrett have predicted 'corporate virtual workspaces' — effectively computer-generated office buildings — which workers will access via their 'home reality engine' console [27]. Within such a scenario, various interesting possibilities start to abound. For example, *every* employee may have the largest office in the building, and may select a different décor every day. Employees will also be able to edit their software body so that they can appear as they wish, and will have the option to make their door selectively invisible to other workers! Whilst such predictions are still largely fictional speculation, they do indicate what is probably a near future in groupware advancement. Perhaps just as significantly, they also suggest that prejudice may cease to be an obstacle in business relationships when gender, age, ethnicity and disability can be masked by computer software.

Current multiple-user business virtual reality systems are not nearly as advanced as those advocated by Pruitt and Barrett. The *Virtuosi* project funded by the DTI CSCW Programme and the SERC in the UK, however, is working toward the realization of virtual organizations supported by networked virtual reality technology. Partners in the research include British Telecom, GEC, and universities in Nottingham, Lancaster and Manchester. One goal of *Virtuosi* is the creation of the 'virtual factory'. Toward this end, virtual meeting spaces have already been prototyped to which remote participants wearing virtual reality headsets can be transported. Participants may all sit down and talk at a desk, or alternatively may walk around and take turns to write on a virtual whiteboard. Colleagues may also join in via video links that will allow them to appear on virtual TV monitors. A second goal of *Virtuosi* is the realization of the 'virtual catwalk'. When this project comes to fruition, designers will create new garments on computer, which will then be modelled by computer-generated mannequins in a fashion show held before buyers who attend in virtual reality [28].

EMBRACING THE NEW MEDIUM OF BUSINESS

To many the concept of virtucommuting, with organizations created in cyberspace, will sound like pure fiction. Yet using e-mail to stay in touch with colleagues around the world *is* a widely accepted concept. We have therefore come full circle, back to the notion that in general people can only embrace technological developments in incremental babysteps. Doing business in virtual reality is merely an extension of using presently accepted groupware software like *Lotus Notes* or holding a video-conference. In ten years the concept will probably be commonplace. As Charles Grimsdale, Managing Director of virtual reality systems supplier *Division* noted at a conference in March 1994, virtual reality today is where multimedia was ten years ago. In five years time, virtual reality will be where multimedia is today. Still developing, perhaps, but most certainly a commonly accepted business tool.

As computer networks based on fibre-optic and satellite-linked digital superhighways proliferate, and the cost of high-specification computer hardware continues to tumble, cyberspace will offer more and more possibilities for remote working. Whilst the majority of employees' lives are not likely to be greatly affected by the virtual organization concept over the next few years, a substantial minority will find themselves working in radically new and hopefully radically exciting ways. Indeed, as more companies become aware of the overhead reductions now possible via a decreased reliance on common office space, many will be *forced* to implement hot-desk systems, hotelling, virtual teamworking, traditional homeworking, and perhaps even virtucommuting, in order to remain competitive. However, we need not fear this trend. It is a natural transition. An evolution of organization. The industrial revolution freed the majority from toiling in poverty on the land, yet the cost was population concentration, pollution, and a large travelling component within the average working day. As we cross the second industrial divide, the ravages of commuting and congestion may be removed from many people's lives. We are indeed passing through a *revolution,* even though we may be too close to appreciate it. And even if three out of four people still regularly travel to a common office, the removal of the fourth from our transportation infrastructure will greatly increase the quality of life for all, not to mention decreasing the building overheads incurred by almost all organizations.

Technology not only tempts business re-engineering and transformation, it also improves the flow of our work and is potentially exciting. When completing a task manually, people are far more likely to be distracted than when working at a computer screen and keyboard. Many, many people have found themselves sitting down at a computer keyboard to work 'for just half an hour', only to look up many hours later to find that the afternoon had passed them by. Like it or not, computers demand and hold human attention. The technology may be complex and deviously frustrating on many occasions, yet few of us fail to be drawn into cyberspace when working with colourful, graphical, user-friendly and highly interactive software applications.

The more we can interact with each other *through* technology, the more *transparent* computers and communications systems will appear, the more we will *forget* we are working through them, and the greater will be the *quality* of the business relationships we may foster across new 'virtual' organizational working patterns. After all, although the tools of cyberspace may be cold, logical and horrendously complex, their application will continue to allow the culture and camaraderie — the battle, the losing and the winning — of business life to be conducted not just more *efficiently,* but also more *effectively.* For as Jean-Louis Gassee reminds us:

> We humans are in love with our tools because they help us become more than we are, to overcome our limitations and extend the boundaries of what it is possible to do with our brains and bodies [29].

REVIEW AND DISCUSSION QUESTIONS

1. Why is there a danger of 'incrementalism' with regard to the application of computer technology within business?

2. Highlight the advantages for organizations of implementing new working practices such as hot-desk and hotelling environments.

3. How are developments in connectivity leading to more organic organizational structures?

4. Discuss what futures may lie in store regarding the evolution of virtual organizational forms.

References

[1] Porter, A. 'Virtual Companies Reconsidered', *Technology Analysis & Strategic Management*, 5(4), 1993.

[2] Baxter, A. 'Virtual Factory Takes Shape', *The Financial Times*, February 8th 1993.

[3] Hamit, F. *Virtual Reality and the Exploration of Cyberspace*, Carmel, IN: Sams Publishing, 1993, pp.266-271.

[4] Davidow, W. and Malone, M. *The Virtual Corporation*, New York: Harper Business, 1992.

[5] Barnatt, C. *Cyber Business: Mindsets for a Wired Age*, Chichester: John Wiley & Sons, 1995, p.184.

[6] Peters, T. and Waterman, R. *In Search of Excellence*, New York: Harper & Row, 1982, p.112.

[7] Miles, R.. and Snow, C. 'Organizations: New Concepts for New Forms', *California Management Review*, XXVII, 1986 pp.62-73.

[8] Morgan, G. *Creative Organization Theory: A Resourcebook*, Newbury Park, CA: Sage Publications, 1989, p.67.

[9] Ibid.

[10] Barnatt, C. and Starkey, K. 'The Emergence of Flexible Networks in the UK Television Industry', *British Journal of Management* 5(4), 1994, pp.251-260.

[11] Piore, M. and Sabel, C. *The Second Industrial Divide*, New York: Basic Books, 1984.

[12] Gibson, W. *Neuromancer*, New York: Ace Books, 1984.

[13] Barnatt, C. op. cit; p.206.

[14] Hayman, S. *The Electronic Frontier*, Transcript of BBC TV *Horizon* documentary, London: Broadcasting Support Services, 1993, pp.6-7.

[15] Kavanagh, J. 'The Groupware Revolution', *Financial Times Review: Software at Work*, Spring 1994.

[16] Wang, C. *Techno Vision: The Executive's* Survival Guide to Understanding and Managing Information Technology, New York: McGraw-Hill, 1994, p.144.

[17] Brown, M. 'BT on the Beam' *Management Today*, January 1994, p.73.

[18] Judkins, P. and West, D. *Networking in Organizations: The Rank Xerox Experiment*, Aldershot: Gower, 1985.

[19] Stewart, T. 'The Information Age in Figures', *Fortune International*, April 1994, p.56.

[20] Barnatt, C. *A Prelude to the Cyber Business*, working paper, School of Management & Finance, University of Nottingham, 1993,XIII, p.14.

[21] *Business Update*, Issue 7, Digital Equipment Corporation, 1993.

[22] Raymond, S. and Cunliffe, R. 'At Home in the Office', *Financial Times*, March 9th 1994.

[23] Sprout, A. 'Moving into the Virtual Office', *Fortune International*, May 2nd 1994, p.67.

[24] Raymond, S. and Cunliffe, R., op. cit.

[25] Lloyd, B. 'Office Productivity — Time for a Revolution', *Long Range Planning*, 23(1), 1990, pp.66-79.

[26] Sprout, A, op. cit.

[27] Pruitt, S. and Barrett, T. 'Corporate Virtual Workspace' in Benedikt, M. (ed) *Cyberspace: First Steps*, Cambridge, MA: MIT Press, 1993.

[28] Benford, S., Bowers, J., Gray, S., Roden, T., Ryan, G. and Stanger, V. 'The Virtuosi Project' in *Proceedings of VR 94*, Virtual Reality Expo (February), 1994.

[29] Laurel, B. *Computers as Theatre*, Reading, MA: Addison Wesley, 1993, cited p.213.

FURTHER READING

Whilst full sets of references are provided at the end of each Chapter and Reading, the following books may be particularly useful for students and lecturers in providing additional material to complement *Management Strategy and Information Technology* in a teaching context:

As a basic introduction to business computing:

- Barnatt, C. (1994) *The Computers in Business Blueprint,* Oxford: Basil Blackwell.

As alternative general 'text' sources:

- Daniels, N.C. (1994) *Information Technology: The Management Challenge*, Wokingham: Addison-Wesley.
- Martin, C. and Powell, P. (1992) *Information Systems: A Management Perspective* , McGraw-Hill: London.
- Peppard, J. (1993) *IT Strategy for Business*, London: Pitman.

As specific guides to key topic areas:

- Barnatt, C. 1995 *Cyber Business: Mindsets for a Wired Age*, Chichester: John Wiley & Sons.
- Hammer, M. and Champy, J. (1993) *Reengineering the Corporation*, New York: Harper Collins.
- Lacity, M.C. and Hirschheim, R. (1993) *Information Systems Outsourcing: Myths, Metaphors and Realities*, Chichester: John Wiley & Sons.
- Trimmer, D. (1993) *Downsizing: Strategies for Success in the Modern Computer World*, Wokingham: Addison-Wesley.
- Wang, C. (1994) *Techno Vision: The executive's guide to understanding and managing information technology*, New York: McGraw-Hill.

INDEX